The Japanese on Trial

The Japanese on Trial

ALLIED WAR CRIMES OPERATIONS IN THE EAST, 1945-1951

By Philip R. Piccigallo

University of Texas Press, Austin and London

Requests for permission to reproduce material from
this work should be sent to Permissions, University of
Texas Press, Box 7819, Austin, Texas 78712.

Library of Congress Cataloging in Publication Data

Piccigallo, Philip R   1949–
    The Japanese on trial.

    Bibliography: p.
    Includes index.
    1. War crime trials—Tokyo, 1946–1948.   2. In-
ternational Military Tribunal for the Far East.   3. War
criminals—Japan.   4. World War, 1939–1945—Atrocities.   I. Title.
JX5438.8.P5   341.6'9   79-13400
ISBN 0-292-78033-8

To my parents, Terry and Sam

Contents

Acknowledgments

I acquired many debts in the course of writing this volume. By far the largest is owed to Hyman Kublin, my thesis adviser at the City University of New York, whose generous bestowal of wisdom and guidance was surpassed only by the boundless inspiration he imparted and concern he showed. I am also profoundly indebted to Arthur M. Schlesinger, Jr., whose careful reading of the manuscript produced numerous constructive suggestions, nearly all of which have been incorporated into the text. I would like to express my sincere appreciation, too, to Louis L. Snyder, Hans L. Trefousse and Telford Taylor. Certainly the work has benefited from their invaluable insight and selective criticism. Numerous individuals throughout the world, most of whom I have never met personally, assisted me in the locating of relevant materials. Nevertheless, a special note of gratitude here is owed to the published and other efforts of Frank Joseph Shulman, George C. Chalou, Robert Donihi and R. John Pritchard, as well as to the many helpful archivists and national librarians of the Allied nations and Japan. For her major contribution to the typing and re-typing of the manuscript, I am sincerely grateful to my sister, Marguerite. A particular debt, beyond words and measure, is owed to Sydney Rosenberg, who first showed me the way. Above all, I am most grateful to my parents, whose unfailing encouragement, patience and love sustained me throughout.

Such assistance notwithstanding, I alone, of course, am responsible for any shortcomings in this work.

A NOTE ON JAPANESE NAMES

Japanese names throughout appear in Western style —that is, the personal names first, followed by the surname.

Introduction

Between 1945 and 1951, Allied military commissions assembled throughout the Far East condemned 920 Japanese to death and sentenced some 3,000 others to prison terms. The accused had been found guilty, in varying degrees, of war crimes. In addition, an International Military Tribunal sitting at Tokyo from 1946 to 1948 tried and sentenced 25 "major" Japanese war criminals—Tojo and company—for plotting and waging the Pacific War. For its contribution to the fields of international history and certain aspects of international law alone, this massive and cooperative Allied effort to bring Japanese war criminals to justice warrants serious study. Yet it has been relatively overlooked, except perhaps in passing, by scholars and jurists alike. The time is long overdue for its emergence from behind the shadow of Nuremberg.

Granted, one cannot realistically expect phrases such as Rape of Nanking, Bataan Death March, Thai-Burma Railway or Sack of Manila to elicit the same kind of response usually associated with mention of Nazi horrors. Terms such as *concentration camps*, *genocide*, *holocaust* and *final solution* immediately focus attention upon one outstanding event of the past three decades: the proceedings of the International Military Tribunal at Nuremberg, held from 1945 to 1946. So, too, with war crimes operations and trials. The overwhelming number of studies—and they are countless—that deal with the subject concentrate solely on those related to Germany. Doubtless, the register of atrocities perpetrated by Nazis between 1933 and 1945 stands unchallenged as a monument to evil, and will forever endure disquietingly in the people's hearts and minds. Nazis, however, possessed no monopoly over the commission of war crimes during World War II.

Throughout the East, Japanese waged an equally, though not as designedly, ruthless and inhumane campaign against opposing military forces and local civilian populations. After 1931, and to an increasing degree after 1937, members of the Japanese army, navy, police and government beat, tortured, burned and massacred Chinese by the thousands. American fliers captured over the mainland, Burma, the Pacific Islands or Japan proper were humiliated, bayoneted and executed without trial. Whole populations of villages of Java, Rabaul, Kuala Lumpur and the Southwest Pacific Islands were slaughtered outright. Japanese military police, the notorious *Kempeitai*, specialized in devising novel methods of eliciting information from captives and causing unimaginable suffering. And they practiced their trade generously. Prisoners of war, the Japanese felt, did not deserve treatment befitting soldiers, as they had shamefully surrendered or allowed themselves to be captured. Often the captors worked them until they died.

Immediately prior to and after the American invasion of the Philippines in late 1944, Japanese naval personnel in Manila and dispersed army contingents in Batangas Province launched a sanguinary assault on local inhabitants. Insensate carnage ensued, resulting in the wanton massacre of thousands of Filipinos. Manila, like so many other cities, towns and villages which had stood in the path of the rampaging Japanese Imperial Army, was razed.

What caused such behavior? Was it attributable to Japanese unyielding adherence to strict discipline or blind obedience to orders? Did it stem from Japanese reliance upon Spartan values or obsessive belief in the need to establish an empire? Perhaps blame rests with uniquely Japanese moral codes or just the infinite madness of war itself. In any event, actions such as these defy simply explanation as surely as they numb the consciousness. Nor will any attempt to explain them be made in the present study. In fact, but for the preceding *mise-en-scène*, direct reference to atrocities will hereafter have merely passing status, and will serve one basic function: to awaken readers to the reality that Japanese, too, perpetrated war crimes and that, not surprisingly, Allied nations held them accountable. This is a study, not of Japanese war crimes, but of the Allied effort to bring to justice those who committed them.

Additional, perhaps more important, reasons necessitate further examination of Allied war crimes operations in the East. First of all, eleven nations participated. Principal burden for investigating, locating, apprehending and prosecuting war criminals fell to the governments of America, Britain, Australia, the Netherlands, China, the Philippines, France, Russia and, to a lesser extent, those of Canada, New Zealand and India. Allied military courts conducted trials, occasionally jointly, at Batavia, Canton, Guam, Hong Kong, Khabarovsk, Kuala Lumpur, Labuan, Macassar, Malaya, Manila, Manus Island, the Marshall Islands, Morotai, Nanking, Port Darwin, Rabaul, Shanghai, Singapore, Yokohama and, of course, Tokyo.

In all respects, then, the Allied war crimes operation in the East was an international effort. Each nation, viewing the trials within its own domestic and international political, economic and social context, outlined and followed, within practical limitations, its own war crimes policy. Put simply, Japanese war crimes trials did not to any great extent determine the course of any Allied nation's major policies; rather, major policies and relative factors determined the course of the trials in each nation. This is another way of saying that Japanese war crimes trials were made to fit into the overall national and foreign policy objectives of each Allied country.

Inasmuch as this is true, the Allied war crimes operation in the East assumes new meaning. Study of it is important not only for a comparison of legal procedures and principles. Its significance also does not lie exclusively in the contribution, particularly that of the International Military Tribunal for the Far East (IMTFE), to international law. Even such questions as whether the Allies afforded Japanese accused fair and impartial trials or whether, as Richard H. Minear and others have suggested, they practiced "victors' justice" are but part of a much larger and more meaningful consideration.[1]

Greater relevance, to wit, may be found in a comprehensive and comparative examination of each Allied nation's policies toward, and treatment of, Japanese war criminal suspects, as well as their relative policies vis-à-vis one another. From this, it is believed, a clearer and more accurate understanding of how and why postwar international relations in the East developed or degenerated as they did in succeeding years will emerge.

A word on the necessarily limited objectives of this study is in order. In many respects, works centering upon broad, relatively unexplored topics can serve introductory purposes at best. So it is in this instance, especially where actual trial coverage is concerned. The present study seeks only to lay the groundwork for, and perhaps stimulate, further inquiry into Japanese war crimes trials. It makes no claim to definitiveness. It offers no attempt to examine exhaustively the thousands of Allied war crimes trials conducted throughout the East. Such an attempt, although ultimately needed, would demand Herculean effort—certainly exceeding the capabilities of one individual—and must therefore await the combined labors of future scholars. Beyond this, that type of project would require many volumes for adequate presentation. Nor are all the materials essential for such an investigation currently or readily available. Moreover, recourse to such materials is not vital to the present study.

By all measures the central feature of this work is the Allied Eastern war crimes operation in its entirety. Sweeping overviews of each nation's war crimes trials program, providing sober and representative portrayals, have been the goal throughout. The actual trials constituted but part of a massive, often extremely complex, international Allied operation spanning much of Asia and the Pacific and Indian oceans. The preponderance of this study, as its title indicates, is devoted to operational aspects of the trials: namely, uncovering of atrocities; transmission of warnings to Tokyo; establishment of national and international war crimes agencies, teams and trial procedures; identification, location, apprehension and incarceration of suspects; collection of evidence, written testimony and witnesses; furnishing of trial personnel, from court presidents and attorneys to interpreters and reporters; preparation and conducting of trials; and pervasive, effective Allied cooperation in accomplishing the foregoing.

Another aim has been to determine the role of Japanese war crimes trials, between 1945 and 1951 and possibly beyond, in each nation's international and domestic perspective. Sections on the trials are intended mainly to provide representative examples of the hundreds of actual trials heard in Allied theaters.

Finally, but by no means of least importance, this work endeavors to rescue lesser Japanese trials from historical oblivion, underscoring in the process the distinctly minor role assumed by the Tokyo Trial in relation to the overall Allied effort. Furthermore, the fact that Allied tribunals at some 2,200 lesser trials applied essentially different legal reasoning than the IMTFE is of major importance and central to this study. The former tried Japanese (mostly military, but some civilian, personnel) exclusively, with rare exceptions, for conventional war crimes: that is, for violations of the laws and usages of war and not—as Tokyo prosecutors did—for crimes against peace. Only so-called "B" and "C" war criminals, those charged with actually perpetrating, ordering or allowing atrocities, stood before lesser tribunals. Class "A" or major war criminals in the dock at Tokyo, on the other hand, stood accused of plotting and waging the Pacific War. This work, it is hoped, goes far in elucidating this fundamental distinction.

Above all, this work is not designed to sit in judgment of the trials, their creators or defendants. Rather, historical objectivity in the Von Rankean tradition has been the author's prevailing goal from start to finish.

The Japanese on Trial

1. Warning and Occupation

Warning

Barely had air raid sirens subsided at Pearl Harbor when reports came of widespread Japanese atrocities against Allied soldiers and civilians. By early 1942 Allied leaders accepted the truthfulness of such accounts, as well as their foreboding potential. Through parliamentary addresses, press statements and official pronouncements, government spokespersons apprised the world of Japanese "acts of barbarism and violence."[1] They also warned the Japanese of the consequences of their behavior.

Initially, Allied authorities expressed their expectations that Tokyo would observe generally accepted norms of civilized behavior and principles of international law. Washington and London, for example, "expected" Tokyo to abide by the provisions of the Geneva Convention of July 27, 1929, relative to the Red Cross and protection of POWs. So explained Secretary of State Hull to the Japanese Foreign Ministry in a note of December 18, 1941.[2] Shortly thereafter, however, the need for more incisive and assertive Allied statements—actually, warnings—waxed evident.

The first formal warning to Japan followed the signing of the Inter-Allied Declaration on *Punishment for War Crimes* in London in January 1942. While the conference dealt primarily with events then taking place in Europe, the Chinese observer directed his message to Tokyo. In "solemnly condemning" the inhumane treatment afforded his compatriots by Japanese, Wunz King pledged China's unswerving commitment to "vindicate" the "elementary principles of justice and morality." All "guilty persons" would be "equally dealt with according to law," assured King; and the "authors" of war crimes would be "held accountable therefor."[3]

On August 21, 1942, Franklin D. Roosevelt delivered his hitherto most explicit admonition to Tokyo. For "some time," he said, the

United States had "been aware" of war crimes committed by the
Axis powers. Future prosecutors would make "appropriate use of
. . . information and evidence in respect to these barbaric crimes of
the invaders, in Europe and *in Asia*," the president, too, assured. In
fairness, he concluded, perpetrators "should have this warning that
the time will come when they shall have to stand in the courts of
law in the very countries which they are now oppressing and answer
for their acts." September witnessed Winston Churchill's "most
particular" desire "to identify the British Government . . . with the
solemn words" of the president. Later that year, in December, Vice-
President Henry Wallace urgently proposed that the United Nations
"make absolutely sure that the guilty leaders [of Germany and Ja-
pan] are punished."[4]

Soon an abundance of Allied pronouncements flowed forth,
each spelled out with greater clarity. This pertained particularly in
later years, as the European war neared its end. Consequently Allied
leaders found increasing opportunity to focus needed attention on
pressing matters in the Pacific. Immediately upon learning the details of the Bataan Death March in late January 1944, Secretary Hull
and British Foreign Minister Anthony Eden issued simultaneous
warnings to Japan. Neither government, they promised, would "forget these acts" or relent in its determination to mete out "just punishment." Eastern war crimes also concerned General Charles de
Gaulle, the head of the French Committee for National Liberation.
"Any" Japanese guilty of mistreating French or Indochinese citizens, he pointedly notified Tokyo in May 1945, would later be held
accountable as a "war criminal."[5]

Through the Swiss minister, Tokyo learned in June 1945 that
the United States possessed a substantial number of Japanese documents "authorizing cold-blooded murder of captured prisoners."
The United States "firmly intended to bring to judgment anyone
who had any part in these acts," warned the Swiss representative.
Moreover, indisputable evidence adduced at the Tokyo Trial revealed that the Allied powers had repeatedly lodged with the appropriate Japanese authorities during the Pacific War a host of "formal
and informal protests and warnings against violations of the laws of
war."[6]

Finally, and most important, the Potsdam Declaration of July
26, 1945, set down "basic policy for the trial and punishment of Japanese war criminals." Issued jointly by America, Britain and China,
and subsequently subscribed to by Russia, the proclamation stated:

"(6) There must be eliminated for all time the authority and influence of those who have deceived and misled the people of Japan into embarking on world conquest. . . . (10) We do not intend that the Japanese be enslaved as a race or destroyed as a nation but stern justice shall be meted out to all war criminals, including those who have visited cruelties upon our prisoners. . . ." [7]

Thus had the Allied powers warned the Japanese government and military of their resolute intention to hold accountable those responsible for war crimes. To the United States Navy war crimes director, Admiral John D. Murphy, the lesson seemed clear: the "presumption that civilized man is conscious of the wrongfulness of vicious brutal acts, especially after the numerous specific warnings, constitutes adequate moral basis for imposition of individual criminal punishment." [8]

In the meantime Allied authorities undertook more practical steps. By virtue of an Anglo-American agreement cemented in December 1942, a United Nations War Crimes Commission (UNWCC) came into being in October 1943. More than any other, this multinational body proved vital to the Allied war crimes operation. The Commission comprised sixteen members, the Soviet Union refusing to join. "Primarily a fact-finding body," the UNWCC dispatched scores of investigation teams to areas in Europe and Asia recently liberated by Allied forces. There they scoured hundreds of miles, unearthing evidence, locating eyewitnesses, interviewing local inhabitants and taking depositions from released POWs. In this manner the UNWCC drew up and forwarded to prosecuting Allied nations lists of European and Eastern war criminals against whom *prima facie* cases appeared tenable. Established in May 1944, a Chungking "Sub-Commission" concentrated exclusively on preparing lists of Japanese suspected of war crimes in the China theater.[9] Such procedure, as well as UNWCC functions, however, generally applied to the trials of lesser Japanese war criminals, and not to the forthcoming trial of "major" war criminals at Tokyo.

Occupation

By signing the Instrument of Surrender on September 2, 1945, Japanese authorities, on behalf of the emperor and government of Japan, accepted the provisions of the Potsdam Declaration. Yet while the Japanese proclaimed their surrender to "the Allied Powers," American influence predominated over the postwar adjustment of Japan. The United States, after all, had shouldered the overwhelming military burden in the Pacific War. Equally important, the long and destructive conflict resulted in the palpable weakening of the traditionally influential powers in the East; only the United States and Russia emerged, in 1945, strengthened. Well before Japan's surrender, American leaders harbored grave distrust of Soviet motives vis-à-vis postwar Japan and East Asia. Certainly, President Truman's decision at Potsdam to exclude the Russians from "any part in the control of Japan" sprang directly from fears that Moscow "was planning world conquest." To fill the Pacific power vacuum, to forestall potential Soviet aggression, to assure American supervision over the occupation of Japan and to restore regional stability as rapidly as possible, then, United States officials felt strongly the need for decisive action.[10]

For these reasons President Truman also decided to entrust leadership of the occupation to General Douglas MacArthur, designated Supreme Commander for the Allied Powers (SCAP) on August 14, 1945. Indeed, Truman directed that MacArthur "be given complete command and control" in Japan. Meanwhile, the "United States Initial Post-Surrender Policy for Japan" of August 29, 1945, became the basis for "all occupation policies." American officials, it is true, assured their Allies of a cooperative effort in the formulation of occupation policies; nevertheless where differences materialized, stated the aforementioned document, "the policies of the United States . . . govern[ed]."[11]

"To formulate the policies, principles and standards" by which the Japanese Surrender Instrument might be effected, the Far Eastern Commission (FEC) was founded in late 1945–early 1946 as the "supreme policy-making body" in the occupation. Here, too, American influences weighed heavily. The FEC, observed its official historian, "generally recognized, respected and followed the lead of the United States."[12] In short, the United States directed and dominated the occupation of Japan.

America's principal role in Japanese war crimes trials ran parallel to its leading role in the occupation. Not only did it spearhead the Eastern war crimes operation, prosecuting more Japanese than any other nation, but it also exercised considerable sway over its Allies' war crimes policies. The Tokyo Trial of major war criminals functioned throughout under the all-pervading shadow of SCAP. Owing to its "predominant contribution" to the defeat of Japan, contended

American prosecutors at Tokyo, "it was the universally admitted right and duty of the United States" to oversee Eastern war crimes trials. Nor, would it seem, did the Allies object: it had been "obvious from the beginning," noted the *China Press*, "that Americans would run the Tokyo Trial." Australians, in fact, expected the United States, with British assistance, to supervise matters.[13]

Occupation policy aimed initially at the demilitarization of Japan. It sought to "eliminate for all time" militaristic elements from Japanese government and society, while simultaneously encouraging moderate elements and inculcating democratic principles. From the start American occupation authorities envisaged war crimes trials as contributing to both these objectives. By removing those militaristic and reactionary forces, they would clear the way for the re-emergence of progressive forces.[14]

Furthermore, the Japanese public would witness firsthand democratic principles in action. Remarkable alone, said SCAP officials, was the fact "that so soon after the cessation of hostilities . . . the victors set up military commissions, not for the purpose of meting out sentences in revenge . . . but for the purpose of ascertaining the guilt or innocence of the accused after a fair and impartial trial. . . ." The entire trial records, they concluded, would stand as "monuments to the fair manner in which the war crimes program in the Far East was handled."[15]

In the meantime more idealistic motives surfaced. Never before in the history of humanity had the reality of global interdependence appeared so marked as with the outbreak of World War II. Vast oceans and land spaces no longer isolated nations from the rest of the world; aerial bombardment made traditional protective measures obsolete. "We are all in the same boat now," President Roosevelt had responded to Winston Churchill's query concerning initial reports of the Japanese assault on Pearl Harbor.[16]

Such sentiments persisted after the war. Only through realization of the concept of "One World," admonished Wendell Willkie, the Republican candidate for president in 1940, could the United States "win the peace" as well as the war.[17] Moreover, Harry Hopkins, FDR's personal adviser, left the Yalta conference of February 1945 convinced that the Allies—"*all* of us, the whole civilized human race"—"could live peacefully" indefinitely. Secretary Hull believed that a new age of international relations had dawned, one freed of traditional power struggles and based upon an identity of interests.[18]

Perhaps of greatest importance was the "vision" of world peace espoused by Franklin Roosevelt. As Franz Schurmann, a distinguished writer on international affairs, commented, "when the President of the United States talks of 'one world,' all listen because he [alone] has the power to attempt to bring it about."[19]

To many, postwar trials represented the "powerful confirmation of the world's faith in justice as the foundation of peace." Certainly not everyone agreed.[20] Undoubtedly, though, the creators and supporters of the Charters of the International Military Tribunals at Nuremberg and Tokyo believed that they acted in the best interests of the whole of civilized humanity. Accordingly, the prosecution at Tokyo strove foremost "to advance the cause of peace and right notions of international law." In this manner it hoped to further enable "men in their international associations, to fashion one world. . . ."[21] That was 1945–1946.

With these factors in mind, we now turn to the most publicized and controversial of all Japanese war crimes trials, that of Hideki Tojo et al.

2. The International Military Tribunal for the Far East: Trial and Judgment

Trial

At Nuremberg major Nazi leaders stood before a military tribunal composed of representatives of the Big Four—America, Britain, France and Russia. By itself, this was not unprecedented; many times in the past victors in a war had held members of the losing side legally and morally accountable for war crimes. What rendered this a truly unique historical and international event, however, was the Allies' expanded definition and application of the term "war crimes." Departing from past practice, the Allies chose not to restrict the term solely to violations of the laws and usages of war or, perhaps more broadly, to offenses against civilian populations. Instead, after some initial disagreement, Allied authorities expanded the definition of war crimes so as to include and underscore the "greatest" crime against world civilization: the plotting and waging of an aggressive war. Moreover, they added, individuals and not merely states or governments could and would be held responsible for this crime.[1]

As many authors have commented on the general similarities shared by the Tokyo and Nuremberg tribunals as have stressed their basic distinctions.[2] Some have discovered substantial significance in the Tokyo Trial, designating it the "Far Eastern counterpart" of the Nuremberg hearing. Not so with others. "The war crimes trials conducted at Tokyo," observed a recent study, "were little more than an echo of the far more famous proceedings held at Nuremberg." Whatever else may be said, one truth cannot be denied: the "objectives" of the IMTFE, in the words of one of the participants, "closely parallel[ed] those of the German trial." Accordingly, the indictment lodged against major Japanese war criminal suspects "followed the general pattern of the Nuremberg document."[3]

Steps toward creating an International Military Tribunal for the trial of major Japanese war criminals began almost immediately after surrender. A United States Joint Chiefs of Staff (JCS) directive forwarded to the supreme commander, General MacArthur, on September 22, 1945, included detailed instructions regarding the prosecution of Japanese war criminal suspects and establishment of such a tribunal.[4]

Within a fortnight of Japan's surrender, SCAP's Legal Section commenced the process of apprehending major war criminals throughout the archipelago.[5] Responsibility for the investigation and prosecution of cases against these individuals devolved upon the International Prosecution Section (IPS) of SCAP, established on December 8, 1945. From the outset this proved a formidable task, as Allied war crimes teams struggled confusedly in their attempt to identify, locate and arrest suspects. The fact that many Japanese, in panic and self-defense, had "destroyed, altered or secreted" incriminating documents just prior to the American landing compounded prosecution difficulties and made the construction of tenable cases that much harder.[6]

President Truman appointed Joseph B. Keenan, a former assistant to the attorney general, as chief prosecutor at Tokyo on November 30, 1945. Keenan, an ardent New Dealer, had earned the label "Joe the Key" in Washington circles. As FDR's "liaison to the U.S. Senate," he had exercised "considerable influence pertaining to financing executive projects (including the Tokyo trial) of importance to Truman following [Roosevelt's] demise." Indeed, "King-Maker" Keenan's talent for "getting things done" had been instrumental in Truman's appointment. Now, as head of the IPS, he operated under "presidential orders of equal weight" to those of SCAP. Under his guidance, American officials hoped, a coherent prosecution staff and case would emerge. In accordance with the JCS directive which ordained that trials of major war criminals be held before an international tribunal, the supreme commander promulgated on January 19, 1946, the establishment of the International Military Tribunal for the Far East.[7]

United States authorities made an attempt to include the other Allied nations in the policy-making process. For one thing, the initial directive to MacArthur had won previous approval "by all nations taking part in the occupation of Japan." For another, Allied action taken at the Moscow Conference in December 1945 led to the founding of the Far Eastern Commission. On April 3, 1946, the FEC approved a policy decision on the "Apprehension, Trial and

Punishment of War Criminals in the Far East." This decision substantially embodied the instructions laid down in the JCS directive. Furthermore, it provided a definition of the term "war crimes" which, *inter alia*, embraced the interpretation of class "A" or major offenses which had been applied at Nuremberg.[8] And concerted Allied efforts, discussed below, produced a positively multinational indictment.

The supreme commander's "special proclamation" of January 19, 1946, also established the Charter of the IMTFE. Like that of Nuremberg, the Tokyo instrument defined the jurisdiction of the tribunal as well as the legal procedure to be followed at the forthcoming trial. Initially drawn up "in its entirety" by American personnel within the IPS, the Charter later underwent amendment to accommodate suggestions offered by Allied prosecutors and the changes "necessitated" by the FEC policy decision. Nevertheless the amended Charter, issued April 26, 1946, contained only minor revisions, most notably an amendment enabling each FEC member to nominate a justice and an associate prosecutor to the tribunal. Thus might non-signers of the Instrument of Surrender, particularly India and the Philippines, be represented.[9]

"For the just and prompt trial and punishment of the major war criminals in the Far East," read the opening article of the Charter, the Allied powers created the IMTFE. Its bench consisted of "not less than six members nor more than eleven members," appointed by the supreme commander. He selected his appointees from names "submitted by the Signatories of the Instrument of Surrender." The supreme commander, in addition, appointed one member (Sir William Webb, Australia) to preside over the tribunal, a secretariat, and all necessary "assistant secretaries, clerks, interpreters, and other personnel."[10]

Six members of the tribunal constituted a quorum. All decisions, "including convictions and sentences," required majority vote "of those members of the Tribunal present." Absence of a judge, even for a prolonged period, did not disqualify him from subsequent proceedings, unless he declared openly an "insufficient familiarity" with events which took place in his absence.[11]

Article 5 of the Charter empowered the tribunal to try and punish Japanese charged with war crimes, including "a. Crimes against Peace: Namely, the planning, preparation, initiation or waging of a declared or undeclared war of aggression, or a war in violation of international law, treaties, agreements or assurances, or participation in a common plan or conspiracy for the accomplishment of any of the foregoing." The IMTFE also exercised jurisdiction over so-called class "B" and "C" offenses: that is, conventional war crimes or "violations of the laws or customs of war"; and crimes against humanity or "inhuman acts committed before or during the war," mainly against civilian populations other than the Japanese. In adopting this definition of war crimes the IMTFE closely hewed to lines drawn by its Nuremberg predecessor. The IMTFE, however, insisted that *only* persons "charged with offenses which include[d] crimes against peace" stand before it; all others were to be tried by national or other courts. The Nuremberg Charter contained "no such exclusive provision."[12]

That he acted in accordance with his "official position" or "pursuant to order of his government or of a superior" did not by itself free an accused from responsibility for crimes alleged. Yet "such circumstances," stated article 6, might "be considered in mitigation of punishment" if so determined as just by the tribunal.

A separate section of the Charter outlined provisions designed "to insure fair trial for the accused." Japanese on trial enjoyed a number of protective guarantees, including the presentation, "in adequate time for defense," of a clearly worded public indictment listing each offense charged; trial proceedings conducted in English and Japanese; translation of all necessary documents and evidence; "the right to be represented by counsel of his own selection," subject to approval by the tribunal, or by court-appointed counsel; and the right "to conduct his defense," including freedom to examine and call witnesses and to request the production of evidence.[13]

Article 13 dealt at length with the question of evidence. At Tokyo as at Nuremberg, the Allies recognized the unique character of war crimes trials and the need, consequently, to relax the ordinarily strict rules of evidence. Thereupon the IMTFE extended its scope beyond the boundaries set by the "technical rules of evidence," adopting and applying "to the greatest possible extent expeditious and non-technical procedure and admit[ting] any evidence which it deem[ed] to have probative value." In brief, it admitted any information which served in any way to prove or disprove the charges. This included any government document or report by the International Red Cross which "appeared" genuine to the tribunal; any affidavit, deposition or signed statement; any diary, letter or statement, sworn or unsworn; copies of the above; and hearsay.[14]

This basic position toward admission of evidence first received expression in a special proclamation by President Roosevelt in July 1942. Military commissions for the trial of war criminals, FDR said at that time, should admit evidence "as would, in the opinion of the President of the Commission, have probative value to a reasonable man."[15] By no means, though, should one conclude that Americans forced or pressured their Allies into accepting this philosophy of admissibility. The reality of the situation disposed of the need for external persuasion.

Rapid demobilization and repatriation of ex-POWs, witnesses and evidence scattered literally throughout the world, wholesale destruction of key documents by Japanese, incredible difficulties in identifying, locating and apprehending suspects in Japan proper and East Asia and other factors combined to render nearly impossible the tasks given to Allied prosecutors. Any attempt to abide meticulously by strict evidentiary rules applicable to municipal courts would have precluded the majority of war crimes trials and delayed interminably those deemed triable. The English perceived this fact. It was one thing to adhere to strict rules of evidence in civil courts, maintained Lord Maugham, an expert on international law "but quite another thing . . . when you have got to get eyewitnesses from all over the Continent who are subject to entirely different ideas of law. . . ." Lord Roche agreed with his parliamentary colleague that war crimes trials should "be bound simply by ordinary opinions of fairness and justice. . . ." Other Allied officials expressed similar views.[16]

Finally, a section of the Charter referred to "Judgment and Sentences." Following a reasoned judgment read aloud in open court, the IMTFE imposed, upon conviction, penalties of death or any other punishment determined just. For a final review, the trial record was transmitted to the supreme commander, who might "at any time reduce or otherwise alter the sentence, except to increase its severity."[17]

Each FEC member dispatched to Tokyo an associate prosecutor, and ultimately a total of seventy-two lawyers served in the IPS.[18] Allied authorities also created an International Defense Staff. From the outset Allied officials assumed that the Japanese defendants would prefer distinguished lawyers from their own country serving as defense counsel. For the most part this proved true. However, unfamiliarity with basic Western legal concepts, Americans felt, would place Japanese lawyers at a definite disadvantage in a trial decidedly Western in procedure and style. To offset this, the United States provided a pool of attorneys "to assist Japanese counsel." Six of the American lawyers resigned in June 1946 because, noted reports, "they had been unable to set up a workable defense organization." Thereafter each American attorney represented one or more defendants.[19] Nevertheless Japanese and American lawyers at Tokyo furnished the accused extraordinarily sound and forceful defenses.

After much deliberation and preparation, Allied prosecutors lodged an indictment against twenty-eight Japanese on April 29, 1946. The document consisted of fifty-five counts, divided into three sections: under the heading "Crimes against Peace" stood counts 1 to 36; under the title "Murder" were counts 37 to 52; and under the title "Other Conventional War Crimes and Crimes against Humanity" fell counts 53 to 55.[20]

Though "largely a British document," the indictment, an American attorney realistically observed, "had to be a compromise between the eleven legal systems represented." "The result," he continued, "was not a document of which an American lawyer would be proud"; still, in the end "it fairly apprised the accused of the offenses with which they were charged."[21] Actually, recalled a former Tokyo prosecutor, "virtually all of the trial counsel [in the IPS] had input into the indictment." Each participating prosecutor, noted Robert Donihi, "had to sign it for his nation"; "Allied concurrence" —not the fiat of any one person, even Keenan or MacArthur—was required for major decisions, such as the selecting of defendants. The "final assemblage" of numerous allied ideas and suggestions into a coherent, operative document by Arthur S. Comyns-Carr, Britain's chief prosecutor, accounted for the indictment's predominantly Anglo-Saxon tenor.[22]

Indicted were twenty-eight Japanese, who had all, with two exceptions, occupied the highest government and military posts at some time between 1928 and 1945. The register of defendants included former officials: four prime ministers, four foreign ministers, five war ministers, two navy ministers, a lord keeper of the privy seal, and four ambassadors, among others. The twenty-eight indicted were: Sadao Araki; Kenji Doihara; Kingoro Hashimoto; Shunroku Hata; Kiichiro Hiranuma; Koki Hirota; Naoki Hoshino; Seishiro Itagaki; Okinori Kaya; Koichi Kido; Heitaro Kimura; Kuniaki Koiso; Iwane Matsui; Yosuke Matsuoka; Jiro Minami; Akira Muto; Osami Nagano; Takasumi Oka; Shumei Okawa; Hiroshi Oshima; Kenryo Sato; Mamoru Shigemitsu; Shigetaro Shimada; Toshio Shiratori; Teiichi Suzuki; Shigenori Togo; Hideki Tojo; and Yoshijiro Umezu.[23]

The Allies spent long hours deciding which Japanese to prosecute. Patently, they perceived, only a symbolic handful could be brought at one time before the international tribunal. Too many defendants would prolong the trial, perhaps indefinitely. War crimes trials policy constituted an integral element of the Allied objective to demilitarize and democratize Japan and to restore stability to East Asia as soon as possible. Swift prosecution and disposition of trials, therefore, became essential.[24]

Above all, to its proponents, the IMTFE—what it represented and what its creators hoped to achieve through it—far surpassed in significance the individuals on trial. From the start the prosecution focused, not merely on punishing the guilty, but upon "the grander and wider aim" of advancing "the cause of peace and right notions of international law." Indeed, said President Truman, "for the first time in history, the legal culpability of war-makers" would be determined at Tokyo as at Nuremberg.[25] Throughout the IMTFE, references to its historical and legal importance emanated from the bench, and from defense and prosecution staffs. Few knowledgeable persons overlooked the trial's potential deterrent effect.[26]

The Tokyo Trial, noted others, served additional purposes. As the most publicized Eastern war crimes trial, it would effectively, if shockingly, "bare" to the Japanese public for the first time the misdeeds perpetrated by their soldiers and leaders. Such exposure, insisted the *Tokyo Shimbun*, was necessary to "dispel militarism from the minds of the people." SCAP officials, too, discerned the urgent need to "educate" a Japanese public hitherto screened from such unpalatable information by more than a decade of official censorship.[27] Beyond this, the *London Times* believed that the IMTFE "should place on unchallengeable record the facts required by history for a moral judgment on the origin and conduct of the war...." To *The New York Times*, the Tokyo Trial transcended in significance the guilt or innocence of any individual. "Actually," it observed, "it is a way of life—the Japanese way—that will go on trial...."[28]

Influenced by such sentiments, the Executive Committee of the IPS selected defendants on the following bases: one, that they could be charged with crimes against peace; two, that they were "representative," both of various organs of the Japanese government (for example, the cabinet, general staff) and of different chronological "phases" in the "conspiracy"; three, that they had assumed positions of "principal" leadership and had had "primary" responsibility for violations charged; and four, that only "negligible" chances of their being acquitted existed.[29] This last point may be regarded as caution and not prejudgment, as some have intimated, on the part of the Allies. An early SCAP policy instructed prosecutors to be "absolutely sure" of a case's tenability before going to trial.[30]

Allied prosecutors excluded from indictment any representative of the Japanese industrial group, or *zaibatsu*. Unable to attribute crimes against peace to the *zaibatsu*, the Executive Committee forwent their indictment despite evidence that certain industrialists had participated in other violations.[31]

Emperor Hirohito, too, escaped indictment. Announced June 18, 1946, this strictly American decision caused perhaps more furor in Allied circles than any other relative to war crimes policy.[32] Immediately after Japan's surrender a multitude of demands that Hirohito be tried as a war criminal inundated, often to the point of embarrassment, SCAP Headquarters and Washington. They flowed from a wide, often disparate, range of sources: government officials in Canberra, Wellington, Chungking, Moscow, Manila and Washington itself;[33] newspapers, such as *The New York Times*, *Straits (Singapore) Times*, and *Stars and Stripes* (Shanghai);[34] private organizations, such as the Institute of Pacific Relations; and the Japanese Communist Party.[35]

Some American officials at first sought to explain or justify this decision by exculpating Hirohito from war guilt: a military clique had "seized the power of Japan and defrauded the Japanese people into believing that the Emperor was behind the war," argued Chief Prosecutor Keenan at the trial. The emperor had been merely a "figurehead," contended an associate prosecutor years later.[36] In more forthright fashion, however, Keenan conceded in an interview given in 1950 that, "strictly legally," Hirohito could have been tried and convicted as a war criminal.[37]

In fact, Americans conceived the granting of immunity to Hirohito as a calculated political decision undertaken in the best interests of the Allied powers. The initial directive ordering the SCAP to set up the IMTFE, *The New York Times* disclosed for the first time in 1949, had "specifically prohibited prosecution of Hirohito." That decision, originating at the highest governmental levels, harmonized "with the course advised by United States experts on Japanese affairs" to Presidents Roosevelt and Truman. General MacArthur, according to this report, had not been consulted "prior to issuance of the order."[38] Still, MacArthur had placed his view of the subject clearly on record: "destroy" the emperor, he asserted forcefully on January 25, 1946, "and the [Japanese] nation will disintegrate."[39]

Abolition of the sacred (to Japanese) institution of emperor, American policymakers reasoned, would have provoked chaos, even violence, among the population. Such reaction would have made a Japanese surrender "impossible" and would have "multipl[ied] the difficulties of the occupation." Necessitated then, said MacArthur, would be a larger occupation force for a longer—perhaps "indefinite"—period of time.[40] More important, United States occupation policy intended to "use the existing form of government in Japan," albeit not supporting it. That is, the Japanese government was to serve as "executor" of American policy.[41]

But in the immediate postwar period, what legitimate Japanese government existed? Apprehension of war criminal suspects and the purging of thousands of former government officials and employees, bureaucrats and industrialists had stripped Japan of much of its leadership. Occupation authorities, indeed, experienced ample difficulty finding an acceptable individual, untainted by past militaristic or reactionary ties, to head the first postwar government. Remove the emperor and not even a symbolic Japanese government around which the people could unite remained. Consequently occupation policy would have been severely crippled from the start. As the *London Times'* Tokyo correspondent put it, Hirohito's "retention on the throne was necessary to prevent an administrative collapse."[42]

Ostensibly, Allied leaders recognized and accepted this reality. For *The New York Times* reported that "all eleven Allies, including Russia, [had in 1946] agreed to exempt Hirohito from prosecution." Alas, it took three years for this "secret" decision to come to light.[43] The Japanese government, noteworthily, at the time and years later, praised the American-sponsored action.[44]

And how, in Allied eyes, did Hirohito's immunity affect the status of those Japanese on trial at Tokyo? Arthur S. Comyns-Carr, the British prosecutor, found "it difficult to understand . . . how the Emperor's absence from the dock can have any bearing upon the cases of those who were there." Beyond that, assessed the *London Times*, "both Japanese and Allied observers" felt that the group arraigned at Tokyo "could scarcely have included a more typical selection of the men who are held responsible for the Pacific War."[45]

In any event, thus composed were the dock, bench, defense and prosecution staffs at the IMTFE. On May 3, 1946, the twenty-eight defendants, looking frail and worn, "shuffled into the renovated auditorium of the War Ministry Building for their arraignment." A courtroom packed with one hundred Allied and Japanese correspondents and five hundred Allied officers of high rank and spectators observed intently. "To our great task we bring open minds both on the facts and the law," announced President Webb. "The onus will be on the prosecution to establish guilt beyond a reasonable doubt." All the accused pleaded not guilty, and the trial was scheduled to begin on June 3.[46]

At this embryonic stage the IMTFE attracted global attention. "History," cautioned *The New York Times*,[47] "will judge these trials wholly by whether the victors themselves adhere to the standards and the laws they impose upon the vanquished. In judging the vanquished, the victors also judge themselves." Justice demanded, averred the *London Times*, "a full hearing, whose absolute fairness neither [those on trial] nor their countrymen can dispute." The "defendants must be considered innocent" until proven guilty, insisted the *China Press;* "every opportunity to clear themselves, if they can do so," must be afforded.[48] Doubtless the prospect of contemporary and future international scrutiny weighed heavily on the consciousness of all concerned with the IMTFE, whether they were members of the prosecution, defense or bench.

Preliminary motions filed by the defendants challenged the jurisdiction of the IMTFE under the Potsdam Declaration and the Instrument of Surrender. Thus raised were "the most fundamental issues of the trial—whether aggressive war was a crime in international law; whether killing in the course of an aggressive war constituted murder; whether there was individual responsibility for international crimes." The tribunal denied the motions, reserving explanation for its final judgment.[49]

Following presentation of its opening statement on May 3, the prosecution began its evidence on June 3, 1946, and closed on January 24, 1947, consuming 192 days in all. Allied prosecutors during this period brought forth 102 witnesses, affidavits from another 1,200 witnesses and an additional 1,000 documents. "Because of the difficulty with Japanese witnesses, the prosecution tried to keep its case as far as possible a documented case on the theory that such a case is best." In fact, the diary of one of the defendants, Marquis Kido, lord keeper of the privy seal, "became the working bible of the prosecution" throughout the trial.[50]

From the very outset language difficulties prolonged the proceedings. A language and clerical staff of 104 Allied nationals and 154 Japanese and special preparation notwithstanding, simultaneous translation proved impossible. Thereupon counsel posed only short, simple questions to witnesses. Later the court approved written presentations prepared in advance.[51] Obviously, such practices severely limited the scope and effectiveness of cross-examination for both prosecution and defense.[52]

In early remarks, prosecutors defined the IMTFE as "no ordinary trial" but rather as "a part of the determined battle of civilization to preserve the entire world from destruction." The accused had taken "the law into their own hands . . . to force their will upon mankind. They declared war on civilization." That their "design" to secure "domination and control of East Asia" and "ultimately the world" "meant murder and the subjugation and enslavement of millions was of no moment to them."[53]

Between 1928 and 1941, contended the prosecution, the accused and others conspired to gain control of the Japanese government. Through this control they prepared and indoctrinated the Japanese people "for a program of aggressive warfare." Evidence adduced at the trial, prosecutors submitted, disclosed irrefutably that "from 1928 to 1941 each change in [the Japanese] government was brought about either to further the common plan or to meet a situation created by some act furthering the plan."[54] Subsequent and concurrent aggressions aimed at China, and later at the other Allies, represented the implementation of the accused's "conspiracy."[55]

Long established in international law, asserted the prosecution, was the right of a belligerent to try members of the armed forces of the losing side for conventional war crimes. In fact, the defense basically conceded this point.[56] Granted, "for the first time in history" individuals were being charged with personal responsibility for offenses "committed while acting in official capacity as chiefs of state." Nonetheless, prosecutors argued, the time had come to free civilized society from the "straightjacket" of precedent and expand the concept of individual responsibility from conventional war crimes to crimes against peace and humanity.[57] Inability to punish persons who had "already . . . brought civilization to the brink of disaster" would render justice "a mockery."[58]

Moreover, in the decades prior to World War II "express" and "implied"—written and customary—"recognitions of the illegality and criminality of aggressive or unjust war on the part of nations" had "accumulated." This "resulted in such a well-established international legal custom as to put the defendants on sufficient notice that their actions were in violation of a norm of conduct which the society of nations might enforce by criminal punishment." Prosecutors cited the Hague Convention of 1907, the Geneva Conventions of 1925 and 1929 and especially the Kellogg-Briand Pact of

1928 as proof of such international recognition. As the war the defendants had practiced had been aggressive and illegal, any deaths attributable thereto constituted "murder."[59] Some may have thought it "strange to include charges of murder in an indictment before an international trial," acknowledged Chief Prosecutor Keenan. Nevertheless, he believed it was "high-time" that "the promoters of aggressive and ruthless war" be revealed "as what they really are— plain, ordinary murderers."[60]

Prosecutors, furthermore, disagreed with the defense's contention that their position contravened *ex post facto* principle. The laws and customs of war, peace and humanity, prosecutors argued, existed well before the Charter of the IMTFE and were "incorporated" into it. The Charter, that is, expressed existing law; it produced no new law. Though "nonstatutory," the defendants' crimes constituted violations of "customary" international law and treaties. Article 10 of the Potsdam Declaration, importantly, referred to "all war criminals," not just those who violated the laws and customs of war. Above all, explained Allied prosecutors, the IMTFE's jurisdiction to try and punish war criminals sprang not from the Potsdam Declaration but from a "body of international criminal law which existed before the acts of the defendants."[61]

Allied prosecutors also assailed the accused for their part in the commission or, more accurately, the allowance of conventional war crimes. Atrocities perpetrated against POWs and civilian populations by Japanese armed forces had occurred on such a wide-scale and regular basis that, prosecution held, the defendants must have or should have known of them.[62]

In its summation, the prosecution piercingly readdressed a major element of the defense case, the claim that Japan had gone to war in self-defense. Chief Prosecutor Keenan argued:

> While there has been much talk by the accused of their having acted in self-defense, it is significant that no one has claimed a threat from any power to attack or invade the Empire of Japan. In these many long months of trial there has been not a single scrap of evidence tendered worthy of the name in support of any such defense. . . . We reject the contention that it is self-defense for a nation to attack another because the latter refuses to supply materials of war to be used against it and its allies.

Keenan thereupon urged the judges to mete out "the sternest punishment known to law" to all twenty-five Japanese on trial (two defendants, Matsuoka and Nagano, had died during the trial; one,

Okawa, had been determined mentally unfit). Repeatedly, he reminded the court of the long-range potential of their verdict in deterring further war. Then the prosecution rested.[63]

On February 4, 1947, the defense commenced its case. It lasted, uninterruptedly, until June 23 of that year. To avoid repetitious evidence "on behalf of two or more defendants and at the same time to preserve the individual interest of each defendant, defense counsel adopted a joint plan of presentation." Such practice, though, buttressed and did not exclude individual presentation.[64]

Existing international law, argued defense counsel Kenzo Takayanagi, "one of the most brilliant minds in Japan," recognized only conventional war crimes. "The punishment of crimes against peace in violation of treaties," he asserted, "has never been known to the laws of nations." Nor had war ever been held illegal. The "thesis that an aggressive war involves criminality either on the part of a responsible State or on the part of responsible individual members of a State" contradicted the "practice of nations." In wars, Takayanagi reasoned, each side invariably labeled the other the aggressor." The epithet, however, stuck to the defeated nation: ". . . will the victor ever admit that it was the aggressor?"[65]

The notion of personal criminal responsibility for the plotting and waging of war in violation of international law constituted, said the defense, "a perfectly revolutionary doctrine." Such interpretation had "been expressly denied by the consensus of international jurists as well as by the customs of nations. . . ."[66] Certainly, then, the prosecution's attempt to expand after the fact the "natural and universally accepted meaning" of the term "war crimes" violated *ex post facto* doctrine as well as all reasonable definitions of justice. Notions of "criminal conspiracy" rested firmly (and uniquely) in Anglo-Saxon, not international, legal tradition, defense counsel purposefully reminded; it clearly did not represent "law at the time of the commission of the alleged acts. . . ."[67]

Also, Japan had not surrendered unconditionally, contended Ichiro Kiyose, Tojo's counsel, but "under the terms of the Potsdam Declaration." Therefore, he proceeded, Japan's leaders warranted different treatment from that afforded German leaders after World War I. For the latter had signed the Versailles Treaty, which specified that the Kaiser would stand trial.[68] Furthermore, Takayanagi charged Allied authorities with failure adequately to forewarn the defendants of their intentions. The Potsdam Declaration referred only to "war criminals"; the defendants obviously assumed, went

this argument, that such allusion embraced exclusively conventional war crimes.[69]

A "major theme" of the defense case revolved around the contention that Japan had acted in self-defense. Generally, ran this assertion, the United States had acted the part of the aggressor, in
its insistence that Japan withdraw from China, in its supplying of
aid to China and in its fortification of Pearl Harbor.[70] "Japan's
planned economy and military and naval preparations prior to the
fall of 1941" Kiyose called "defensive in nature and . . . not undertaken in anticipation of the Pacific War." He stressed the "iron
ring of encirclement thrown around Japan by the several powers"
and the devastating effects on Japan's economy of the Allies' freez-
ing of its assets. Above all, he censured the inflexible and unsympa-
thetic American negotiating demands which ultimately frustrated
"Japan's will to peace, Japan's sincere effort to attain peaceful settlement. . . ."[71]

Prime Minister Tojo, in a 50,000-word written statement and,
impressively, under cross-examination, echoed these sentiments.
He accepted full responsibility for his and Japan's actions. In fact,
to use *The New York Times'* phrase, Tojo "indicted" the Allied nations for their economic blockade and military encirclement which,
he accused, had brought Japan in 1941 "to the point of annihila-
tion" and compelled it to fire the first shot in order to preserve
its "national existence."[72]

Along similar lines, American defense counsel argued that Allied behavior in the prewar period had not departed fundamentally
from Japan's. Continual and widespread disregard of treaties and
international agreements, particularly the Kellogg-Briand Pact, rendered these documents practically "worthless." "Pacts may fall into
desuetude by repeated violations," emphasized Major Ben Blakeney.
And the Kellogg Pact, explained Takayanagi, recognized the right of
sovereign nations to act as necessary in self-defense and also that
each country remained the "sole judge of what constituted self-
defense."[73]

Prosecution's notion of a fourteen-year criminal conspiracy,
countered the defense, rested on absurd assumptions and was rid-
dled with inconsistencies. Not only had the accused disagreed at
times with one another, but many had vigorously opposed certain
acts or the war itself. Many events coincidental to the collapse of
fifteen different Japanese cabinets between 1928 and 1941 occurred
fortuitously or unrelatedly, and concerned innumerable persons

with broadly divergent interests. To theorize about an "organized plan," challenged the defense, defied all reason.[74]

So, too, with charges of conventional war crimes. Atrocities, maintained Takayanagi and Kiyose, "were the sporadic acts of local officers of inferior rank." "Had such a central or overall policy existed," as the prosecution suggested, "it would have been applied uniformly and always everywhere" instead of "merely in a few isolated places."[75] Additional defenses presented at Tokyo included that of superior orders, which held that obedience to lawful orders did not constitute a crime, and that it extended beyond the capacity of victor nations to afford the vanquished a fair trial.[76]

If the acts of Japan's political leaders "constitute criminal offenses" under international law, then, advised Takayanagi, "American, British and Soviet leaders in similar situations should also be subjected to penalties. . . ." "Unless it is proved beyond a reasonable doubt that they committed some criminal offense known to the established law of nations," he continued, the accused "must be declared innocent." This, basically, constituted the defense case. On April 16, 1948, "the last word was said . . . in history's longest trial." Indeed, the transcript of the record by then consumed over 48,000 pages. The IMTFE adjourned for deliberation.[77]

Judgment

Not for seven months did the world learn the Judgment at Tokyo. On November 4, 1948, the eleven international jurists, after analyzing the enormous collection of evidence introduced at the trial, reconvened the IMTFE to render their decision on Japan's twenty-five major war criminals.

After reading aloud in court the lengthy majority opinion, President Webb announced the verdicts on November 12. All twenty-five defendants were found guilty. Tojo, former Foreign/Prime Minister Hirota and five generals received death sentences. Sixteen defendants received life imprisonment. One, former Foreign Minister Togo, received twenty years' confinement; another, former Foreign Minister Shigemitsu, seven years' confinement. In addition, five separate opinions emerged. Despite "vigorous protest" by defense counsel, the tribunal refused to read in open court the three dissenting opinions.[78]

The Judgment comprised 1,218 pages, of which the bulk, some

Bench of IMTFE. August 5, 1946. National Archives. Neg. no. 238–FE–46–66827.

1,050, was devoted to a detailed historical survey of Japan from 1928 to 1945. The actual judgment of the accused covered 7 pages and the reasoning behind individual verdicts, 82 pages.

From the outset the tribunal addressed defense challenges concerning jurisdictional matters, especially such issues as the unprecedented nature—and therefore invalidity—of the IMTFE and several of the charges in the indictment. The IMTFE, it stated, "derives its jurisdiction from the Charter. . . ," and the law of that instrument "is decisive and binding on the Tribunal." Such action did not represent an "arbitrary exercise of power on the part of the victorious nations," held the majority; nor had any new law been created as a result. Instead, here quoting its Nuremberg predecessor, the tribunal maintained that the Charter merely expressed "international law existing at the time of its creation." [79]

It mattered not that never before had individuals been held criminally responsible for acts of state, or for plotting and waging a "war of aggression." "The maxim *'nullem crimen sine lege'* [there is

Prisoners' dock and defense section at IMTFE. May 14, 1946. National Archives. Neg. no. 238–FE–46–65691.

no crime if there is no law]," the tribunal held, "is not a limitation on sovereignty but in general a principle of justice." In fact, averred the tribunal, "far from it being unjust to punish [those deemed guilty] it would be unjust" if they "were allowed to go unpunished."[80]

The majority accepted the prosecution's contention that a body of international law, customary if not statutory, had evolved in the decades prior to World War II. Japan had "voluntarily incurred . . . obligations designed to further the cause of peace" by participating, to varying degrees, in a host of international treaties, agreements and conferences, especially the Kellogg-Briand Pact of 1928. By signing, while not ratifying, the latter Japan had accepted "the solemn renunciation of war as an instrument of national policy."[81]

Surely, stated the majority, "the Japanese Government, who advised the acceptance of terms of surrender," understood the term "war criminals" as it applied in the Potsdam Declaration to mean Japan's highest political and military leaders. Here the Judgment cited an entry of August 10, 1945—four days prior to the surrender

Full court reconvenes for reading of IMTFE Judgment. November 4, 1948. National Archives. Neg. no. 238–FE–48–9115.

—in the Kido diary. Then the emperor had told Kido, "I could not bear the sight . . . of those responsible for the war being punished . . . but I think now is the time to bear the unbearable."[82]

Furthermore, the tribunal concluded that Japan had launched aggressive wars against certain Allied powers. Certainly, it reasoned, those initiated on December 7, 1941, against Britain, the United States and the Netherlands constituted aggressive wars, "whatever may be the difficulty of stating a comprehensive definition" of that phrase. "Unprovoked attacks, prompted by the desire to seize the possessions of these nations"—as these were—"cannot but be characterized as such."[83] And because "the waging of aggressive war was unlawful killing," determined the majority, defendants convicted under counts 39 to 52 of the indictment were guilty of "murder."[84]

The tribunal also discarded certain defendants' claims to special treatment under the Geneva Convention of 1929. Here it cited at length the United States Supreme Court in re the appeal of General Yamashita, that said Convention applied only to "judicial proceedings directed against a prisoner of war for offenses committed while a prisoner of war."[85]

Arguments that Japan had acted in self-defense the Judgment dismissed outright. Measures taken by the Allied powers to restrict Japanese trade were intended to induce Japan to abandon a course of aggression and expansion embarked upon years before. As such, the tribunal found Allied actions justifiable. Going further, it pointed out that Japanese aggression had well preceded any Allied economic countermeasures.[86]

A substantial portion (over 130 pages) of the Judgment dealt with conventional war crimes. Here several key factors were underscored. First, of 235,000 American and British POWs taken by German and Italian armies during World War II, 4% died in captivity; of 132,000 taken by the Japanese Army, 27% died in captivity. Second, the Allies and Protecting Powers had lodged with Japanese governmental authorities numerous "formal and informal protests and warnings against violations of the laws of war" during the Pacific conflict. Granted, determined the tribunal, Japan had only signed, not ratified, the 1929 Geneva Convention on the Protection of POWs. Nevertheless, in 1942 Foreign Minister Togo had assured the Allied powers that, "while not formally bound by the Convention, Japan would apply" its provisions "*mutatis mutandis.*"[87]

Such an overwhelming amount of indisputable evidence had been presented to it, concluded the tribunal, that it proved "atrocities committed in all theaters of war on a scale so vast, yet following so common a pattern in all theaters, that only one conclusion is possible—the atrocities were either secretly ordered or willfully permitted by the Japanese Government or individual members thereof and by the leaders of the armed forces."[88]

After redefining much more narrowly the chief conspiracy charge (count 1 in the indictment) the tribunal found "that the existence of the criminal conspiracy to wage wars of aggression as alleged in Count 1 . . . has been proved."[89] In perhaps its most pointed rebuke of the accused the tribunal asserted that Japan's

> far reaching plans for waging wars of aggression, and the prolonged and intricate preparation for a waging [of such wars] were not the work of one man. They were the work of many leaders acting in pursuance of a common plan for the achievement of a common object. That common object, that they should secure Japan's domination by preparing and waging wars of aggression, was a criminal object. Indeed no more grave crimes can be conceived of than a conspiracy to wage a war of aggression or the waging of a war of aggression, for the con-

spiracy threatens the security of the peoples of the world, and the waging disrupts it. The probable result of such a conspiracy, and the inevitable result of its execution is that death and suffering will be inflicted on countless human beings.[90]

Of the seven defendants sentenced to death by hanging (Doihara, Hirota, Itagaki, Kimura, Matsui, Muto and Tojo), the tribunal convicted all on at least one of the conventional war crimes charges.[91] In fact one, Matsui Iwane, acquitted on all counts save 55, still drew a death penalty. Matsui had been commanding officer of Japanese forces in Central China from 1937 to 1938. The tribunal found him guilty of "disregard of duty" and failure "to prevent breaches" of the laws of war in permitting the infamous Rape of Nanking.

Along with Matsui, only one other defendant (Shigemitsu) escaped conviction under count 1. He nevertheless was found guilty on five counts of aggressive war and one conventional war crimes count. He received seven years' imprisonment. Two other defendants, Hata and Koiso, drew guilty verdicts on conventional war crimes counts yet escaped the death penalty. They received life imprisonment. Two others, Oshima and Shiratori, were acquitted on all counts, save count 1; they received life imprisonment. No discernible sentencing pattern emerged. Ostensibly, the tribunal took into account many peripheral factors in determining an accused's relative guilt. For example, it convicted career diplomat and former Foreign Minister Togo on the same counts (1, 27, 29, 31, 32) as General Umezu, former commander of the Kwantung Army in Manchuria. Togo, however, received twenty years' confinement; Umezu, life.

Eight of eleven judges supported the Judgment *in toto*. Two of the majority, Justices William Webb (Australia) and Delfin Jaranilla (Philippines), submitted separate opinions. Webb fundamentally disagreed with the tribunal's concept of conspiracy. While recognizing the existence of crimes of conspiracy in Anglo-American and other legal systems, he perceived no basis in international law for the offense of "naked conspiracy." To prosecute individuals for such a generally groundless offense, he proceeded, would amount to "nothing short of judicial legislation."[92] Beyond this Webb took issue with the punishments meted out by the majority. Noting the Nuremberg Tribunal's imposition of life sentences on several accused convicted of plotting and waging aggressive war, Webb urged his brethren to follow suit, in consideration of "the fact that aggressive war was not universally regarded as a justifiable crime when [the defendants] made war."[93] Finally, what some considered the most "sensational" aspect of Webb's statement centered about the emperor's legal status. While he forwent a personal indictment of Hirohito, Webb clearly implied that the emperor's unquestioned authority in the period before, at the start of and during the war could conceivably have led to his prosecution. In all, however, Webb recorded no dissent.[94]

Jaranilla's sole disagreement with the majority judgment focused on the issue of punishments. He found a "few" of the penalties "too lenient, not exemplary and deterrent, and not commensurate with the gravity of the offense or offenses committed." "In fact," Jaranilla believed, "if any criticism should be made at all against this Tribunal, it is only that the Tribunal has acted with so much leniency in favor of the accused and has afforded them, through their counsel, all the opportunity to present any and all pertinent defenses they had, thus protracting the trial."[95]

Justices Henri Bernard (France) and Bernard V. A. Röling (Netherlands) presented partial dissents. Both upheld the IMTFE's "constitutionality" as well as the Allied nations' right to create it. To Bernard the IMTFE derived its jurisdiction from that "natural or universal law" which "exists outside and above nations." The "victorious powers," Röling determined, "are bound by the provisions of existing international law."[96] Both also praised Allied leaders for affording the vanquished a judicial proceeding rather than subjecting them to "mere political actions, based on the responsibility of power."[97]

Such sentiments notwithstanding, Bernard nevertheless found the IMTFE procedurally defective. Contrary to Continental legal procedure, no official and independent inquiry had preceded the trial. Beyond this, Bernard reproached the prosecution's "unequal and unjustified" effort, here pointing an accusing finger at the emperor, "whom the trial revealed could have been counted among the suspects and whose absence from the trial . . . was certainly detrimental to the defense of the Accused." Finally, Bernard criticized the IMTFE judges' failure to deliberate aloud and jointly prior to reaching their individual decisions.[98]

Thereupon Bernard concluded: "A verdict reached by a Tribunal after a defective procedure cannot be a valid one." Consequently, and even while conceding the responsibility of several accused for commission of conventional war crimes, Bernard reserved all judgments.[99]

Röling doubted whether the Kellogg-Briand Pact of 1928 or any other international resolution criminalized war "in the ordinary sense."[100] Yet, Röling submitted, crimes in international law "can also indicate acts comparable to political crimes in domestic law, where the decisive element is the danger rather than the guilt, where the criminal is considered an enemy rather than a villain, and where the punishment emphasizes the political measure rather than the judicial retribution." "In this sense," he believed, "the crime against peace, as formulated in the Charter [of the IMTFE], is in accordance with international law." Nonetheless Röling, citing in this instance the action taken by the Nuremberg Tribunal, felt that "no capital punishment should be given to anyone guilty of the crime against peace only." Only accused found guilty of conventional war crimes, he believed, deserved the death penalty.[101]

Röling thereupon approved eleven of the sixteen life imprisonment terms. Three of the accused who received life sentences, Oka, Sata and Shimada, Röling thought "should have been found guilty of conventional war crimes" and thus deserved the "supreme penalty." He "respectfully agree[d]" with all death penalties pronounced, save for that awarded Hirota, the diplomat and only civilian condemned. As foreign minister, Hirota "certainly had no knowledge whatsoever and could have had no knowledge, while he certainly could not have prevented . . . atrocities." Röling felt he "should have been acquitted."[102]

Similarly, Röling maintained that Hata, Kido, Shigemitsu and Togo should have escaped conviction. In Röling's mind, for example, Shigemitsu had done his best as foreign minister to prevent or halt atrocities by forwarding all relevant protests to the "proper authorities."[103] Moreover, it had been "proven beyond doubt," asserted Röling, that Togo had entered the Tojo cabinet in October 1941 with the purpose of preventing a Pacific War. Yet Togo understood that failure would result in his being forced to support the government, out of loyalty, in war. An individual who joins a government "for the sake of promoting peace," but "is forced to vote for war," Röling concluded, "cannot be accused of aggressive intent."[104]

By far the most piercing and comprehensive dissent lodged against the majority judgment flowed from the pen of Justice Radhabinod Pal of India. Pal adopted completely defense counsel's contention that no authoritative and "binding" body of international law existed prior to World War II and that no statutory or customary law had been declared or made war unlawful. Instead, it remained a "recognized rule of international life" that sovereign nations insisted on retaining complete freedom of action concerning questions vital to their existence; so, too, that nations freely resorted to "war as a legitimate instrument of self-help" whenever peaceful solutions failed.[105]

The prosecution's attempt to prove individual Japanese defendants guilty of conspiring to wage, and waging, "aggressive war" Pal deemed "preposterous" and an exercise in "victors' justice." Had not, he pointedly inquired, the USSR and the Netherlands "attacked Japan"? Were those wars aggressive? "Perhaps at the present stage of International Society the word 'aggressors' is essentially 'chamelonic' [*sic*] and may only mean the leaders of the losing party."[106]

Events leading to the Pacific War, Pal reasoned, had unfolded "gradually." He censured the tribunal's misguided attempt to prove a conspiratorial plot to capture control of the Japanese government: "the story here has been pushed a little too far, perhaps, to give it a place in the Hitler series."[107] Nor, said Pal, had "any common plan or conspiracy" existed in respect to atrocities. Violations of the laws and customs of war, even wide-scale examples such as the Rape of Nanking and the Bataan Death March, he determined, had been "all stray incidents."[108] Indeed, Pal added, "if there was anything approaching" direct orders to commit atrocities, "it is the decision coming from the Allied powers to use the atomic bomb."[109]

Pal fully accepted defense's argument that Japan—a "have-not" nation—and the defendants had acted in justifiable "self-defense." The defendants had been "really driven to take action" against Anglo-American economic measures and fortification of Pacific territorial possessions which, they truly believed, threatened Japan's survival.[110]

To Pal, international law required "unanimous agreement" among the parties concerned. It "serve[d] no useful purpose" to conduct war crimes trials of vanquished only. Such practice added nothing to "the risk of defeat" and merely served to underscore the notion of "might makes right." "If it is really law which is being applied," he advised, then also prosecute culpable "members of the victor nations."[111] Pal thereupon recommended "that each and every one of the accused . . . be found not guilty on each and every one of the charges in the indictment."[112]

Representatives of the Allied Council for Japan, General MacArthur presiding, reviewed and confirmed the IMTFE verdicts and sentences on November 24, 1948. After a brief additional review, in which he discovered no cause "to warrant [his] intervention," MacArthur directed the appropriate military authorities "to execute sentences as pronounced by the Tribunal."[113]

A final act, however, remained. On December 6 two defendants, Doihara and Hirota, won the right to a preliminary hearing before the United States Supreme Court. Less than three weeks later the Court, by a 6–1 count, rejected petitioners' central argument that the IMTFE was essentially national in character. "We are satisfied," stated the majority, "that the tribunal which sentenced these petitioners is not a tribunal of the United States," but rather an Allied creation. Thus, the Court concluded, American courts "have no authority to review, affirm" or otherwise alter its judgment or sentences.[114] Three days later, on December 23, 1948, the seven condemned Japanese were executed at Sugamo prison in Tokyo.

And so the IMTFE passed into history. Before moving on, however, several summary and other observations are in order.

Having adopted their Nuremberg predecessors' reasoning, Allied prosecutors and jurists at Tokyo elected to try major Japanese governmental and military leaders, as individuals, for violations hitherto unclearly defined in international law: specifically, for crimes against peace (that is, plotting, initiating and waging a war of aggression) and conspiracy to commit the foregoing. Japanese also stood before the IMTFE, it is true, charged with conventional war crimes and crimes against humanity. Nevertheless we must not underestimate the historical and international legal significance of the principal, that is, class "A," offenses introduced and dealt with first at Nuremberg and then at Tokyo—a significance engulfed in controversy, as dramatized by clashing views of prosecution and defense staffs, and the majority Judgment vis-à-vis dissenting opinions.

Yet, for all its importance, the IMTFE constituted but a small part of a much larger process: even prior to the Tokyo Trial's opening session, additional, related Allied war crimes efforts—by far exceeding in scope and ambition those of the IMTFE, pursued in part independently and in part jointly—were underway throughout the East. These efforts continued well beyond the IMTFE's termination, concluding in 1951. The Tokyo Tribunal, in short, was a constituent part of the entire Allied Eastern war crimes operation, albeit the most celebrated, longest, most discussed and, some felt, most important single component. Beyond that, so-called minor trials conducted elsewhere contained several features which essentially distinguished them from the IMTFE.

Allied military commissions assembled outside of Tokyo sat in judgment of Japanese accused only of class "B" and/or class "C" war crimes. While differences in national legislation arose, this definition generally comprised: (B) violations of the laws or customs of war, for example, murder; ill-treatment of civilian populations, POWs, civilian internees or hostages; plunder of public or private property, and the like and (C) crimes against humanity, such as murder, extermination, enslavement, deportation and other inhumane acts directed against civilian populations before or during the war. For practical purposes, then, classification "B" meant actual perpetrators of war crimes; classification "C," those superior officers who had formulated the plans or given the orders for, or failed to prevent, war crimes.

Allied officials in Yokohama, Singapore, Rabaul, Batavia, Manila and elsewhere beyond Tokyo forwent prosecuting class "A" war criminals, even though in most cases they were empowered to do so. Save for rare exceptions—most notably at some Chinese trials —Japanese stood before lesser tribunals charged with universally recognized, conventional war crimes as set forth in the Hague (1907), Geneva (1929) and other conventions, official Allied army manuals on the rules of land warfare, and respected texts (Hall, Oppenheim, Lauterpacht) on international law. Violations more theoretical or strictly Anglo-American in nature—such as crimes against peace and conspiracy—were generally discarded by lesser Allied military commissions. Hence those Japanese tried at the latter, so-called "small fry" war criminals, stood in marked distinction from the major, or class "A," suspects tried and convicted by the IMTFE.

And while the Tokyo hearing doubtless consumed an inordinate amount of Allied time and effort, the hundreds of Allied lesser trials involving thousands of Japanese accused consumed far more— and, therefore, are deserving of far greater attention than they have received to date. To them, and the Allied operation which enabled them, we now turn.

3. United States: Procedure and Machinery

The United States, as noted, spearheaded the investigation, apprehension and trial of Japanese war criminals. Its leaders, beginning with FDR in August 1942, were among the first explicitly to warn the Japanese that perpetrators of war crimes would be punished after the war.[1]

Meanwhile the United States joined in the creation of the UNWCC in October 1943. Later, Americans actively engaged in the founding and subsequent activities of the Chungking-based Far Eastern Sub-Committee on war crimes.[2] Under United States direction, the Far Eastern Advisory Committee (FEAC) convened in Washington in October 1945. "Recommendations" emanating from this body resulted in the "formulation of policies, principles and standards" by which Japan fulfilled its obligation of surrender.[3]

In December the FEAC was reconstituted as the Far Eastern Commission. Among its varied purposes, the FEC had due concern for the question of war crimes. A special "Committee No. 5: War Criminals" embraced all elements of the subject for consideration: identification, apprehension and trial of Japanese suspects as well as punishments for those convicted.

Later on, in April 1946, the FEC issued a "Policy Decision" designed, ostensibly, to outline if not direct Allied Eastern war crimes policy. Besides granting the SCAP and "the military command of any" Allied nation power to convene military courts for the trials of war criminals, the FEC policy decision also offered a broad definition of "war crimes" which included reference to violations generally known as "crimes against peace" and "crimes against humanity."[4]

Unlike their Allies, Americans based their jurisdiction to create military commissions for trying war criminals on statute law. Such commissions had long existed in American law, even preceding the

Constitution.[5] Their legality had recently been upheld by the Supreme Court in the so-called Saboteur case, *ex parte Quirin* (1942). The Court's decision in this case laid the foundation upon which future American military commissions—and their decisions—rested.

All congressional and presidential powers derived from the Constitution, the Court reaffirmed in its decision. This included congressional authority to "define and punish . . . offenses against the Law of Nations," of which the law of war constituted a part. Furthermore, said the Court, Congress had by statute—the Articles of War—acknowledged the military commission as a legal tribunal for the trial and punishment of violations against the law of war.

Presidential executive power, the Court further determined, provided authority to conduct such commissions. The president, as commander-in-chief of the armed forces, or any field commander competent to appoint a general court-martial, could convene a military commission.[6] President Roosevelt even declared in July 1942, by special proclamation, that any perpetrators of war crimes against the United States or its citizens "shall be subject to the law of war and the jurisdiction of military tribunals."[7]

United States authorities drew up different war crimes trials regulations for different theaters. Distinct provisions, that is, applied to the Mediterranean, European and Pacific territories. To further complicate the matter at hand, American authorities often amended Pacific regulations or superseded them with additional or later statutes.

Under the auspices of General MacArthur, the United States Armed Forces, Pacific, issued initial regulations on September 24, 1945. These rules prevailed at two of the earliest American trials, and particularly that of General Yamashita. Shortly after, however, on December 5, 1945, a new set of SCAP Regulations supplanted those of September.

Close examination of both sets of rules revealed their basic similarity. Only in their respective definitions of war crimes and in the time periods covered by their respective jurisdictions did they differ significantly—and these differences covered mainly form, not substance. Regulation 5 of the September rules provided a broad definition of war crimes. It lumped into a single definition a long list of offenses which embraced many aspects of international law, namely, crimes against peace, crimes against humanity and violations of the laws and usages of war. It gave no time limits for the crimes covered under its jurisdiction.[8]

Obviously, these rules had been drawn up in haste. American officials, like their British and Australian counterparts, exerted every effort to launch their war crimes operation as soon as possible. The December SCAP Regulations thus benefited from additional time and thought. In what became the basis for all future United States trials in the East, these regulations defined war crimes more specifically, and in language nearly exactly the same as that used in the FEC policy decision of April 1946 and in article 5 of the Charter of the IMTFE:

> (a) The planning, preparation, initiation or waging of a war of aggression or a war in violation of international treaties, agreements or assurances or participation in a common plan or conspiracy for the accomplishment of any of the foregoing.
> (b) Violations of the laws or customs of war. . . .
> (c) Murder, extermination, enslavement, deportation and other inhuman acts committed against any civilian population before or during the war. . . .

United States military commissions, then, tried Japanese for crimes against peace, conventional war crimes and crimes against humanity. Moreover, American tribunals had jurisdiction over "but not limited to" the above offenses.[9]

"All persons charged with war crimes" and "in the custody of the convening authority at the time of the trial" were subject to United States military jurisdiction under the December regulations. Americans had jurisdiction over war crimes committed during a broad time period. In fact, an "offense need not have been committed after a particular date to render the responsible party or parties subject to arrest, but in general should have been committed since or in the period immediately preceding the Mukden incident of September 18, 1931."[10]

In most other respects the regulations of September and December 1945 resembled one another. Primary concentration, therefore, will be focused on the later set of rules.

Power to convene military commissions devolved upon General MacArthur, the SCAP, or any field or military commander so authorized by him. Similarly, power to appoint members to such commissions fell to MacArthur or his delegates.[11]

United States military commissions consisted of at least three members. Required qualifications for appointment to a commission included, *inter alia*, professional competency and strict impartiality. Members of any of the service branches, as well as civilians, could sit on a commission; rarely, however, were non-military personnel selected. SCAP rules prescribed, furthermore, that "one specially qualified member" be designated "law member." His ruling was "final" as concerned all matters relating to the admissibility of evidence. He need not be, and seldom was, a lawyer.[12]

Majority vote decided all rulings and findings, save those relating to admissibility of evidence and conviction and sentence. The latter required "the affirmative votes of not less than two-thirds of the members present." Presiding members, either appointed by the convening authority or assuming the position by virtue of superior rank, headed all commissions. Americans made allowance for the establishment of "international military commissions consisting of representatives of several nations or of each nation concerned." Mixed inter-Allied commissions tried cases involving violations against one or more nations.[13]

In an effort to guarantee all accused a fair trial, United States regulations permitted public sessions, "except when otherwise decided by the commission." Also, each commission produced a complete and clear record of the proceedings for presentation after the trial to the convening authority. Beyond this, Japanese accused enjoyed additional legal and procedural safeguards including the rights to: obtain a copy, clear and complete, of all charges and specifications preferred against them well in advance of trial; be represented, "prior to and during the trial," by court-appointed counsel, counsel of their own choice or themselves; testify in their own behalf, present evidence, rebut prosecution evidence and cross-examine "each adverse witness" at the trial; and "require the production of documents and other evidentiary material." From the start American regulations directed commissions to "confine each trial to a fair, expeditious hearing" on germane issues only.

United States military commissions awarded, upon conviction, the following punishments: "death by hanging or shooting, imprisonment for life or any less term, fine or such other punishment" determined proper. This included confiscation of any property of a convicted accused.[14]

All sentences required approval by the convening authority prior to execution. First, though, an initial appellate review of every case took place. A special staff of reviewers, "all mature lawyers of extensive experience," and about equally divided between military and civilian personnel, examined the trial records. After ascertaining that "no error prejudicial to the accused (whether claimed by the accused or not) had been committed," they forwarded their reports and recommendations to the staff advocate general.

This officer then analyzed the trial record, offered further recommendations and, ultimately, sent the entire record to the commanding general or convening authority. Thereupon this individual might "approve, mitigate, remit in whole or in part, commute, suspend, reduce or otherwise alter the sentence imposed." If he discovered an inconsistency or iniquity in the trial record, the convening authority could "remand the case for rehearing before a new military commission." Under no circumstances, significantly, could he "increase the severity of the sentence." All death sentences demanded confirmation by the SCAP—General MacArthur himself —prior to execution.[15]

Like their Allies, American authorities recognized the unique character and necessities of war crimes trials. Consequently they decided to relax the ordinarily strict rules of evidence applicable in criminal courts. Recounted elsewhere in this study, the merits of this matter need not detain us here. Adhering to the same principle which governed the admissibility of evidence at the IMTFE, United States commissions admitted "such evidence . . . as in the commission's opinion would have probative value in the mind of a reasonable man." Military courts implemented the rules of evidence, accordingly, "with the greatest liberality to achieve expeditious procedure."

In this manner American tribunals permitted the introduction as evidence of a wide range of documents, reports (official and unofficial), "affidavits, depositions or other signed statements," letters, sworn or unsworn statements, copies of the above, "facts of common knowledge" and hearsay.[16]

Supplementing the preceding regulations were additional "Rules of Procedure," promulgated February 5, 1946. Basically, these elaborated and specified official trial procedure. In minute detail they outlined, for example, the types of questions ("short, simple") to be asked, and those ("long, complicated") to be avoided; the precise seating arrangement for all court personnel; and the oaths to be administered.[17]

Further amendments to United States war crimes regulations followed in December 1946. These new regulations, worthy of special note, deleted reference to war crimes committed by "units and organizations." The original September regulations had authorized

American courts to try criminal groups—as units, not individuals—for specific offenses. By December 1946, apparently, American officials realized that such provisions, which proved applicable in some European war crimes trials (against members of the Gestapo and SS, for example), had no similar application in the East.[18]

None of the Allied nations' war crimes regulations completely absolved from guilt an accused who pleaded "superior orders." Those of the Commonwealth nations, it will be shown, contained provisions similar to the following American principle: while such a plea in itself "shall not constitute a defense," it "may be considered in mitigation of punishment if the commission determines that justice so requires."[19]

While not prohibited from doing so, American war crimes courts refrained, as a practice, from delivering reasoned judgments—that is, carefully spelled out statements explaining why and on what evidence they based their decisions and verdicts. Only on rare occasions did they and their British counterparts depart from this norm, as in the Yamashita (chapter 4) and Gozawa (chapter 6) cases. Here American behavior was not extraordinary. French, Dutch and Chinese military commissions alone, in fact, "provide[d] in varying degrees of fullness, the reasons for decisions arrived at." As it developed at United States–supervised trials, noted the UNWCC, it frequently proved impossible "to determine with certainty on what ground" a commission based its judgment. Nonetheless in most cases penetrating insights into a trial's relevant facts, its judgment and the law applied thereat may be found in the subsequent remarks of a SCAP Review Board.[20]

American judge advocates at war crimes trials performed fundamentally different duties than their Commonwealth brethren. The British judge advocate, that is, served as an impartial adviser to the court, "whereas his United States counterpart prosecute[d] in the name of the United States and prepare[d] the record of the trial."[21]

Finally, American officials issued yet another set of regulations exclusively for the China theater on January 21, 1946. While resembling closely the September regulations, the new China statutes nevertheless contained a few notable distinctions: for one, they authorized American commissions operating in China to prosecute Japanese for crimes against humanity and conventional war crimes, but not for crimes against peace—that is, for "planning, preparation, initiating or waging a war of aggression"; for another, they made no allowance for creation of mixed inter-Allied military tribunals.

Doubtless this latter provision reflected Washington's recognition of Chungking's determination to prohibit war criminal prosecutions on its soil by any nation which had not actually fought on Chinese territory.[22]

A central agency to deal with Eastern war crimes, the War Crimes Office of the United States War Department in Washington, opened on October 7, 1944. Under the supervision of the judge advocate general, the agency collected "evidence concerning cruelties, atrocities and acts of oppression committed" by Japanese "in violation of the laws of war." American investigation teams explored all avenues in search of possible evidence. Then they analyzed, sifted and arranged all accumulated material.

A Pacific War Crimes Branch, part of United States General Headquarters, Army Forces Pacific, came into being in April 1945. With purposes similar to the War Crimes Office, it conducted independent investigations, forwarding all additional files of evidence and records against Japanese suspects to the central agency in Washington for additional collation.[23]

A United States JCS directive of September 1945 established the principal American war crimes agency for the Far East at SCAP Headquarters in Tokyo. Direct responsibility devolved upon the supreme commander, General MacArthur. Approved by all nations participating in the occupation of Japan, the directive ordered the investigation and arrest of all suspected war criminals. Moreover, it enabled the SCAP "to appoint special international courts and to prescribe rules of procedure for them." It also gave the military commander of any Allied nation authority to create special military courts for the trial of war criminals.[24]

Soon after, MacArthur formed two offices for the prosecution of war criminals. The International Prosecution Section (see chapter 2) dealt exclusively with major war criminals scheduled for trial before the IMTFE. Another office managed all matters concerning the apprehension and trial of other Japanese suspects. Before long, this latter office passed under the control of the Legal Section of SCAP, which subsequently set up two branches. The first, in Yokohama, took charge of trials in the Japanese mainland itself, and the second, at Manila, handled Japanese accused of committing crimes against American forces in the Philippines. When Legal Section, Manila, closed on January 1, 1947, Philippine authorities assumed responsibility for the disposition of all remaining cases.[25]

During October and December 1945 SCAP elevated Legal Section, Yokohama, as a Special Staff Section of General Headquarters. Responsibility for "advising" General MacArthur on general war crimes policies and procedure fell to the section chief, Colonel Alva C. Carpenter. Assigned to this section was a variety of functions, including: further investigation of war crimes and collection of evidence; preparation of cases; establishment and maintenance of a central registry for war criminal suspects and making recommendations concerning their apprehension and trial; and recommending appointments to war crimes commissions.

Besides the one at SCAP Headquarters, three additional regional war crimes agencies were created in China, India and the Pacific Islands. A Shanghai War Crimes Branch operated at the headquarters of United States Forces, China theater. Another, located at New Delhi, operated at the headquarters of United States Forces, India-Burma theater. The third, established at Guam, operated at the headquarters of United States Navy, Pacific Ocean Area. Direct supervision of all three branches emanated from the Central War Crimes Branch in Washington.[26]

Allied cooperation (except Russia, see chapter 8) throughout the Eastern war crimes effort was encouraged and, in many aspects, realized. The governments of Australia, Britain, Canada and China dispatched special divisions to SCAP's war crimes agency. A French liaison officer operated there during 1947. Allied war crimes teams, working both independently and in concert with the Legal Section's investigation teams, built up cases against Japanese involving their own nationals.

In turn, the United States maintained its own war crimes section at the headquarters of Southeast Asian Command's (SEAC) Central War Crimes Branch, in Singapore. Here and in Hong Kong Japanese accused of victimizing American personnel stood before British military courts, a United States officer assisting in the prosecution.[27] Similarly, American authorities left "primary responsibility" for war crimes trials in the India-Burma theater to SEAC. America limited its participation there to "furnishing members for commissions and prosecution staffs" in cases involving United States nationals. At trials concerning American victims held in Java, Thailand, French Indochina, the Celebes, Malaya and Sumatra, United States authorities relied heavily on "joint American, Dutch and Australian evidence" to construct tenable cases.[28]

Whence came the personnel to implement this vast undertaking? Rapid demobilization immediately after the war decreased significantly the pool of human sources from which the United States might have been expected to staff its war crimes operation. Personnel shortages, then, appeared from time to time and in certain theaters. Still, throughout its existence, America's war crimes operation remained a function of the military. As such, it always enjoyed a substantial, even if severely reduced, source of personnel to draw upon. And it had the financial backing of the United States government. While obstacles to providing qualified legal personnel at Eastern trials often cropped up, rarely, if ever, did such hindrances prove insurmountable.

Take, for instance, the situation in the Pacific Islands, where mounting responsibilities and acute personnel shortages nearly brought to a halt the United States Navy War Crimes Trials Program by March 1946. Hitherto only two regular navy officers—the director war crimes, USN, and the president of the navy's then sole functioning military commission—had been permanently assigned to the war crimes team at Guam. For months a makeshift, "meager" staff comprised of temporarily assigned, hastily indoctrinated and heavily overworked reserve officers had carried the burden. Requests for assistance had gone, up to that time, unanswered amidst the more pressing demands of demobilization, occupation and repatriation. Conditions changed dramatically, however, after January 1947 when the secretary of the navy and judge advocate general, USN, decided definitely to pursue the navy war crimes program to its conclusion. Thereafter the Bureau of Naval Personnel furnished an ample number of qualified lawyers, judge advocates, reporters, interpreters and clerical workers. Personnel shortages no longer impeded the navy's war crimes duties.[29]

United States war crimes staffs operating in the Philippines and China likewise overcame sporadic shortages of qualified personnel. In Manila, for example, Philippine scout officers, "all graduates of the United States Military Academy and two being law graduates," after 1946 served alongside American officers as law members of various military commissions. Personnel of the Judge Advocate General Section, United States Forces, China, "carried out almost completely" the American war crimes program in Shanghai. Nevertheless the program's successful completion was ultimately assured through the "excellent cooperation" of, among others, the United States Air Force, SCAP, and "certain of the Chinese ministries" which provided supplemental personnel at key junctures.[30]

Only qualified and experienced American lawyers served at Eastern war crimes trials. While military personnel frequently acted as prosecution and defense counsel, many cases were tried by civilian attorneys employed by the United States government. This applied particularly to trials conducted at Yokohama: of some forty lawyers employed by the defense division there, only five were from the military.[31] Cases heard in places such as Guam, Manila or Shanghai, however, where it proved more difficult to attract civilian personnel, witnessed qualified navy and army officers serving as prosecution and defense counsel. In fact, as noted, entire war crimes staffs were transported to such overseas locations: several career officers, all legal specialists, to coordinate the program and serve on military commissions; trial lawyers; administrative and investigative personnel; interpreters; security guards; and stenographers and reporters. Authority for all assignments emanated from Washington.[32]

American personnel usually "handled entirely" the prosecution of trials. Frequently Japanese lawyers, paid by the Japanese government, assisted American defense counsel. Should an accused so request, these positions were obligingly reversed: that is, the American served in an "advisory" capacity. In most cases, especially those at Yokohama, American counsel "handled the bulk" of defense duties, although United States Navy trials in the Pacific Islands saw, after May 1946, "leading Japanese civilian counsel . . . detailed from Japan through SCAP and the Japanese Government" share defense duties with Americans in all cases. Not infrequently such Japanese civilian attorneys volunteered their services to an accused compatriot, working without financial compensation. A special body of reviewers, "all seasoned and experienced lawyers" in private practice and mostly civilians (at Yokohama, at least), were provided from throughout Far Eastern outposts or from the United States. Finally, qualified American language officers acted as interpreters, supplemented by Japanese interpreters "recruited on a volunteer basis from . . . disarmed military personnel and later from the Japanese Government."[33]

American authorities, as indicated, brooked few delays in commencing their war crimes operation. Like their Allied counterparts, their motivation derived, partly at least, from increasing revelations of "grim tales, yet unfinished," of Japanese tortures, beatings, inhumane conditions and "atrocity campaigns" perpetrated upon American soldiers. "Aroused by the pitiable condition of many" recently released American and Allied POWs, observed the *London Times*, four American teams "systematically" scoured the Yokohama and Kawasaki districts in search of evidence against Japanese suspects.[34]

Americans, nevertheless, did not view so-called minor war

crimes trials, any more than they did the IMTFE, as a means of exacting vengeance upon a fallen foe. Rather, they perceived as a principal responsibility, *The New York Times* commented editorially, the removal of Japan's "ability to do any more evil." Arrest and punishment of Japanese war criminals, they reasoned, would contribute well to the demilitarization of Japan.[35]

Furthermore, the trials had to serve to "educate" the Japanese public, screened from an impartial reporting of facts and world crises by way of an overbearing system of censorship for nearly a decade. General MacArthur, therefore, directed that the "stark facts of Japanese atrocities be told to the Japanese people." At SCAP's suggestion several representatives of Japanese newspapers agreed to publish explicit reports of the wartime behavior of their compatriots.[36]

Americans intended, too, to reinforce existing international law and to deter individual criminal behavior in future wars. Through their participation in the "administration and enforcement" of civilized society's established "fundamental laws and customs of war in accordance with the principles of humanity," they believed, the international law of war would "take tangible form and deterrent effect to warn potential wrongdoers that society will punish those who violate the laws and customs of war." America's involvement in a just but stern war crimes program, indeed, would help to make international law a "guardian of peace" by furthering its evolution into "a definite and positive reality, both in its character and its consequences."[37]

Above all, Americans conducted war crimes trials "not for the purpose of meting out sentences in revenge . . . but for the purpose of ascertaining the guilt or innocence of the accused after a fair and impartial trial." Finally, about its "moral justification" and pressing obligation to perform this service the United States had no reservations. Embodying perfectly this belief, and therefore worthy of extended citation, are remarks contained in the judge advocate's opening statement in the American navy trial of Vice Admiral Hara at Guam:

> It was and is the duty of the Allied Powers, the United Nations, to enforce the standards of international law and society, and to punish those who had violated the law and custom of war. It is the duty of the victor to do this, just as it is the duty of the police and the courts to apprehend, to confine, to try and to punish those who violate domestic criminal law. It is specious reasoning that contends that it is unfair for the conqueror to try the vanquished. The police,

"the forces of law and order," must be stronger than the criminals. If not, the power of society to punish for wrongdoing would perish, for the criminal and his kin do not apply the standards of lawful society to punish the wrongdoer—as we found out in Germany after World War I. If the force of law and order ceases to be stronger than those who violate the standards of society, either revolution or chaos inevitably results. Therefore it is natural and proper that the victor nations, the "law and order" nations of international society, should punish those individuals who have violated the laws and customs of international society, the laws and customs of war.[38]

The actual process of rounding up Japanese suspects began on the day of Japan's surrender, September 2, 1945. SCAP Headquarters ordered the Japanese government "to furnish complete information" regarding the location of POW camps; names of all Allied POWs; all Japanese military and civilian personnel; and all other "relevant" data.

Much incriminating evidence and many useful documents had been "deliberately" destroyed by panicky Japanese soon after the surrender.[39] But enough had escaped destruction to enable the apprehension and arrest of suspects by SCAP forces. The initial order, listing former Prime Minister Tojo as the first to be arrested, went out September 10. A deluge of arrest orders—for members of the "Pearl Harbor Cabinet," former foreign and other governmental ministers, leading military and civilian figures, and thousands of "small fry"—ensued shortly. Many Japanese, as elsewhere in the East, committed suicide upon learning of their imminent seizure. Occasionally SCAP instructed the Japanese government itself to "arrest and deliver" designated suspects. In the fall of 1947, in fact, several Japanese detectives were assigned for this purpose. Later the National Rural Police assisted them. In the end, the Japanese government and its agencies proved reasonably cooperative and efficient in carrying out SCAP's search and arrest orders.[40]

By the end of 1945 American authorities had charged some 600 Japanese with war crimes. A list of approximately 2,000 additional suspects had been drawn up, but no action had yet been taken. Such caution, not delay, stemmed from MacArthur's instructions to army prosecutors: before they began to prepare a case for trial, they should be "absolutely sure" that a tenable case existed. "Every suspect," he therefore ordered, should receive a "thorough screening" prior to arrest and thereby "reduce the possibility of an acquittal once the trial begins."[41] Efficiency became a keynote of the United States operation: as of July 1, 1948, SCAP had ordered 2,636 Japanese arrested, of whom all but 34 were apprehended or otherwise accounted for.[42]

Much occurred between 1945 and 1949 to alter American leaders' view of the world situation. Hopes for broader and deeper Soviet-American friendship and cooperation vanished amidst burgeoning Cold War frictions. "Mutual trust," a by-product of wartime unity, had degenerated into "mutual terror," a by-product of Washington-Moscow rivalry.[43]

So, too, had visions of "one world" dissolved. In May 1947 James F. Byrnes, secretary of state, noted the Soviets' firm determination to see the world divided into two fixed spheres of influence. Subsequent events unfolding in Europe, the Middle East and Asia furthered this Russian objective. Indeed, by early 1949, American press journalist William L. Ryan observed perceptively, "the one world dream . . . ha[d] faded before a new concept which may mean two worlds and perhaps someday a third."[44]

These and other factors caused a significant and radical reshaping of American attitudes and policies toward Japan. In September 1945, for instance, General MacArthur promised that Japan would never again be a world power and that its punishment, "just beginning, will be long and bitter." Yet a year and a half later MacArthur, acclaiming the remarkable achievements of the occupation, declared Japan ready for an early peace treaty.[45]

Japan had undergone pervasive "transformation," General Robert Eichelberger asserted publicly in late 1947. It had become a "reservoir of friendship which might, in future years, deter any enemy who considered striking at the United States." Japan's future loomed particularly important to United States security as Communist forces pushed inexorably toward victory on the Chinese mainland throughout 1948. Thereupon George F. Kennan, director of the state department's policy planning staff, recommended in February 1948 that the United States concentrate on securing Japan against Communist "penetration and domination."[46]

As a result autumn of 1948 witnessed the "focus" of occupation interest begin "to shift from reform to economic recovery." Many occupation reforms had already proven, or potentially were proving, successful. American authorities therefore reasoned that the time had come to promote Japan's economic rehabilitation, as a means both of relieving pressure on American coffers and of strengthening Japan against external and/or internal threats.[47]

War crimes policy, in this as in other instances, ran parallel to occupation policy. Demilitarization and democratization, the original occupation objectives, for the most part had been or were in the process of being realized. Allied forces had already tried and convicted many war criminals. In virtually every Allied nation by 1948, public and private discontent over the prolongation of war crimes trials, especially the IMTFE, mounted as steadily as interest in them declined.[48]

United States authorities, in accordance with Kennan's advice, recognized the need to stabilize Japan, politically and economically, and to "win" that nation to its side in the Cold War. An early and moderate peace treaty with Japan, they discerned, would be most constructive in this respect. But according to the Tokyo edition of *Stars and Stripes*, "any discussion of a peace treaty with Japan," the state department decided in autumn 1948, had to *follow* the termination of all Eastern war crimes trials. Later, treaty negotiations held in January 1951 between John F. Dulles and Prime Minister Shigeru Yoshida indicated the validity of such a view. At that time, the parties agreed that any peace settlement should exclude "further additions to the list of war criminals."[49]

Pursuant, then, to its revised goals the United States pressed its Allies to accept the following measures: an early end to Japanese reparations payments; rapid conclusion of a peace treaty; and, after 1948, swift disposition of all remaining war crimes trials.

SCAP itself began to "wind down" war crimes operations in March 1948, urging its Allies to "expedite" trials in November of that year.[50] Shortly after the IMTFE, in December 1948, SCAP released all remaining class "A" Japanese war criminal suspects held since autumn 1945 who had not been tried at Tokyo. A "unanimous" FEC Policy Decision of February 24, 1949, sanctioned, somewhat belatedly, the unilateral American action of the preceding December: it stated that "no further trials should be initiated" against class "A" suspects. Finally, a FEC "recommendation" of March 31, 1949, rang down the curtain on Eastern war crimes trials. In it Allied nations were encouraged to conclude, "if possible," all Japanese trials by September 30 of that year.[51] The manner in which each of the Allied countries reacted to such United States "suggestions" and "recommendations" fills much of the following pages.

While it has been necessary to present the preceding background on changing American attitudes and policies toward Japan and Eastern war crimes trials, nevertheless we have run well ahead of our basic story. To that, we now return.

United States military courts sitting in the Philippines, China, the Pacific Islands and Japan conducted 474 trials, involving 1,409 Japanese accused. Obviously, no comprehensive study of the trials can be attempted here. Rather, a sweeping overview of American-held trials will be the objective of the following two chapters. Trials embracing special personages, legal principles, occurrences or outcomes will receive proportionate attention. Featured, above all, will be the most remarkable or most important trials in each theater. Subsequent chapters, examining Allied trials, will adhere to a similar pattern.

4. United States Trials— Yamashita and Homma: The Philippines

No account of United States, indeed Allied, Eastern war crimes operations would be balanced without special treatment of the case of General Tomoyuki Yamashita. Aside from the IMTFE in Tokyo, it was the most celebrated and controversial Eastern trial. Not accidentally, Yamashita was also the first Japanese tried by any Allied power. The Yamashita trial set the tone, and several significant legal precedents, which characterized many succeeding American and Allied tribunals. In certain ways, soon to be discussed, it stood as the most legally influential, and therefore potentially important, war crimes trial of World War II.

Yamashita attained the title "Tiger of Malaya" in February 1942 when troops under his command conquered the long-established British bastion of Singapore. In a remarkable occurrence, 100,000 British troops surrendered to Japanese forces numbering less than a third that amount. Before long, however, the fortunes of war turned against Japan. Throughout the Southwest Pacific and Southeast Asia Japanese forces steadily retreated before continual American advances. Following the capture of Saipan and Pelelieu in July and September 1944, United States forces prepared to invade the Philippines.

Supreme command over the Japanese 14th Army Group, and all *Kempeitai* (military police), in the Philippines devolved upon General Yamashita on October 7, 1944. Count Terauchi, the supreme southern commander, maintained control over all army forces in the Islands. As navy forces there operated under a completely separate command, any joint army-navy operations required Terauchi's supervision.[1]

On October 18, 1944, ten days after Yamashita arrived in Manila, American forces invaded Leyte, in the central Philippines. In

November Terauchi transferred his headquarters to Saigon, thus further complicating any joint army-navy operations, which still had to be channeled through him.[2] Gradually, between December 1944 and February 1945, command over all Japanese fighting forces in the Philippines passed to Yamashita. This included "at least technical command" over some 20,000 naval land forces in the Manila area which had been "assigned to the army for tactical command only during land fighting."[3]

Yamashita meanwhile had been forced to retreat into the mountains of northern Luzon. Japanese troops spread throughout the Islands, at the same time, prepared to confront overwhelmingly powerful American forces as they advanced northward from Leyte. In a fit of either rage, desperation, insanity or a combination of all three, Japanese troops waged a systematic campaign of brutality, terrorism and murder against the Filipino population. Untold thousands, including women, children, even infants, the elderly, the sick, priests and nuns, fell victim to the Japanese onslaught. Property damage everywhere in the Philippines was immeasurable. Manila was razed.[4]

Yamashita surrendered to American forces on September 3, 1945. He was charged as a war criminal on September 25, and arraigned October 8. His trial commenced three weeks later. The indictment against him charged that he

> between 9 October 1944 and 2 September 1945, at Manila and at other places in the Philippine Islands, while commander of armed forces of Japan at war with the United States of America and its allies, unlawfully disregarded and failed to discharge his duty as commander to control the operations of the members of his command, permitting them to commit brutal atrocities and other high crimes against people of the United States and of its allies and dependencies, particularly the Philippines; and he, General Tomoyuki Yamashita, thereby violated the laws of war.[5]

At the arraignment American prosecutors submitted a list of sixty-four sets of crimes committed by Japanese troops at various locations in the Philippines. Responsibility for all the violations included in this "bill of particulars," said prosecutors, rested with Yamashita. Yet as defense counsel pointed out, "at no place [in the bill of particulars] was it alleged that the accused ordered, condoned, or actually knew anything about these things, or in any manner sanctioned their commission. . . ."[6] Another bill of particulars, introduced on October 27, charged Yamashita with fifty-nine further violations.

A five-man military commission, appointed by Lt. Gen. Wilhelm D. Styer, commanding officer, Western Pacific, tried Yamashita. None of the members of the commission—three major generals and two brigadier generals—was a lawyer by training. Not even the president, designated "law member," had civilian legal experience. Still, as an army spokesperson later observed, all the members of the commission "had broad legal experience in that throughout their service they had participated on innumerable occasions in the trial of military offenders as prosecutor, counsel and member of the court."[7] Lieutenant General Styer also appointed a battery of six men, all lawyers, to defend Yamashita. Harder-working, more dedicated counsel Yamashita could not have found had he chosen them himself.

Upon being served the supplemental bill of particulars two days before the trial, the defense moved the court for a "reasonable continuance."[8] Motion was denied, and "the first major war crime trial of World War II" opened as scheduled before a courtroom packed with notables: high-ranking officers and civilians; Filipinos, Chinese, Americans and Europeans; and international newspaper correspondents. Klieg lights burned, cameras rolled and flashbulbs flashed.[9] According to one critic, "the courtroom atmosphere had a grotesquely carnival air."[10]

In his opening address Chief Prosecutor Robert M. Kerr branded Yamashita as a "common criminal." The prosecution then set the pattern which it followed throughout the trial: it proceeded to introduce witness after witness (mostly Filipinos) who, in simple, sometimes dramatic but always deeply moving, fashion described the horrors perpetrated upon them, their families and neighbors by troops under Yamashita's command.

Women wept uncontrollably as they described how their infants had been tossed into the air and caught on Japanese bayonets. Nuns told of being raped and bayoneted. Young children recalled how their parents had been bludgeoned or burned to death in their presence. Witnesses recounted mass executions by decapitation. On it went, interminably it seemed, consuming some 2,900 pages of trial evidence.[11]

Newspaper coverage of the trial was as sensational as it was extensive. Reputable newspapers frequently overstepped the bounds of objective reporting, not only emphasizing the macabre and sanguinary aspects of testimony and evidence, but often offering unwarranted conclusions as well. "Like the lurid details of a much publicized murder case," wrote the *Stars and Stripes*, "Yamashita's moral guilt is a matter of general information. . . ."[12] It was one thing for a military newspaper to make such a prejudicial statement during a trial, quite another for the *New York Herald Tribune* to feature such misleading headlines as "Yamashita Rule Gave Internees Starvation Diet" or "Yamashita Men Sacked Manila at His Orders." In both instances the reader had to proceed further into the story to learn that such headlines referred to allegations made by witnesses, not proven facts.[13]

Day after day, for more than a month, some of the world's leading newspapers featured lurid and melodramatic coverage of the trial. Typical lead stories read: "Girl, 11, Stirs Yamashita Hearing by Stories of Stabs, Parents' Slaying" (*The New York Times*); "Convent Girl's Ordeal. More Evidence at Yamashita Trial" (*London Times*); "Killing Said Ordered by Yamashita" (*China Press*); "Screams at Yamashita, 'You Dirty Jap'" (*Straits Times* [Singapore]).[14] *Time* magazine erroneously linked Yamashita to the infamous Bataan Death March by dubbing him "The Beast of Bataan."[15] Actually, Yamashita was stationed in Manchuria at the time of that incident.

Basically, the prosecution contended that: "various elements, individuals, units, organizations and officers" under the command of Yamashita committed "a wide pattern of widespread, notorious, repeated, constant atrocities of the most violent character." These violations occurred throughout the Philippines. Due to the excessive notoriety and flagrancy of these offenses, as regarded both their "scope" and "inhumanity," Yamashita "must have" known of them "if he were making any effort whatever to meet the responsibilities of his command." If he did not know of these acts, "notorious, widespread, repeated, constant as they were, it was simply because he took affirmative action not to know." "That," concluded Chief Prosecutor Kerr, "is our case."[16]

Counsel for the defense countered with a basic argument. After an initial unsuccessful challenge to the jurisdiction of the military commission, the defense centered its case on Yamashita—his character, the precarious conditions he confronted in the Philippines and his genuine efforts to control the behavior of troops under his command. No attempt was made to disprove charges of atrocities by Japanese forces in the archipelago; the defense sought only to extricate their client from legal responsibility for those misdeeds.

Defense counsel stressed Yamashita's dignified character and sought to "disassociate" him, in the minds of the court, from the "extreme Japanese Military Class."[17] Most significantly, defense counsel underscored the "insurmountable difficulties [Yamashita] faced upon his arrival" in the Philippines: divided command, which precluded direct military control over all army, naval, marine and air forces in the Islands; the "low" morale and discipline of the troops; the poor state of supplies and ammunition; and a communications system so inferior and devastated by American pre-invasion bombing that he "could not" have known or learned of atrocities committed by Japanese troops.

Yamashita, argued defense, had not had time for training or even inspecting troops under his command. In fact, he never came into physical contact with most of the units; they merely passed under his "tactical command" as the battle proceeded.[18] Former aides and subordinates, on the witness stand, buttressed defense's contention that Yamashita "was too busy with the details of combat supply and reorganization of Japanese forces . . . to know what was going on outside his own headquarters." Lt. Gen. Akira Muto swore that Yamashita had instructed Japanese troops to "be fair in all dealings" with Filipinos.[19]

Naval troops in Manila and dispersed army regiments in Batangas Province committed practically all the atrocities in those places. The former had completely ignored Yamashita's orders to withdraw from the city, defense counsel pointedly asserted; similarly, Yamashita wielded "no power" over the latter. Responsibility for most of the violations descended upon war-crazed and drunken soldiers who, "knowing that they had only a few days at best to live . . . went berserk, unloosed their pent-up fears and passions in one last orgy of abandon."[20]

Yamashita ultimately proved the most impressive and, in his own manner, eloquent speaker at the trial.[21] Yamashita's testimony basically repeated the defense argument: he had confronted "constant" and mounting American attack forces; he was "unfamiliar" with the Philippines; he had suffered poor communications and a system of divided command, rendering "impossible" his attempt to "unify" Japanese forces. He concluded by saying:

> I believe that under the foregoing conditions I did the best possible job I could have done. However, due to the above circumstances, my plans and my strength were not sufficient to the situation, and if these things happened, they were absolutely unavoidable. . . . I absolutely did not order [any atrocities] nor did I receive the order to

do this from any superior authority, nor did I ever permit such a thing . . . and I will swear to heaven and earth concerning these points. That is all I have to say.[22]

"Although subjected" to intense, "rapid-fire cross-examination," reported the press, Yamashita "clung tenaciously to his story. . . ."[23]

In short, concluded the defense, "Yamashita did all in his power to control his troops, but . . . the effectiveness of American military operations against him was so great that he was prevented by those operations, and those operations alone, from effectively controlling his troops." "The history of General Yamashita's command in the Philippines is one of preoccupation and harrassment from the beginning to the end."[24] Defense counsel wisely stressed the fact that "of the hundreds of thousands of Japanese military documents adduced by the prosecution," none of the evidence proved that Yamashita ordered, condoned, sanctioned or even knew of the atrocities.[25]

On December 7, 1945, the military commission found Yamashita guilty and sentenced him to hang. "The crimes were so extensive and widespread," it ruled, "that they must either have been wilfully permitted . . . or secretly ordered by the accused." A Military Review Board of the Judge Advocate's Office shortly after confirmed the commission's findings.[26]

Obviously disturbed by the judgment, counsel for defense took extraordinary action. They filed an appeal, first with the Philippines Supreme Court and then, after that court refused to hear the case, with the United States Supreme Court (the Philippines was still a territorial possession of America).[27] The latter, "desired to hear argument." The defense based its application for writ of *habeas corpus* and prohibition on, *inter alia*, the following grounds: "that the military commission which tried and convicted petitioner was not lawfully created. . . ."; "that the charge preferred against petitioner fails to charge him with a violation of the law of war"; that procedure at the trial permitting the admission as evidence of "depositions, affidavits, and hearsay and opinion" "deprived petitioner of a fair trial in violation of the due process clause of the Fifth Amendment."[28]

Before the United States Supreme Court attorneys for Yamashita emphasized that, at Nuremberg, charges against German accused alleged "knowledge and participation" in atrocities in every case, whereas charges against Yamashita specified only that troops under his command had perpetrated atrocities. Prosecutors conceded the lack of direct proof of Yamashita's guilt. But, they argued,

Yamashita had failed to perform a universally recognized duty. As in criminal law, therefore, he was liable on grounds of "criminal negligence," similar to the offense of "manslaughter."[29]

The Court, read the majority opinion, was "not concerned with the guilt or innocence" of Yamashita. It could consider "only the lawful power of the Commission" to try him for the crime charged. Military tribunals, stated Chief Justice Stone, "are not courts whose rulings and judgments are made subject to review by this Court." Military authorities "alone," not the courts, are "authorized to review" the military commission's decision.[30] By a 6–2 vote, the Court denied Yamashita's appeal; the military commission's ruling stood.

General MacArthur confirmed the commission's finding and sentence of death on February 4, 1946. He had "reviewed the proceedings in vain search for some mitigating circumstances" on Yamashita's behalf, but could "find none." Yamashita, MacArthur added, had "failed his duty" as a soldier, and "to his country, to his enemy, [and] to mankind." "No new or retroactive principles of law, either national or international," unfolded in the case, declared MacArthur; rather, it was "founded upon basic fundamentals and practices," "immutable" and "standardized." "The results," he concluded, "are beyond challenge." A final plea for commutation of sentence was rejected on February 8.[31] General Yamashita was hanged on February 23, 1946.

If, as MacArthur averred, the results of the Yamashita trial were "beyond challenge," why then did so many people disagree or feel uneasy with the final judgment? And was the judgment truly devoid of any "new or retroactive principles of law, either national or international"? Let us begin with the second assertion.

Army prosecutors, and most international jurists, believed that the legal principle applied in the Yamashita decision—that is, command responsibility—rested "on a just and sound foundation." The Military Review Board held that "the doctrine that it is the duty of a commander to control his troops is as old as military organization itself. . . ." An eminent international legal expert, Quincy Wright, agreed that "it would appear that international law holds commanders to a high degree of responsibility for the actions of their forces." Even critics of the decision conceded the existence of the principle in military law.[32]

Nevertheless there can be no gainsaying that this "marked the first time in history that the United States as a sovereign power had tried a General of a defeated enemy nation for alleged war crimes." Put simply, never before had a victorious nation actually applied the principle of command responsibility against a defeated officer of such high rank. Clearly then, as universally recognized, the Yamashita case was "unprecedented" in military or international law.[33]

On this basis, therefore, criticism has been registered. Besides counsel for defense, some individuals suggested "that those who were responsible for this trial felt that the eyes of the world were upon them and that a precedent should be established." American prosecutors perceived, insisted these critics, that the Yamashita decision would "determine the precedent for future war criminal prosecutions."[34]

Others, too, and for a variety of reasons, deemed aspects of the trial challengeable. Defense attorneys, for example, during and after the hearing repeatedly complained that Yamashita's trial was "rushed" by the prosecution or by superior forces behind it (MacArthur, reports indicated, had urged "haste" upon the military commission) and that they were deprived of ample time to prepare an able defense and, specifically, effectively to counteract the introduction of fifty-nine additional offenses on the eve of the trial.[35]

Several prominent figures, most notably United States Supreme Court Justices Rutledge and Murphy, concurred with these defense contentions. "In view of all the facts," Justice Rutledge stated in his dissent, the burden placed on the defense "in the short time allowed for preparation" rendered their task "an impossible one." Such action, combined with other violations, declared Justice Rutledge, "deprived the proceeding of any semblance of trial as we know that institution." Justice Murphy's dissent reproached the "needless and unseemly haste" of the proceedings. And an American prosecutor at Nuremberg later observed, with relief, that "nothing remotely resembling the speed" of the Yamashita trial occurred in Germany.[36]

To this censure, one might respond that the sheer enormity of SCAP's task dictated a policy of expedition: by November 1945, 2,000 Japanese already awaited trial before United States military commissions. Faced with rapid demobilization, and the government's desire swiftly to re-establish stability in the postwar Pacific, SCAP, it could be argued, had to rush the trials if it expected to complete them within a reasonable time.[37]

Criticism more substantive in nature alleged that Yamashita had been deprived, procedurally, of a fair trial. Defense counsel consistently charged that the admission as evidence of depositions, statements (some unsigned), documents and hearsay (occasionally three times removed) violated the due process clause of the Fifth Amendment and divested the trial of any semblance of fairness.

Many agreed. Courtroom observers, especially British and Australian reporters covering the trial, expressed "shock" at the "loose interpretation of the evidence." Some even doubted whether an actual trial was taking place. American reporters, too, questioned trial procedure.[38] Justice Perfecto, of the Philippine Supreme Court, registered a fiery dissent against trial procedure, labeling such practice a "denial of the due process of law."[39] Justices Murphy and Rutledge, in piercing and eloquent dissents, reached similar conclusions. The protection of the individual's rights, stated the former, "including those secured by the due process clause of the Fifth Amendment," "belong to every person in the world, victor or vanquished. . . ." The subjection of a fallen foe to an "unfair trial," he added, was "unworthy of the tradition of our people."[40]

Others maintained that Yamashita had been "prejudged" before the trial; that the members of the military commission entered the courtroom with "closed minds"; that Yamashita, as the first Eastern war criminal to be tried, and as an admired hero of the Japanese, "had to" be convicted in the minds of Allied leaders; that he had been tried, not for war crimes, but for his crushing victory over Western forces in Singapore in 1942; that the trial actually exonerated Yamashita, but the American military judges condemned him anyway. These critics pointed to the results of a poll taken at the trial's conclusion by twelve international correspondents. They voted then 12–0 in favor of Yamashita's acquittal.[41]

On the other side, however, assembled the trial's proponents. Concerning trial procedure, these persons pointed to the fact that the military commission which tried Yamashita was just that: a military commission—whose constitutionality, they stressed, had recently been upheld by the Supreme Court in *ex parte Quirin* (1942). Accordingly, the supporters explained, military procedure and discipline prevailed at military trials. Those who complained of improper evidentiary and other procedure "seemed to confuse the difference between domestic civil courts and military commissions."[42]

Far more, it cannot be overestimated, was at stake in the Yamashita case than the fate of one man. Acceptance of the critics' views concerning improper procedure could possibly open to question the validity of every Allied war crimes trial conducted in the East or in Europe, for all such trials were heard by similar military courts, according to similar military procedure.

Several years later Justice Robert H. Jackson, former chief prosecutor at Nuremberg, provided a clarifying voice. In the *Eisentrager* case, argued in 1950, Jackson observed that "American citizens conscripted into the military service are thereby stripped of their Fifth Amendment rights and as members of the military establishment are subject to its discipline, including military trials for offenses against aliens or Americans." "If this Amendment invests enemy aliens in unlawful hostile action against us with immunity from military trial," he proceeded, "it puts them in a more protected position than our own soldiers." Concluding, Jackson truly captured the gist of the matter: "It would be a paradox indeed if what the Amendment denied to Americans it guaranteed to enemies."[43]

Moreover, a substantial number of newspapers and legal scholars supported the trial's findings, and deemed the proceedings "fair." Included in this group were *The New York Times* and *New York Herald Tribune*, as well as the *Nippon Times*, the *Yomiuri Hochi*, and the *Mainichi*. Typical of these organs, the *Tribune* later added that, through a "meticulous legal process," "all the avenues of American and international law had been explored in his [Yamashita's] behalf."[44] Also, a host of American army and navy officers attested to the trial's "fairness and legality."[45] Beyond this, while from the day of the surrender he clearly expected to be convicted and executed, Yamashita nonetheless in December 1945 "thanked" the commission for granting him a "fair trial." So, too, did Mrs. Yamashita express gratitude for the "admirably fair" method of American justice afforded her husband.[46]

In commencing the Eastern war crimes trials operations with Yamashita's case, surely Allied leaders aimed at setting a model—a precedent—for future hearings and rulings. At issue stood not only the legality of employing military procedure at war crimes trials, but also the validity of the principle of command responsibility: some prosecuting nations, among them China and the Netherlands, had explicitly defined violation of such principle as a war crime in their trial regulations.[47] And nearly all prosecuting Allied nations later based convictions on the Yamashita ruling.[48]

Furthermore, as at Nuremberg and Tokyo, legal principles espoused and established at the Yamashita trial were—ideally at least—intended to serve as guideposts for future international and individual behavior and accountability, including those of the Allies.[49] Under article 6, clause 2 of the United States Constitution, for example, all validly ratified international law becomes part of the "supreme law of the land." And in 1956 United States authorities embodied the principle of command responsibility in their army field manual, *The Law of Land Warfare*.[50]

The Yamashita decision, then, had potentially long-range ramifications, even beyond significance for Eastern war crimes trials. In fact, the most disquieting of all criticism leveled at the Yamashita judgment centered about the practical wisdom—not legality—of the ruling. The trial result, submitted an army colonel and lawyer, Kenneth A. Howard, "rests uneasily upon the international conscience." For, he continued, it "assumes the fact that the actual war crime was committed by the subordinate but would not have been committed had appropriate restraining action been taken by the commander."[51] Such an assumption, discerned Justice Murphy, implied that "no one in a position of command in an army, from sergeant to general," could escape responsibility for the actions of subordinates. Conceivably, "the fate of some President of the United States and his chiefs of staff and military advisers may well have been sealed by this decision." Judge Röling, the Dutch representative at the IMTFE, drew similar conclusions regarding the possible fate of European leaders.[52] In a notable and more recent instance, distinguished legal experts such as Telford Taylor and Richard A. Falk implied that the Yamashita "standards" might have been legally applied to the actions of high-ranking American military leaders in Vietnam.[53]

Should one accept the legality of the Yamashita trial—in itself, not an unreasonable assessment—certain bothersome issues still remain. It is difficult, for one thing, to ignore the moving assertions of defense counsel, Justices Murphy and Rutledge and others that political realities—Yamashita's great prestige among Asians, the Allied desire to establish a strong, implementable precedent and SCAP's preoccupation with "haste," *inter alia*—unduly influenced the trial. It is equally difficult, however, to ignore the inescapable implications of this argument: that is, that all those involved in the trial's judgment and subsequent reviews, either consciously or unconsciously, were more influenced by political pressures than by their duty to uphold fundamental principles of justice. Consider the following: apart from the five-man military commission that tried Yamashita, as Brig. Gen. Courtney Whitney explained:

> the legal adequacy of the record to sustain Yamashita's conviction and sentence was passed upon first by the Judge Advocate of General Styer's headquarters and thereafter by General Styer himself as the reviewing authority in the first instance. . . . because the death sentence was involved . . . the trial record was again subjected to meticulous review by a board of five senior officers of the Judge Advocate General's Department in General MacArthur's headquarters and subsequently referred to General MacArthur himself. . . . [Relevant issues were then] argued before the nine Justices composing the Philippines Supreme Court and thereafter heard by the eight members of the United States Supreme Bench.

Of these thirty men "who intervened to hear and pass upon one phase or another" of the Yamashita trial, only three supported Yamashita's defense.[54] Allegations of political motivation or undue political influence, therefore, necessarily impugn the judicial and/or personal integrity and competence of twenty-seven reputable military officers and jurists—a charge not lightly made or easily sustained.

Perhaps one must search elsewhere, beyond the political realm, in an attempt to understand the Yamashita trial and judgment. Noteworthily, convincing evidence exists that, even had Yamashita been acquitted in Manila, he would have been re-tried by the British for alleged war crimes committed against Chinese and British personnel in Singapore in 1942.[55] Or, believed his Japanese biographer, had Yamashita remained and been captured in Manchuria, he would have been tried and executed by Soviet forces; better that he died in Manila, concluded Shuji Oki.[56]

Two factors, it may be suggested, militated against Yamashita's acquittal. First, Allied determination to establish unequivocally that violation of the legal principle of command responsibility constituted a criminal and punishable offense. It has already been shown that such principle had long standing in military and international law. SCAP (and later Allied) officials, however, in the Yamashita case extended the principle beyond its traditional application— namely, to lower-grade field officers—and carried it to its fullest potential: a top-ranking general.

In judging Yamashita according to such high standards SCAP officials violated no existing principles of law. "The purpose of defining activity as criminal," commented Falk, "is to draw an outer boundary around what is permissible."[57] This the Yamashita judges and reviewers, within the generally accepted framework of military and international law, sought to accomplish. Moreover, these individuals were prepared, then, to hold themselves and members of their armed forces to equally high standards. "However history may ultimately assess the wisdom or unwisdom of the war crimes trials," asserted Telford Taylor, "one thing is indisputable: At their conclusion the United States Government stood legally, politically and morally committed to the principles enunciated in the charters and judgments of the [Nuremberg and Tokyo] Tribunals"—and to the Yamashita decision.[58]

This brings us to the second point which seemingly played a large role in Yamashita's conviction and ultimate fate: the human element. The author of a recent study of the Nuremberg Trial, Bradley F. Smith, observed that the members of the tribunal "made their decision at a time and in a place where one could literally touch the death factories of Auschwitz and Treblinka." "They were a victorious Allied court," Smith wrote further, "an instrument of rightful wrath, without time or inclination for endless review and reconsideration."[59]

Aside from geographical differences, nearly the same could be said of those who decided and reviewed the Yamashita case. They, too, with the obvious exception of the eight United States Supreme Court justices (whence came two of the three dissenting voices), "made their decision at a time and in a place" of immeasurable death, suffering and destruction. (Manila, the site of the trial, was the second most devastated city of World War II, after Warsaw.) While definitely argued before a victorious court, "an instrument of rightful wrath," the Yamashita trial patently received adequate "review and reconsideration."

Beyond this, less than two months had elapsed since Japan's surrender when the Yamashita trial opened. Wartime passions doubtless still ran high among natives and Americans in the Philippines; and Yamashita, reported journalist Paul Katona, was then the "most hated man" in the Islands. Also, Yamashita's hearing "was the *first* of its kind after many years of a bitter war."[60]

Whether and to what degree such factors influenced the individuals who judged and reviewed the Yamashita case—their professional training and detachment notwithstanding—is impossible to ascertain. But a strong case, it would appear, can be made as regards the sentence awarded. Conviction alone would have satisfied the Allied goal of establishing a sound legal precedent. Certainly evidence of extenuating circumstances surfaced at the Yamashita trial. The death penalty, therefore, appears superfluous and reflective of an inability or unwillingness to understand the precarious situation which Yamashita had confronted.

An attempt at explaining—not justifying—imposition of the death penalty may be offered. Perhaps in October to December 1945 it was, as *The New York Times* perceived, "too soon" to bury past hatreds; "too soon" to forget recent injuries; and "too soon" for even the strongest-willed and most righteous people to overcome powerful—possibly subconscious—emotions. Sentencing patterns, as they may be gauged, support this thesis: several nations demonstrated a "marked" decline in severity of punishments as war crimes trials progressed, and as "wartime memories recede[d] farther and farther."[61]

"My one regret," Lieutenant General Muto, Yamashita's trusted aide, wrote in December 1945, "is that the General [Yamashita] is the first of all Japanese officers to be tried by any Court Martial or Military Tribunal." Because, he continued, "regardless of how fair all concerned try to be in this first trial, everyone is so mentally or perhaps emotionally disturbed that justice may be lost sight of by some."[62]

Again, there is no way of determining with certainty to what extent, if any, external and psychological factors influenced the twenty-seven military officers' and jurists' decision to confirm Yamashita's conviction and sentence. Nonetheless one vital observation, in postscript fashion, commands attention. The next American trial in the East examined the wartime behavior of General Masaharu Homma. In recommending that the death sentence awarded Homma be executed, a SCAP Review Board reasoned as follows: "During the commission of the gravest of these atrocities, accused was not a vanquished commander of a defeated army whose mind was filled with operational details, whose communications were shattered by rapid retreat or enemy activity, or whose troops were disorganized and spurred to excesses by disruption. He was rather riding the crest of victory. . . ."[63] Might not this review, by implication, be construed as belated recognition that extraordinarily difficult and precarious conditions somewhat mitigated the culpability of commanders—such as Yamashita—whose troops committed atrocities? Or—and this is hard to accept—had reviewers in the Homma case unwittingly undermined the majority position in the Yamashita case?

General Tomoyuki Yamashita on trial, Manila. October–December 1945. U.S. Army.

"The second major war crimes trial in the Pacific" opened in Manila in late December 1945. Again, the legal principle of command responsibility arose. Charges against the accused, Lt. Gen. Masaharu Homma, included, *inter alia*, responsibility for the "bombing of Manila after it was declared an open city"; the infamous Bataan Death March of 1942; POW camp "abuses"; and "refusal to grant quarter to Major General [Jonathan M.] Wainwright's troops on Corregidor" in 1942.[64] Homma had been commander-in-chief in the Philippines from December 8, 1941, to August 15, 1942.

Through the testimony of witnesses, circumstantial and other evidence and, ultimately, a partial admission by the accused, prosecutors established that Homma had known of some of these viola-

War criminal Mikio Taneichi, flanked by his American defense counsel and *Nisei* interpreter, is sentenced to death by U.S. military commission in Manila. June 4, 1946. National Archives, Neg. no. WPA–
46–1388.

tions at the time of their occurrence. Homma's headquarters, for
example, stood less than 500 yards from the Death March road.
Under intense cross-examination Homma conceded that he had
"witnessed part" of the Bataan march and had even driven along
the road occasionally. But, he insisted, he had seen there "nothing
of concern," that is, he saw no bodies or dying men, only men who
"looked tired and haggard." As for the bombing of Manila in December 1941, Homma testified that "poor communications" had prevented his learning that MacArthur had proclaimed it an "open
city."[65]

A battery of six attorneys defended Homma. One, Harvard-
trained George A. Furness, challenged the jurisdiction of the military tribunal. Furness stressed the fact that General MacArthur had
convened the court, appointed defense and prosecution counsel and
would eventually have to confirm any death sentence. Since the
alleged offenses had taken place "in a campaign in which Homma
had defeated forces under MacArthur's command," Furness argued,
an impartial trial was impossible.[66]

Basically, American prosecutors charged Homma "with responsibility for the actions of his troops" and that "he knew or should
have known" of their commission of widespread and brutal atrocities. Homma accepted "moral responsibility for anything that hap-

Marine Corps Captain John Hamas, former POW, arrests Dr. Sukashi Sakurai, suspected war criminal, in Tokyo. October 14, 1946. National Archives. Neg. no. WPA–46–68228.

pened." Nevertheless, he maintained, Japanese commanders operated under severe handicaps, most notably the system of divided command and tenuous communications. He swore that he had not learned of the Death March and other atrocities until after their occurrence. In a moving plea, counsel for defense appealed to the five-man military commission "not to judge this Accused by the standards of our own army," but—in all fairness—"by the standards established by the Japanese Army." Furthermore, defense counsel urged that special significance be accorded the accused's character: his testimony "had the ring of truth"; his "sincerity and integrity" rendered the battery of defense lawyers "proud to have represented him."[67]

The commission found Homma guilty on February 11, 1946, of failure "to control the operations of the members of his command, [and] permitting them to commit brutal atrocities and other high crimes" against American and Filipino people. It sentenced him to be shot.[68] As noted, a SCAP Review Board confirmed the verdict and sentence. Again, as in the Yamashita case, counsel for defense petitioned the United States Supreme Court for a rehearing on the grounds that their client's Fifth Amendment rights had been abridged. Again, the Court upheld the decision with Justices Murphy and Rutledge registering equally stinging dissents. And again, MacArthur validated the proceedings and punishment, issuing a personal condemnation of the accused. On April 3, 1946, reported *The New York Times*, the "originator" of the Bataan Death March, "which killed 17,200 American and Filipino captives," was executed.[69]

This trial, significantly, attracted far less criticism than Yamashita's. This may be attributed to the prosecution's success in establishing some direct connection between Homma and the actual commission—or in this instance knowledge—of war crimes. Many, particularly Filipinos, lauded the ruling. Finally, apparently General MacArthur viewed this and Yamashita's trial as "major" war crimes trials. "As our forces were being demobilized in the Philippines," he later wrote, "the remaining United States cases *of this kind* were tried by the International Tribunal in Tokyo."[70]

American military authorities in the archipelago concentrated on bringing to trial Japanese accused of serious crimes, usually those which carried a penalty of death upon conviction. Indeed, more Japanese received death sentences at Manila trials than in all other American theaters combined (see the statistics at the end of chapter 5). Such severe sentencing, though, may be attributable in no small part to the fact that Philippine trials were among the first heard by American (and Allied) military commissions. Accordingly their judgments inevitably reflected a greater intensity of wartime passions, and less tempered compassion, than trials held at a later date. This ran parallel to sentencing patterns in other nations, as will be shown. American reviewers at Yokohama trials conducted from 1947 to 1949, for example, confirmed only 51 of 124 death sentences meted out.

American commissions, then, regularly convicted Japanese of mistreating, beating and torturing or "murdering" by "beheading and bayoneting" United States military personnel captured in the Islands. One trial saw a Japanese civilian, a former interpreter, sentenced to hang for participation in the "raping, torturing and kill-ing" of civilians in Cebu City in March 1945.[71] The number of de-fendants tried simultaneously at Manila trials ranged anywhere from one (Yamashita, Homma) to fourteen (Hikotaro Tajima et al.). Military commissions frequently imputed varying degrees of guilt to accused at mass trials and thus often handed out disparate pun-ishments. Sentences awarded at the Tajima trial, for instance, ranged from five years' imprisonment (two) to death (one); most, however, exceeded twenty years (seven).[72] Philippine trials usually lasted be-tween four and twelve days, although Yamashita's and Homma's took thirty-four and thirty days, respectively. The shortest trial re-quired less than one day's hearing, and seven trials lasted but two days.[73]

American prosecutors relied substantially upon the precedent established in the Yamashita and Homma cases. Most notable in this regard was the trial of Lt. Col. Seiichi Ohta, former commander of military police in the Philippines. Despite a strong effort by court-appointed defense counsel, the United States commission adjudged Ohta guilty "for a systematic series of crimes committed over a peri-od which became definite." The court rejected defense pleas that Ohta had not actually committed the offenses, as well as the plea of "superior orders." Specifically, the commission ruled that he had "unlawfully disregarded and failed to discharge his duties as a com-mander to control the operations" of troops under him. Involved in this case, the press correctly observed, were "the same legal points" as in the Yamashita case.[74]

The United States War Crimes Branch, Manila, closed on Janu-ary 1, 1947. Americans officially assisted in the preparation of re-maining trials until April 30, 1947, although evidence of individual American participation beyond that date may be found. Responsibil-ity for the disposition of remaining trials, involving non-American victims, thereafter devolved upon Filipino authorities. Final statis-tics for United States trials held in the Philippines are as follows: cases held, 97; defendants tried, 215; convictions, 195 (90.7%); ac-quittals, 20 (9.3%); death sentences, 92 (47.4% of total accused convicted).[75]

5. Other United States Trials: China, the Pacific Islands and Yokohama

The Doolittle Fliers Trial: Shanghai

In December 1944 Secretary of War Henry Stimson ordered the establishment of a war crimes branch in the Judge Advocate Section of China Theater Headquarters, Shanghai. Unlike in the Philippines, which until July 1946 remained a territory of the United States, Americans did not maintain an independent War Crimes Branch in China; Chinese sovereignty precluded such action. As a result all investigative and prosecution activities of United States personnel in Shanghai required the prior "acquiescence of the Chinese [Central] Government"—so stated a Joint Chiefs of Staff directive of July 1946.[1]

Actually, Sino-American cooperation in creating and managing effective Japanese war crimes programs in China had been worked out in a previous agreement between the two Allies. According to it American and Chinese military authorities would apprehend and hold suspects "separately or for the other." In fact, Americans formally received the "go ahead" from Chungking to apprehend suspects in China as early as October 1945. Furthermore, the agreement prescribed that each would try Japanese for war crimes directed exclusively against its own nationals.[2]

Chiang Kai-shek's Nationalist Government granted United States forces in China "temporary authority" to conduct war crimes trials on its soil for several reasons. First, suggested the ranking officer, China Theater, Judge Advocate General Branch, Colonel Edward H. Young, it did so, "as a matter of policy," which is another way of saying that Washington would have it no other way. The United States position, revealed flatly during the latter stages of the war, held that "in the absence of any agreement to the contrary," an invitation to a foreign military force to enter the country and repel an enemy "includes" the right and duty to conduct war crimes trials operations. Chiang really had no choice but to accept and work within this resolutely stated American policy decision if he wished to remain in Washington's good favor after the war. Second, the "close and friendly Sino-American relationship" which had developed during the war years required such cooperation.[3] Third, Chinese authorities clearly recognized the advantages of United States assistance. As one, Dr. Wang Shih-chieh, minister for foreign affairs, put it, "Allied justice could more effectively be served" by active American participation. No doubt these individuals recalled the vital assistance provided by an American judge advocate in organizing the Chinese National War Crimes Office in 1944, as well as in carrying out the preliminary functions of the UNWCC Pacific Sub-Commission.[4]

Allied cooperation, to be sure, manifested itself throughout America's Shanghai operation. The Judge Advocate Section, China Forces, kept close contact with the Southeast Asia Command of Chinese, British, French and Dutch authorities. American and Chinese war crimes personnel participated in joint investigations, sometimes shared quarters or office space and assisted each other in transporting personnel or suspects. And United States forces constructed a courtroom on the top floor of a modern Shanghai jail, made available to them by Chinese authorities.[5]

Beyond this, Chinese authorities depended wholly on United States forces, particularly those of SCAP, to effect the extradition of suspects or witnesses from Japan for trials in China.[6]

Meanwhile United States war crimes teams "rushed through the preparations" for trials. By January 21, 1946, a separate set of war crimes regulations had been drawn up for the China theater (see chapter 3). Already at that time cases against "more than 100" Japanese suspects awaited prosecution in Shanghai. Nearly all of the early trials conducted by United States authorities in China dealt with Americans who had been shot down over the mainland during the war. Once captured, these fliers had invariably been "tried" by makeshift Japanese courts-martial under the "Enemy Airmen's Act" of 1942. This "law" held "that anyone who took part in raids against non-military targets or violated international law would be sentenced to death."[7] Japan's leaders had enacted it in response to the famous Tokyo air raid of April 1942 conducted by Lt. Col. James H. Doolittle.

The "Hankow Airmen" trial opened in Shanghai in January 1946. Charged with the humiliation, beating, torturing and, ultimately, "cremation" of three American fliers stood eighteen members of the Japanese gendarmerie. Upon the defense's plea for "additional time" to prepare its case, the president of the five-man military commission adjourned the trial until February 7. The prosecution did not oppose. Such behavior did not go unnoticed. "In direct contrast from Japanese mock courts-martials [*sic*] and trials committed during the war," perceived the *China Press*, the present court "observed all the rules of democratic justice." [8]

In final argument defense attorney Major Maurice Levin asked the commission to acquit his clients on the grounds of superior orders—"illegal though those orders were." He stressed that in the Japanese military code orders assumed a "sacred" character, and Japanese soldiers regarded them as emanating from the emperor himself. Besides this "moral compulsion," pressed Levin, over the head of every Japanese soldier hung the threat of "physical compulsion": that is, failure to carry out orders might mean "death or punishment." Another defense counsel, Lt. Col. E. M. Hudgins, insisted that "those really responsible"—five unlocated high-ranking officers—"were missing."

In his rejoinder the prosecutor held all accused "to be implicated and guilty and cognizant" of their violations of the "accepted rules of land warfare governing POWs." "Not one," he emphasized pointedly, had "lifted a finger" to help any of the American airmen. Responsibility for the deaths, he charged, belonged to all involved, "directly or indirectly." After two weeks of "intense hearings" the trial closed on February 27. [9]

On March 1 the commission presented its findings. All accused save one (a sergeant) were found guilty as charged. Thereupon the commission awarded five death sentences and twelve sentences of imprisonment ranging from eighteen months to life. Without a reasoned judgment there is no way of ascertaining exactly why the court ruled as it did. However all United States war crimes trials, as noted, underwent review by higher military authorities to determine whether they conformed to the appropriate rules and regulations and to assure that the evidence supported the conclusions of the court. The theater commander had final say over all verdicts and sentences.

Lt. Gen. A. C. Wedemeyer, theater commander for China, administered the final review in the Hankow Airmen trial. "That the commission carefully weighed the sentences adjudged" seemed "abundantly clear" to him. He had "searched in vain" for reasons to grant clemency, but guilt "had been shown beyond a reasonable doubt." The trial had been conducted, and the opportunity afforded defendants to secure a just trial, "conscientiously and fairly." Indeed, the defendants had expressed their gratitude to the court for granting them a "fair trial." Wedemeyer approved the sentences.[10]

"What may yet prove to be the most sensational war crimes trial in Shanghai," in the words of the *China Press*, commenced February 27, 1946, at the Ward Road Jail Courtroom. There allegations against four Japanese officers centered about the execution of eight United States airmen of the famous Doolittle raid, shot down over China in 1942. So significantly did American officials view this trial that Joseph Keenan, chief prosecutor at the IMTFE, and five assistants sat as "observers" during its opening sessions. This "test case," such officials thought, might later prove useful "as a precedent" at the Tokyo Trial. The notion of "attaching liability to the highest levels of the Japanese government and army" for "this barbarous treatment" of American POWs concerned them most.[11]

Charges against Maj. Gen. Shigeru Sawada, former commanding general of the Japanese Imperial 13th Army in China, read, *inter alia*, as follows: in August 1942 he did "at or near Shanghai . . . knowingly, unlawfully and wilfully and by his official acts cause" eight members of American forces "to be denied the status of POWs and to be tried and sentenced by a Japanese Military Tribunal in violation of the laws and customs of war." Two other accused had sat as members of the "unlawful" military tribunal. American authorities charged them with "knowingly, unlawfully and wilfully" trying to "prosecute and adjudge" the eight men "to be put to death in violation of the laws and customs of war." Charges against the fourth accused, who had commanded and carried out the execution of three of the airmen, included unlawfully causing their deaths "in violation of the laws and customs of war." All accused pleaded not guilty.[12]

On the witness stand Sawada testified that he had carried out all executions "in accordance with direct orders from Prime Minister Tojo" in Tokyo. The American fliers, he insisted, had received a fair trial; all evidence adduced against them had been "fair and accurate" and proved, for example, that the Americans had definitely "bombed" schoolchildren at Nagoya. Refusal to grant the Americans defense counsel at the trial, Sawada explained, "accorded with [Japanese] military regulations."[13]

Court-appointed American defense counsel demonstrated in this case an energy, a competence and a sense of dedication every bit equal to those of lawyers for Yamashita and Homma. Despite prosecution objections (overruled), the defense introduced, and the court admitted, as evidence affidavits by General Shunroku Hata (commanding officer, Chinese Expeditionary Force; IMTFE defendant) and Prime Minister Tojo. According to these documents Sawada had "acted in accordance with military regulations and law": "full responsibility for the trial and its outcome lay with the War Ministry." Tojo stated emphatically that Sawada had "no choice" but to obey. Defense counsel went even further, introducing affidavits by American and Japanese personnel of primary schools in Nagoya which sought to establish that the Doolittle fliers had indeed, "contrary to international law," bombed innocent civilians.[14]

The United States military commission's finding, delivered April 16, 1946, surprised many people. All accused were guilty, it held, but extenuating circumstances existed in each instance. Sentences thus ranged from five (Sawada) to nine years' imprisonment at "hard labor." To be sure, as the press observed, the "comparatively light sentences . . . indicated a reversal" by the commission of the prosecution's argument that the accused "had exercised direct responsibility." In a rare departure, the commission pronounced, albeit briefly, a reasoned judgment: "The offenses of each of the accused resulted largely from obedience to laws and instructions of their Government and their Military Superiors. They exercised no initiative to any marked degree. [Others, not they, were responsible for] the enactment of the *Ex Post Facto* 'Enemy Airmen Law.' These circumstances . . . do not entirely absolve the accused from guilt. However, they do compel unusually strong mitigating consideration. . . ."[15]

Japanese defendants offered the defense plea of superior orders more frequently than any other at Eastern war crimes trials, as the UNWCC remarked. Few better examples may be found of the substantial weight given this plea by a military commission than the preceding decision in the "Doolittle Fliers Trial." Equally important here was the discreet influence exerted by the Yamashita precedent on the decision. While Sawada's "wrongful acts or omissions" may have stemmed from "negligence rather than design," the commission still judged him guilty. For, noted the UNWCC, the Yamashita trial had established "that a Commanding General has the affirmative duty to take such measures as are within his powers to protect POWs from violations of the laws of war."[16]

Trials involving similar issues—in this case, "denial of a fair trial during a war"—sometimes evinced substantially different results. Considering that the composition of military commissions, the Japanese on trial, and the specific facts and circumstances varied from case to case, this was to be expected. Analogous patterns, indeed, often appeared in civil criminal trials.

Take, for instance, the trial of Lt. Gen. Harukei Isayama and seven other officers, tried at Shanghai between July 1 and July 25, 1946. Each accused, read the indictment, did at Taihoku, Formosa, wilfully, unlawfully and wrongfully, commit cruel, inhuman and brutal atrocities and other offenses against certain [fourteen] American POWs, by permitting and participating in an illegal and false trial and unlawful killings of said POWs, in violation of the laws and customs of war."[17] All of the accused, who pleaded not guilty, had taken part in the "trial," either as chief judge, judges or prosecutors.

Evidence adduced at the hearing revealed that the American POWs had been denied the opportunity to obtain evidence or witnesses on their behalf; that no documents, besides the charges, had been interpreted to them; that they had not been provided defense counsel. Trials of all fourteen Americans had been completed in one day. Counsel for defense argued, fruitlessly, that such trials constituted "normal" procedure according to the Japanese military code. The commission found all accused guilty, sentencing two to death, two (including Isayama) to life imprisonment, and the rest to forty, thirty, and twenty years, respectively. Reviewing authorities later commuted one of the death sentences to life.[18]

Although charges in the Isayama case closely resembled those in the Doolittle Fliers Trial, sentences awarded Lieutenant General Isayama et al. were palpably more severe. This discrepancy may be attributed, indirectly, to the major political importance imparted the Doolittle raid by Japanese leaders themselves. Tokyo obviously considered the trial of the captured Doolittle "miscreants" so important that it issued to subordinates in China—Sawada and company—direct orders pertaining to its performance and disposition. Evidence of direct governmental influence upon Sawada et al. came to the attention of the military commission, whereas no similar mitigating evidence surfaced in the case against Isayama et al.

Similar conclusions surrounded the trial of General Hisakasu Tanaka and five other officers. American prosecutors charged Tanaka et al. with offenses nearly identical to those preferred in the Isayama case, except in this instance the crimes occurred in Hong Kong. A United States military commission convicted five of the defendants, again pronouncing harsh sentences: two (including Tanaka) received death, two received life imprisonment and one received fifty years' confinement. (The Confirming Authority, however, later commuted the death sentences to life, approved one life sentence, and reduced the two remaining sentences to ten years.)[19]

Many United States–conducted trials in China concerned mistreatment of Americans in POW camps. One hearing witnessed a Japanese major sentenced to thirty years' imprisonment at hard labor for torturing an American naval officer in a prison camp. The trial lasted one day. In another case, a Japanese senior civilian interpreter, employed by the Japanese army at two POW camps, was charged with "maltreating" American POWs. And a former superintendent of a POW camp in Mukden received twenty-five years' confinement at hard labor after his conviction for "brutal and inhuman" atrocities against American captives. His actions, said the court, caused over two hundred deaths and incalculable suffering.[20]

As in other theaters, cases in China frequently hinged almost solely on documentary evidence, that is, affidavits and depositions. This leads to a final observation: court-appointed defense counsel on numerous occasions contended forcefully and creatively on behalf of Japanese defendants. Besides those defense strategies described above, others included the assailing of court procedure, which admitted documents as evidence and thereby precluded cross-examination—a practice one attorney called in court "grossly unfair"; the insistence that there existed "insufficient proof" to convict; and outright challenge of the "right" of United States commissions to try cases on Chinese soil.[21]

Final statistics for trials held in China are as follows: cases tried, 11; defendants involved, 75; convictions, 67 (89.3%); acquittals, 8 (10.7%); death sentences, 10 (14.9% of total accused convicted).[22]

United States Naval Trials: the Pacific Islands

Naval authorities supervised all United States war crimes trials in the Pacific Islands, "the first and only . . . ever conducted" by the navy. The secretary of the navy had made known the navy department's intention to participate in such trials as early as January 1945. In April of that year, following a proposal by the judge advocate general of the navy, Guam became the administrative headquarters of the program.

Under the program the National War Crimes Office and its Navy Division assisted local commanders, who were urged to "prosecute their own programs." Thus encouraged, area commanders executed massive investigations of war crimes throughout the Marianas, Marshall, Gilbert, Palau, Bonin and Caroline Island groups. As in other theaters, a war crimes staff in Guam sifted, collated and analyzed mountains of documents, affidavits and other evidentiary material gathered by investigative teams. Slowly but surely legal personnel molded this amorphous matter into tenable, coherent cases. Moreover, a cooperative effort soon developed, "including Army, Navy, British, Australian, Indonesian, and native authorities, in the exchange of information, extradition of prisoners, and even the trial of prisoners accused of war crimes against the nationals of other governments."[23]

From the outset several elements, some procedural and some operational, distinguished navy trials from those held under army jurisdiction at Manila, Shanghai and Yokohama. Of greatest significance were distinctions pertaining to jurisdiction and rules of evidence. Military commissions convened by the navy, for example, "were governed by the provisions of Naval Courts and Boards, except when authorized by the convening authority to relax the rules for naval courts to meet the necessities of trial and to use such SCAP rules of evidence and procedure as necessary to obtain justice." In other words, SCAP war crimes trials regulations of September and December 1945 did not apply at navy trials, save where naval authorities deemed their use advisable. While thus possessed of "considerable discretion" in certain cases, naval authorities often found evidence "clearly admissible under the provisions of the SCAP rules" inadmissible before navy commissions.[24]

Navy trials also differed procedurally from those of the army. As laid down in "Commander Marianas Trial Procedure," it became "standard practice to require . . . normally seven and never less than five officers as members" of a navy commission. Most of the time a rear admiral, but occasionally a navy commodore, marine corps colonel or navy captain, sat as court president. Complete trial records were referred for review "as to legal features," first, to the director war crimes, USN. He then "proposed necessary actions" to the commander, Marianas Area, as convening authority, and commander-in-chief, Pacific Fleet as reviewing authority. The judge advocate general of the navy thereupon examined, "completely and separately," each case before presenting the case to the secretary of the navy for "final action."[25]

Navy war crimes trials were unique, too, in that they featured abundant instances of voluntary Japanese assistance. Rear Admiral John D. Murphy, director war crimes, USN, commended the numerous Japanese "who came forward without expectation of individual gain to lend assistance" to navy authorities. This included not only Japanese government officials, who generally cooperated in locating and apprehending war criminals, or those Japanese who performed as defense counsel and interpreters, but also those Japanese who, in greater numbers than any other nationals, served as witnesses.[26]

Despite these distinctions, navy authorities operating in the Pacific Islands also had experiences and applied legal precedents at war crimes trials similar to those of their army counterparts elsewhere. For instance, "Practical limitations of time and personnel [at navy trials] required special effort to confine the prosecution of the war crimes program to the more serious crimes and offenses." Indeed, serious offenses involving murder or neglect of duty resulting in murder "constituted 96% of the [navy] cases tried after October 1945." Also, navy commissions generally rejected the plea of "superior orders" as an absolute defense, although they considered it in mitigation of punishment where applicable. Yet, significantly, the secretary of the navy promulgated a policy in December 1946 "that all sentences of death adjudged as to persons who committed offenses in accordance with orders of higher authority and who did not commit such offenses on their own initiative, would be mitigated."[27]

Pacific Island trials, like those in other American theaters, frequently handled cases involving violation of the legal principle of command responsibility. Likewise, navy trials commonly saw Japanese civilians, former teachers, interpreters and government officials brought forth as war criminals and nationals other than Americans—British, Australian, Philippine, Spanish, French, Swiss, Marshallese, Guamanian, Rotanese, and so on—as victims.[28] And, to be sure, the principle that ignorance of the law, whether international, local or common, does not exculpate a violator of such law received expression at navy war crimes trials as forcefully as anywhere else. Admiral Murphy said in this regard:

> The fact that numerous individuals may not have been familiar with the earlier precedents for such [individual] criminal punishment, or with specific pertinent criminal laws or treaty provisions, is legally and morally immaterial. In civilized society enforcement of law cannot be made to depend upon proof that the individual violators were

aware of the existence, and import of the specific laws involved. . . .
particulary where the acts committed were of an inherently wrongful
or uncivilized nature. (But actual ignorance may properly be made a
basis for mitigation.)[29]

Under the authority of the commander, Marianas Area, navy
officials established military commissions for war crimes trials at
the United States Naval Air Base at Kwajalein Island (Marshall Islands) and Guam (Marianas Islands). On December 7, 1945, the
Kwajalein commission heard the navy's first case, one of three it
would try. The remaining forty-four navy war crimes trials of Japanese took place at Guam.

Rear Admiral Nisuke Masuda and four lesser officers of the
Japanese Imperial Navy were charged, in this initial case, with
"murder." Specifically, the prosecution alleged that "on or about
10th March 1944, on the Island of Aineman, Jaluit Atoll, Marshall
Islands . . . [the accused did] wilfully, feloniously, with malice afore-
thought without justifiable cause, and without trial or other due
process, assault and kill . . . three [captured and unarmed] American
fliers . . . in violation of the dignity of the United States of America,
the international rules of warfare and the moral standards of civilized society."[30] Actually, Masuda did not attend the trial, having
committed suicide before its commencement. Prior to his death,
however, he had written a statement in which he confessed having
ordered the aviators' execution.

In the main the defendants did not dispute the reporting of
facts; they admitted their participation in the execution. Nonetheless they pleaded not guilty. To begin, the defense challenged the
jurisdiction of the commission, but was overruled by the latter.
Upon the plea of superior orders, then, defense counsel predicated
their entire argument.

To one defense attorney, himself a former lieutenant-command-
er in the Japanese Imperial Navy, fell the task of explaining how
each Japanese soldier had been taught to adhere to "absolute discipline and obedience." To this effect, he quoted from an Imperial
Rescript: "Subordinates should have the idea that the orders from
their superiors are nothing but the orders personally from His Majesty the Emperor." Furthermore, he stressed, failure to obey an
order could have resulted in punishment, even death, for a Japanese
soldier. Pointedly, a co-counsel noted that each of the accused had
asked to be relieved of the execution duty. But how could they—

a lieutenant, two ensigns and a warrant officer—refuse "when emphatically ordered by Masuda, a man of strong character," and a rear admiral?

One of the two prosecutors began his rebuttal by citing "the universally recognized and accepted rule" contained in article 23c of the 1907 Hague Convention: "It is particularly forbidden," it stated, "to kill or wound an enemy who, having laid down his arms . . . has surrendered at discretion." Buttressing this contention, his colleague quoted from the Geneva Convention of 1929 (article 2, part 1). All POWs, it provided, "shall at all times be humanely treated and protected, particularly against acts of violence. . . ." Regarding, specifically, the plea of superior orders, the prosecution referred to a dictum in a case found in "Court Martial Orders 212-1919:" "Soldier is bound to obey only the lawful orders of his superiors"; orders to execute "unlawful acts, he is bound neither by his duty or by his oath" to obey.

On December 13 the commission found all accused guilty, issuing in the process three death penalties. One accused, named Tasaki, a custodian of the POWs who had handed the American fliers over to the executioners, received ten years' imprisonment. Partially acknowledging that Tasaki had merely acted in accordance with Masuda's commands, the court showed mercy because of the "brief, passive and mechanical participation of the accused."[31]

Evidence brought forth at the trial of Lt. Gen. Joshio Tachibana and eleven others clearly supported principal prosecution charges of "murder." Navy lawyers alleged additional offenses, however, which combined to render this one of the more outstanding Pacific trials. Specifications preferred against Tachibana et al. included the charge that, in February 1945, on Chichi Jima, Bonin Islands, he had wilfully, premeditatedly and unlawfully beheaded an American POW. Furthermore, after the killing, read the charges, he did "eat the flesh and viscera of the body" of said POW. Charges preferred against other accused comprised, variously, murder, unlawful mistreatment, neglect of duty in violation of the laws of war and prevention of honorable burial.[32]

The Tachibana case highlighted the significance of accurately worded charges. Notwithstanding admission by the accused that they had engaged in acts of cannibalism—it "makes me strong," said one—navy prosecutors refrained from relying substantially or specifically on that charge; instead they alleged cannibalism merely as an aggravating factor, basing their case on other, more universally recognized and long-held offenses. No precedents existed in modern international law to deal with such a primitive violation. Rather than risk an adverse verdict by some future student of the trial records, United States naval authorities in Guam elected to forego charging cannibalism as a "war crime."[33] Interestingly, Australian authorities in Wewak, New Guinea, handled a similar situation differently: a supplemental list of war crimes drawn up by their own War Crimes Commission had included reference to the violation of "cannibalism," thereby enabling prosecution on that ground (see chapter 7).

Notably, too, the Tachibana trial underscored the decisive influence exerted by the Yamashita precedent. As mentioned, American prosecutors lodged a diversity of charges against the accused. Nevertheless the naval commission adjudged all guilty on, *inter alia*, one count, that is, "Neglect of Duty in Violation of the Laws and Customs of War." All the defendants, it ruled, had "neglected and failed to discharge" their duties as superior officers "to control members of their commands. . . ." Hence this decision reinforced the thesis that a higher officer's failure to restrain troops under his control rendered him accountable for war crimes "when his omission" led to the "commission" of such crimes.[34]

"The 'most spectacular' trial ever conducted by the Navy in the Pacific," so termed by Rear Admiral Arthur G. Robinson, ended in Guam in September 1947. Evidence and testimony introduced at the two-month trial, presided over by Admiral Robinson, related a tale of diabolical sadism. Captain Hiroshi Iwanami, former fleet surgeon and commanding officer of a naval hospital on Truk Atoll, and eighteen co-defendants stood accused of torturing to death eight American POWs at Truk in 1944. Iwanami, witnesses testified, had "devised and ordered" the executions, carried out "by inhuman experimental use of bacteria, dynamite, and bamboo spears."[35]

Additional evidence disclosed that Iwanami and several other doctors had performed shock experiments on four POWs by placing tourniquets on their arms and legs for long periods. Upon removal of the tourniquets after seven hours, two of the POWs died immediately from shock. Iwanami had injected four other POWs with streptococcus bacteria to cause blood poisoning. The deceased POWs were later dissected, their heads severed and subsequently boiled by Iwanami for specimens. Beyond this, the trial featured several remarkable twists—the committing of *hara kiri* by three Japanese witnesses who chose death over testifying against their former com-

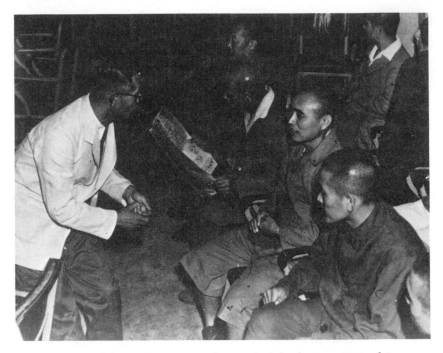

Japanese defense attorney confers with defendants at United States Navy trial of General Tachibana et al. Vice Admiral Mori, IJN, an accused in this bizarre cannibalism trial, reads an American newspaper account of the proceedings. U.S. Naval Historical Center.

manders, for one. In the end the five-man commission convicted Iwanami of "murder" and "violating the laws of war" and condemned him to be shot. Sentence was duly executed. The remaining eighteen accused received sentences ranging from ten years' imprisonment to life (only one).[36]

The largest group to face a war crimes court in Guam comprised twenty Japanese servicemen. The accused, eighteen of whom later drew convictions, were charged with the "atrocity slaying" of ten civilians on Babelthaup Island in the Palau Island group during the war.[37] In another notable instance, a naval court condemned eleven Japanese to hang, including Rear Admiral Shigematsu Saikaibara, and sentenced five others to prison terms extending from ten years to life. All had been found guilty of the mass execution of ninety-eight Pan American Airways civilian employees on Wake Island in 1943. Prior to delivery of verdict, Saikaibara reproached the court,

Prosecution and defense counsel, assisted by interpreters, frequently conferred on matters of procedure and law at Allied war crimes trials in the East. U.S. Naval Historical Center.

suggesting that those "who planned" and employed atomic bombs "should be regarded in the same light as we."[38]

An unusually large percentage of navy war crimes trials concerned charges of "punishment as spies without trial." The United States Supreme Court (*ex parte Quirin*, 1942) had defined the spy as an unlawful combatant, not entitled after capture to the same protection guaranteed a POW. Still, the Court ruled that the universally accepted law of war secured certain legal safeguards to alleged spies, particularly the right to a fair trial. In such Pacific Island cases, Japanese stood charged with having punished or executed without a fair trial native inhabitants, such as Marshallese or Rotanese, as spies. Navy commissions generally held Japanese highly accountable in these instances, often convicting an accused, first, of murder (if a death resulted) and, second, of violation of the laws and customs of war. Harsh sentences, death or life imprisonment, were common.[39]

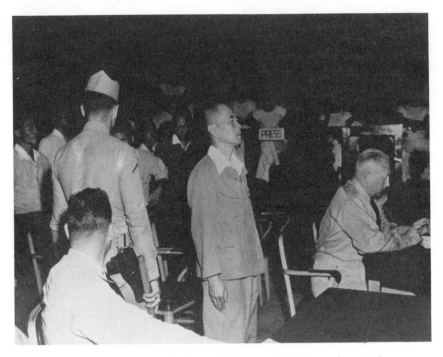

Former Surgeon Captain Hiroshi Iwanami, IJN, stands quietly at attention as United States Naval Commission at Guam sentences him to death. U.S. Naval Historical Center.

Finally, in August 1948 Japanese and American authorities in Tokyo successfully concluded a two-and-a-half-year search for a Japanese medical corpsman suspected of war crimes. Allegedly, Tadashi Teraki had dissected the bodies of three American POWs and removed their livers for experimental use. The accused, later tried by a joint navy-marine-army military court on Guam, had eluded investigators by authoring a spurious suicide note in 1946.[40]

Trial operations in the Pacific Islands terminated May 21, 1949. While "virtually nothing has been published" concerning the Pacific trials, one authority who has studied them, George E. Erickson, Jr., concluded that the "procedures adopted on Guam followed the same high standard of justice as prevailed at Nuremberg." To Admiral Murphy the navy war crimes program "demonstrably acted in harmony with the highest traditions of judicial dignity and impartiality."[41] Final statistics for trials held in the Pacific Islands are as follows: cases tried, 47; defendants involved, 123; convictions, 113 (91.9%); acquittals, 10 (8.1%); death sentences awarded, 30

(26.6% of total accused convicted); death sentences executed, 10 (8.8% of total accused convicted); life sentences, 36 (after commutation of death sentences). "All of the death sentences and all except one of the life imprisonment sentences were adjudged for murder convictions."[42]

United States Eighth Army Trials: Yokohama

Lt. Gen. Robert L. Eichelberger, commanding general, Eighth Army, Yokohama, received orders from SCAP on December 6, 1945. He was instructed to "establish facilities for the confinement, interrogation, and safekeeping of war crimes suspects [and] unfriendly witnesses"; also, to "appoint military commissions for the conduct of trials" soon to begin. Duties were to be divided among Legal Section, Yokohama, and members of the Eighth Army. The former, that is, "would provide personnel for investigation and prosecution of cases," while the latter "would appoint" members of military commissions, defense counsel, court reporters, interpreters, translators and court orderlies. Later on SCAP issued orders authorizing theater commanders to transfer "all convicted Japanese war criminals whose origin is Japan" to the custody of commanding general, Eighth Army, for confinement in Sugamo prison in Tokyo.[43]

United States–conducted trials in Yokohama are of specific significance for at least two reasons. First, they constituted the bulk of American Eastern war crimes trials: of 474 trials, 319 took place in Yokohama. Second, and of greater weight, Yokohama trials assumed, technically, an international nature as opposed to, say, national trials conducted by the British in Singapore or by the Dutch in Java. As the official SCAP historian put it, Yokohama military commissions were "appointed by authority delegated through normal army channels from and by the Supreme Commander for the Allied Powers who represents all the occupying nations." While American army authorities appointed commissions, "they are nonetheless International Tribunals since the prime authority for their creation stems from S.C.A.P." Others, too, have commented on the "international character" of the Yokohama trials.[44]

Yokohama trials, in any event, "covered every type of war crime," from "misuse of Red Cross gift parcels to the most brutal atrocities." "No less spectacular were the personages involved"—some of them women—professional soldiers, from the highest to lowest rank, sailors and admirals, interpreters, farmers, teachers,

doctors, nurses, government officials, Shinto priests and college pro-
fessors.[45] By late 1945 SCAP personnel had drawn up a list of some
two thousand Japanese suspects. To manage this enormous burden,
Eighth Army authorities classified Yokohama trials into separate
categories, depending on the crime involved. They devised seven
groups: "POW Command Responsibility Trials"; "POW Camp Trials"; "Trials for Ceremonial Murders"; "Airmen Atrocity Cases";
"Denial of a Fair Trial"; "Trial for Acts of Revenge"; and "Trials
for Medical Experiments on POWs."

As suggested by these category headings, many Yokohama trials involved offenses or legal principles dealt with in previous chapters. Those trials in the "POW Command Responsibility" group,
for instance, followed closely the outline, procedure and outcome of
the Yamashita and Homma trials. In such cases, SCAP prosecutors
usually charged former area commanders of Tokyo POW camps
with "violating the laws and customs of war" by "unlawfully dis-
regarding and failing to discharge their duties." Often prosecutors
lodged hundreds of specifications against Japanese defendants, alleging specific offenses, such as failure to provide POWs with sufficient
food and sanitary conditions, or participating or acquiescence in the
torture and beating of POWs. Mainly, however, Yokohama tribunals
held POW camp commanders responsible for the misdeeds of personnel under their control.

Defense counsel at these trials invariably sought to prove that
"camp commanders could not help reflect the higher command's"—
Tokyo's—attitude toward treatment of POWs or that prison guards,
not their clients, perpetrated and were therefore responsible for atrocities. Often defense attorneys produced numerous copies of written
orders issued by Prime Minister Tojo and other governmental authorities directing the defendants to perform "misdeeds." On the
other hand, prosecutors generally attempted to demonstrate that
the accused either knew of, or partook in the commission of, war
crimes. Often, as in the Homma case, prosecutors stressed the prox-
imity and visibility of an accused's headquarters vis-à-vis the actual
site of prison camp atrocities. The fact that former colonels and
camp commanders Kaname Sakaba and Kunji Suzuki, for instance,
occupied headquarters enjoying unimpaired views of prisoners' quarters and the entire campgrounds spoke poorly of their failure to
restrain prison guards' excesses. Both received life imprisonment
terms. More often than not, in truth, command responsibility trials
resulted in conviction of, and awarding of heavy sentences to, the
accused.[46]

A typical "POW Camp Trial" concerned a Japanese major and former commander of Kokura prison camp No. 3 in the Tokyo area. Charges preferred against Yaichi Rikitake included, *inter alia*, abuse, torture, starvation and improper medical care of POWs, resulting in the deaths of approximately 150 of them. At the hearing Rikitake testified that he "had not abused" any POWs; he had merely "slapped some," a procedure, he quickly pointed out, quite common in the Japanese army. Of course, he assured them, he had clearly ordered all camp personnel to "protect" POWs. Living conditions for the prisoners, he insisted, "were as good or better" than those for the Japanese guards and officers.

A seven-man military commission adjudged Rikitake guilty and sentenced him to fifteen years' imprisonment at hard labor. However some members, revealed the court president, "favored suspension of sentence," believing the prosecution had failed to prove sufficiently that Rikitake was responsible for "personally committing atrocities." Moved by the recommendation, Rikitake waxed emotional in praise of a judicial system which would seemingly exonerate him for the excesses of his underlings. "I would like to spend the rest of my life educating the Japanese people in the American ways of democracy and justice," he said immediately after the trial. Perhaps he later altered his views. This case, like so many others, saw the reviewing authority wield decisive power. After a meticulous examination of the proceedings, the reviewer concluded that evidence at the trial, indeed, substantiated the accused's guilt: Rikitake "had personally struck POWs, witnessed beatings" and refused to arrest or alleviate mistreatment. Soon after, a staff judge advocate concurred with this opinion, submitting further that, in the pursuit of justice, Rikitake deserved a "harsher" penalty. Punishment thereupon was approved.[47] All early Yokohama trials pertained to POW camp atrocities and to direct or indirect responsibility for such misdeeds by camp commanders.[48]

At the outset some Eighth Army officials apparently misconceived the sheer immensity of their assignment. One, Colonel Robert V. Laughlin, a judge advocate, formed an unwarranted conclusion when, in December 1945, he "expected all the [Yokohama] trials to be over within six months." The stark realities of the situation soon disabused individuals of such notions. To Colonel Alva C. Carpenter and others it soon became obvious that SCAP's only realistic hope of disposing of all the trials within a reasonable length of time rested in conducting "common" or "mass" trials. Such proceedings combined into one the trials of varying numbers of accused charged either "collectively" or individually with identical or similar offenses. Evidence, like the accusations, introduced at common trials usually "overlapped considerably," noted Colonel A. R. Browne, Eighth Army judge advocate; prosecution and defense efforts, respectively, were joint. The number of Japanese tried simultaneously generally ranged from three to twelve, but often rose to fifteen to twenty and, occasionally, to as many as forty-six. SCAP and Eighth Army officials—indeed, all the Allied nations—regularly held mass hearings principally because they expedited war crimes trials operations and spared military commissions the burden of evaluating endless streams of repetitious and superfluous evidence and testimony.[49]

Common trials, in any event, began in late February 1946 and quickly became a normal mode of procedure. Military commissions, in such cases, judged accused according to their specific involvement in the crimes alleged. Yokohama tribunals frequently heard cases where a subordinate, say a corporal, received a heavier sentence for his part in brutalities committed against POWs than several of his immediate superiors at the same prison camp. A typical case saw American prosecutors charge nine Japanese, in varying degrees, with responsibility for the deaths of thirteen hundred Allied POWs. All "alleged crimes had occurred on the hell ship," *Oryoko Maru,* en route from the Philippines to Japan in 1944. Death penalties were meted out to Lieutenant Junsaburo Toshino, commander of the guards aboard the prison ship, and his second in command and interpreter, Shusuke Wada. Four others received prison terms ranging from ten to twenty-five years; and two, both army privates in the ship guard, were acquitted. Notably, during the trial the Eighth Army commission dropped the charges against, and acquitted, the captain of the ship, Shin Kajiyama. It based its actions on the grounds "that it was not in his power to have prevented the atrocities. . . ."[50]

Cases centering about the issue of "denial of a fair trial" reproduced, basically, scenarios akin to those depicted in the China "Doolittle Airmen" trials. Major Notuo Ito and three other officers, in one instance, stood before a Yokohama commission charged with "violations of the laws and customs of war"; specifically, that in July 1945, "during the course of illegal, unfair, false and null proceedings" before a military tribunal they "did wilfully and unlawfully sentence to death" eleven American POWs. The Americans, fliers returning home from a bombing raid on Nagoya, had crashed over Japan in May 1945.

Ito, evidence revealed, had "pre-instructed" the interpreter at the POWs' trial to falsify the translation. When the Americans testified, for example, that they had bombed exclusively "military installations," he was to add "and adjacent areas." The makeshift Japanese trial lasted about an hour and a half. Only partial translation (and the veracity of that, obviously, is questionable) was afforded the defendants. They had no defense counsel, and no witnesses appeared on their behalf. The Americans learned only after the verdict that the accusation carried a penalty of death upon conviction. Ito testified to the "accuracy" of the facts, but nevertheless insisted on the legality of the eleven airmen's execution by beheading, as it had been carried out "by order of the Army Commander."

Ito, as organizer of the trial and execution, drew a death sentence. The remaining three accused, as judges at the "trial," received twenty, twenty and fifteen years' imprisonment, respectively. Relevant factors stressed by a SCAP Review Board were: Ito's "failure to permit review of trial sentences, as dictated by Japanese [military] law"; the brevity of the trial; and "failure to protect the rights of accused." "As far as the record discloses," stated the Board, "the three judges read no documents and heard no evidence, but sentenced eleven men to die upon the statements and arguments made by Ito." It upheld the sentences. The trial, however, did not end there. A staff judge advocate, in an "addenda review," concluded that Ito had carried out "the indicated desires of his superiors." This "slight element of compulsion," he therefore decided, justified "a sentence less than death." Commutation of Ito's punishment to life imprisonment ensued shortly thereafter.[51]

Yokohama trials now and then ballooned to unwieldy proportions. A military commission in one case convicted and sentenced twenty of twenty-two Japanese to confinement ranging from one to thirty years at hard labor for crimes perpetrated against Allied POWs at Narumi prison camp. Interestingly, a civilian received the harshest penalty for "beating, burning, mistreating and abusing" the POWs. In another, charges of "violations of the laws and customs of war" as set forth in 184 specifications were brought against twenty-seven members, including the chief for all Japan, of the *Kempeitai*. Through beheading, shooting or poisoning, assailed the prosecutor, the accused had killed fifty-five American fliers at *Kempeitai* headquarters in Osaka. After a long trial (over five months), the sentences awarded reflected the military commission's attribution of widely varying degrees of guilt to each defendant: of the fifteen convicted, five got life imprisonment; one, forty years; seven, from two to seven years; and two, one year. A Review Board later acquitted the latter two accused.[52]

The largest United States mass trial also witnessed, observed the *Sydney Morning Herald*, "the highest number sentenced to death at any one time since the war crimes trials began in the Far East." Forty-six Japanese stood charged with involvement in the torture, bayoneting and decapitation of three United States Navy airmen in 1945. Forty-one of the accused originally drew death sentences. "After painstaking review of thousands of words of testimony," however, the commanding general, Eighth Army, one year later commuted twenty-eight of the death penalties to prison terms ranging from five years to life. Presently a final SCAP reviewer commuted six of the remaining thirteen death penalties to prison terms.[53]

Yokohama trials bared certain types of war crimes hitherto unconsidered in other United States theaters. Japanese, Eighth Army officials soon learned, for example, occasionally executed captured Americans strictly for purposes of revenge. A typical trial of this nature concerned five Japanese seamen charged with the "wilful and unlawful" murder of five Americans aboard the vessel *Nitta Maru* in 1942. The victims were among a group of approximately twelve hundred American POWs being transported to safer areas for incarceration following the Japanese conquest of Wake Island. Having chosen the five Americans at random, the accused then informed them that, for "killing many Japanese soldiers on Wake Island . . . you are now going to be killed for revenge." So testified several former Japanese personnel aboard the ship. A reviewing authority, shortly after the trial, deemed "excessive" the life sentences meted out to the accused. "Mitigating circumstances"—accused had been ordered by superiors to carry out the execution—existed; the reviewer thereupon commuted the sentences to ten years' imprisonment. However, a staff judge advocate, strongly disagreeing with this reasoning, later recommended that the life sentences be validated. "Said killings aboard the *Nitta Maru*," he emphasized, "were ceremonial" and pervaded entirely by "an overtone of deadly revenge." The convening authority, apparently concurring with the latter review, approved the original sentences.[54]

Uniquely, too, Yokohama courtrooms heard additional, even more diabolical types of crimes. Several trials saw large numbers of highly trained Japanese medical and scientific personnel accused of performing medical experiments, often resulting in death, on American POWs. Principal charges preferred against thirty former servicemen and faculty members of the Medical School of Kyushu

Imperial University, for instance, read that "accused, acting jointly and in pursuance of a common intent, did, in conjunction with others . . . wilfully and unlawfully kill approximately 8 of 12 American POWs . . . by vivisecting them, mutilating and dissecting and removing parts from and otherwise desecrating the bodies of said prisoners."[55]

The briefest trial where the defendant pleaded not guilty occupied less than one day. On the other hand, complicated, multi-issue mass trials frequently persisted beyond five months (not counting the reviewing procedure). In April 1948 an Eighth Army commission tried its first woman accused, Shigeko Tsutsui, a former army nurse. Charges brought against her included that she had participated in "merciless medical experiments" upon captured American fliers in 1945.[56]

General MacArthur personally ordered the "first retrial" of a Japanese convicted at Yokohama in May 1949. The Eighth Army commission that had convicted First Lieutenant Tetsutaro Kato, SCAP headquarters learned afterwards, had "admitted prejudicial evidence which impaired Kato's rights."[57]

United States spokespersons commonly pointed to SCAP's liberality and generosity, which "spared no" expense or effort in its endeavor to provide Japanese defendants "every opportunity to defend" themselves. Perhaps no case better manifested such resolution than that of five former lieutenants general, including Tadakazu Wakamatsu, Tojo's vice-minister of war. In order "to ensure the defendants . . . a fair trial," the Eighth Army in August 1948 authorized and paid for two American lawyers to fly more than half way around the world gathering defense evidence. "Virtually the whole of Southeast Asia" was to be combed, and over a thousand witnesses screened in the search.[58]

Noteworthy, in conclusion, are the details of a truly unique case—for it commenced in Yokohama as a war crimes trial and wound up in Los Angeles as a hearing for treason.

Originally, in May 1948, a Yokohama commission instituted war crimes charges against American-born Tomoya Kawakita. Kawakita, it was alleged, had mistreated American and Canadian POWs at a Japanese mine near Osaka during the war. When a former POW in Los Angeles recognized him, American authorities arrested him and brought him back to Japan for trial. During a hotly disputed hearing, a Yokohama military commission finally conceded Kawakita's point that he had maintained "dual citizenship" during the war and that as an American "national," he therefore had the right to an American civil trial. Kawakita, in any event, fared no better at his Los Angeles hearing. A federal judge found him guilty of "treason" in October 1948 and sentenced him to hang.[59]

Yokohama trials ended in October 1949. Final statistics for trials held in Yokohama are as follows: cases tried, 319; defendants involved, 996; convictions, 854 (85.7%); acquittals, 142 (14.3%); death sentences awarded, 124 (14.5% of total accused convicted); death sentences confirmed and executed, 51 (6.0% of total accused convicted). Of the remaining death sentences, the following action was taken by the confirming authority: 3 were reversed and acquitted; 34 commuted to life; 17 reduced to twelve to forty-five years; 12 reduced to ten years; 5 reduced to five years; 2 retried and sentenced to a term of years.[60]

United States War Crimes Operations in the East: A General Survey

What general conclusions respecting American Eastern war crimes trials may be drawn from the preceding material? First, United States trials in the Philippines differed, in one respect, from those held elsewhere. That is, Philippines trials featured generous testimony by live witnesses, mostly native inhabitants. Witnesses were occasionally flown, when practicable, from various parts of the globe to testify at trials in Shanghai, Guam and Yokohama. For the most part, though, cases heard at these locations rested heavily—and usually hinged—upon evidence documentary in nature. Not unusually prosecutors presented military commissions with more than four hundred affidavits, records, depositions and other materials. As one reviewing authority expounded: "It was necessary to use affidavit evidence because more than 23,000 [former POWs] were processed and started on their way to the United States during the first three weeks of the occupation."[61]

Some prominent individuals criticized America's conduct of Japanese war crimes trials. The preponderance of this criticism, significantly, focused on American application of military procedure at the trials. Most notable in this regard stands the censure leveled by dissenters in re the Yamashita and Homma decisions. As previously indicated, such verbal assaults attracted no paucity of equally forceful, cogent rejoinders. Therefore the reader is referred to the appropriate section (in chapter 4) for futher examination of this matter.[62]

United States Navy judge advocate conducts a cross-examination of a witness in the war crimes trial of Hidesaku Furuki at Guam. U.S. Naval Historical Center.

Beyond this, however, consider the nearly complete absence of any published criticism aimed at the quality of American court-appointed attorneys and, moreover, the consensus of opinion, offered by contemporary observers and authorities who have studied the subject, that the quality of American defense counsel was "excellent." These individuals determined that American defense teams tried cases zealously, "just like 'the boys back home.'" Characterized frequently by "much bickering and discussion between prosecution and defense counsel," Eastern war crimes trials "were regular 'knock-em down and drag-em out' affairs."[63] Commonly prosecution and defense exchanged "heated" words, attacks and accusations. To one authority, John Appleman, such behavior demonstrated "how seriously defense counsel took their duties, and how intensely they represented the interests of their former enemies." The director war crimes, USN, Rear Admiral John D. Murphy, believed that "these American defense counsel ably carried out their defense duties with initiative, courage and devotion to their professional

Colonel Kikuchi Tada, examined by a Japanese defense counsel, testifies in his own behalf. His co-defendants, including Lieutenant General Inoue, sit beside him in the dock. U.S. Naval Historical Center.

obligation to exert every legal effort in behalf of the accused."[64]

Notwithstanding a score of obstacles confronting them—the most formidable being the ubiquitous language barrier—American lawyers performed admirably, concluded a professor of law, Robert W. Miller; upon further study, he felt, "the legal profession will say of defense counsel—'well done.'"[65] Joining his colleagues in praise, one reviewer at the Yokohama trials, Paul E. Spurlock, pointedly referred to the virtually unanimous expression of gratitude from the accused to defense counsel, "irrespective of the verdict." Japanese accused manifested full satisfaction with court-appointed counsel "in almost every instance" at Guam trials, noted another firsthand observer. A host of others concurred with these sentiments.[66]

Not everyone, though, interpreted positively the zealousness exhibited by American lawyers. One scholar, R. John Pritchard, censured the "wretched partisanship shown in many of the American trials" by prosecution and defense counsel. Pritchard, noteworthily,

Defendant Hiroshi Fujii (second from left), accused of practicing medical surgery without anesthetics on Allied servicemen at the Omori POW camp, surrounded by his American and Japanese defense counsel, Yokohama. September 30, 1946. National Archives. No neg. no.

predicated his judgment in the main on a comparative study of the courtroom behavior of British lawyers, well known for their traditionally undemonstrative deportment. Actually, only one truly derogatory observation regarding the quality of American civilian defense attorneys—and that on an isolated incident—has been uncovered in this study. Colonel Edward L. Supple, executive officer, Philippine-Ryukyus Command, charged the Civilian Personnel Section, War Department, with failing "to screen civilian employees" prior to hiring them as defense attorneys. Consequently, he proceeded, a minimum of five incompetents, including "three habitual drunkards," were attached to the Defense Section, Manila. In mitigation, it should be mentioned that the three heavily drinking individuals were, shortly after their discovery, returned to the United States.[67]

The efforts of Japanese defense counsel who served at minor United States war crimes trials, too, won praise. Such individuals,

The accused, Isamu Yokoyama, is sentenced to death by a five-man United States Eighth Army commission at Yokohama. Kyodo Photo Service.

"well established and highly respected in their profession in Japan," wrote Admiral Murphy, "displayed exceptional skill, knowledge, devotion and untiring energy in their efforts. . . ." The same applied, he added, to the performance of American and Japanese interpreters at the trials. While snags in translation frequently arose, Admiral Murphy encountered not one instance of insurmountable language difficulties at navy trials in the Pacific Islands. An equally complimentary appraisal of translation facilities at minor Eastern war crimes trials was offered by the UNWCC.[68]

Many of those who assessed positively the achievements of defense counsel at the trials, abetted by additional voices, also viewed favorably the trials themselves. Certain supporters underlined the unquestioned impartiality of a system which provided an elaborate review process in every case. The Yokohama Review Branch, they remarked, at its peak comprised twenty-eight lawyers, mostly civilians and each a member of his own state bar. The legal experience of this group ranged from ten to thirty-seven years. Reviewers, said one reviewer, Albert Lyman, tended to be lenient.[69] He obviously alluded to the fact that SCAP reviewers at Yokohama confirmed only 51 of 124 death penalties meted out, and reduced sentences in 48 other cases.

Advocates submitted that United States military courts "were all composed of human beings, who acted in a conscientious and fair-minded manner, striving earnestly to do their best." Perhaps the most balanced opinion came from Appleman. To him, "an examination of the trial records themselves disclose[d], with a few exceptions, remarkable consistency in procedure and fairness in the rulings" of American tribunals. Despite occasional "slight slips from the high standards of justice sought," Appleman concluded, "upon the whole," the trials were "exceedingly fair." Other eminent individuals—diplomat and statesman George F. Kennan and constitutional historian Charles Fairman, among others—attested to the fairness of the trials.[70]

"The greatest legitimate criticism which can be made" of the United States trials in the East centered about the conducting of mass trials. Censure in this regard was quite general, even among trial supporters. Critics decried such practice, which prevented even capable and earnest defense counsel from adequately representing Japanese accused. Frequently a lawyer defending several Japanese simultaneously "was forced to attack one defendant in order to exculpate another"—particularly in cases involving the plea of superior orders.[71]

It should be borne in mind, first, that all of the prosecuting Allied nations regularly held joint trials. Moreover, SCAP and state department officials discerned relatively early that only through expedition of the trials might they ever hope to dispose of their enormous burden within a reasonable time, and thereupon dedicate themselves to concluding a workable, non-punitive peace treaty with Japan.

Final total statistics for United States–conducted trials in the East reveal the following:[72]

	Yokohama	China	Manila	Pacific Islands	Total
No. of cases	319	11	97	47	474
Defendants tried	996	75	215	123	1,409
Convictions	854	67	195	113	1,229
Acquittals	142	8	20	10	180
Death sentences	51	10	92	10	163

6. Britain

Procedure and Machinery

While Britain, along with the other Allied nations, basically followed America's lead at the international proceedings at Tokyo, a different logic determined its part in the location, apprehension and prosecution of suspected Japanese war criminals elsewhere. There Britain maintained a position more befitting its reputation, as it stood in 1945, as a great global power—albeit a reputation already in question and soon to enter a period of steady decline.

Early in the course of the war British officials assumed an active role in the investigating and reporting of Japanese atrocities committed against Commonwealth citizens.[1] Such concern led to British association, beginning in September 1942, with official American warnings that, after the war, perpetrators of war crimes in the East would receive just punishment. Britain joined in the establishment of the UNWCC in October 1943, and shortly thereafter London became the organization's headquarters.[2]

As the war neared its conclusion, the subject of war crimes trials increased in importance. The time would soon be at hand, government leaders realized, when official declarations and proposals would be rendered obsolete; the need for specific and operable solutions would soon grow urgent. Lively public debate ensued, covering all major aspects of the problem: apprehension of suspects, location of trials, composition and jurisdiction of the courts and who and what types of crimes to prosecute. Above all, British officials evinced determination to see embodied in Eastern war crimes trials the highest traditions of British justice. At stake stood "much more than mere retaliation," declared the lord chancellor (Lord Simon) in a House of Lords debate in March 1945. The advance of civilization, he argued, depended upon the universally equitable and impartial application of law, especially international law.[3]

Indeed, high and often meticulous regard for justice according to law and, particularly, for the maintenance of "British standards of justice" is a dominant theme in the story of British-conducted war crimes trials in the East.[4] More on this point will be found in the following pages. Here it is significant to note that the sentiments expressed by some leading British figures in the immediate postwar period—demanding outright military executions of major war criminals—were completely absent in the trials of minor Japanese war criminal suspects.[5] The clearest and most convincing testimony to this fact, aside from the actual trial records themselves, is the document upon which the British based the jurisdiction of their military courts to try war criminals.

On June 14, 1945, the War Office, by "Special Army Order," issued the Royal Warrant. Based on the Royal Prerogative which, in English law, is "nothing else than the residue of arbitrary authority which at any given time is legally left in the hands of the Crown," the Royal Warrant established regulations governing war crimes trials. His Majesty, stated the warrant, "deems it expedient to make provision for the trial and punishment of violations of the laws and usages of war" committed during any war "in which he has been or may be engaged at any time after the 2nd September 1939."[6]

The Royal Warrant defined "war crime" narrowly, as a violation of the laws and usages of war committed during any war in which Britain participated after September 1939. As "these regulations applied to all British Military Courts in all theatres and territories under British control and occupation," the Warrant therefore circumscribed the scope of crimes subject to British military jurisdiction. Thus "leaps to light," in the words of Viscount Maugham, an authority on international law, the glaring omission of any mention of jurisdiction to punish "crimes against peace" or "crimes against humanity." Britain, then, departed from the list and definition of war crimes laid down by the IMTFE, as well as by the United States in its regulations. British authorities prosecuted only Japanese believed guilty of actually perpetrating war crimes, *stricto sensu*. In adopting a narrower jurisdiction the British, added Maugham, based their prosecutions and convictions squarely on the "well-established laws and usages of war" and rules of international law.[7]

Other sections of the Warrant dealt with the convening and composition of British military courts. One regulation conferred upon certain senior officers the power to convene military courts for the trials of suspected war criminals.[8] Another directed that military courts consist of not fewer than two officers in addition to the president; also, that of these members, at least one should have "legal qualifications." If practicable, the president appointed "as many officers as possible of equal or superior rank to the accused." Similar reasoning applied to the appointing of officers of the same service branch—for example, naval or air force—as the accused.[9]

Provisions were included for the creation of mixed inter-Allied military courts. Where deemed "desirable," the convening officer appointed as a member of the court, "but not as President, one or more officers of an Allied Force serving under his command or placed at his disposal for the purpose," provided that at least half the court, including the president, consisted of British officers. A mixed court remained, under the Warrant, a British municipal court.[10]

An outstanding feature of the British (and other Commonwealth nations') military court system revolved around the functions of the judge advocate. The Warrant permitted his deputation to assist a military court if deemed necessary or desirable by the convening officer. As the legally qualified member of the tribunal, the judge advocate mainly "advised the Court on matters of substantive and procedural law." Unless he and the court thought it unnecessary, his duties included the summing up of evidence prior to the court's deliberation. Above all, the judge advocate endeavored to "be careful to maintain an entirely impartial position." He had no voting powers. Nor were the members of the court obliged to accept his advice. If the convening authority decided against appointing a judge advocate, he was nevertheless under orders to appoint at least one officer having legal qualifications, "unless in his opinion no such officer is necessary."[11] British judge advocates contributed significantly to the securing of justice at Eastern war crimes trials. More courts than not had judge advocates who, in most instances, represented the sole legal authority on an otherwise lay tribunal. And as one British author and the UNWCC noted, he often assumed the essential role of a balancer—the impartial presenter and, indirectly, weigher of evidence.[12]

Under the Royal Warrant, British military courts for the trials of war criminals adhered to the rules of procedure found in the British Army Act, and applicable in a field general court martial of the British army.[13]

The Royal Warrant also extended to British military courts the rules of evidence relating to courts-martial. Contained in section 128 of the Army Act, these consisted of the rules applicable in English civil courts—that is, courts of ordinary criminal jurisdiction in England. Among other things, these rules embraced a number of generally accepted principles, including the provision that an accused is innocent until proven guilty, and the English practice of affording an accused the option of testifying on his or her own behalf as a witness under oath.[14]

Britain and most of its Allied counterparts sought to secure for suspected Japanese the highest degree of traditional judicial safeguards practicable. The unique character of war crimes trials and the many organizational difficulties involved, however, required "a certain relaxation of the rules of evidence otherwise applied in English Courts."[15] Therefore the Royal Warrant departed from the normally strict rules of evidence applicable in English courts and made allowance for the admission of certain types of evidence hitherto excluded: namely, "any oral statement or any document appearing on the face of it to be authentic"; affidavits or written statements given under oath; any report of the International Committee of the Red Cross; "any depositions or any record of any Military Court of Inquiry"; information contained in diaries or letters; and secondary evidence of statements made (commonly known as hearsay) or secondary documentary evidence (copies of original documents). The probative value of evidence introduced at British trials constituted the sole determining factor in a court's decision to admit or exclude: if the evidence appeared "to the Court to be of assistance in proving or disproving the charge," it was admissible; if not, it was rejected.[16]

Enough has already been said in chapters 2 and 3 about the reasoning behind, and the general opinion toward, the decision to relax traditional rules of evidence in war crimes trials. It may be said in fairness that Britain, America and other Allied nations that followed suit did so for reasons identical to those which resulted in the adoption of such practice at the IMTFE.[17] One contemporary British jurist asserted: the British actions represented "an attempt to secure" a fair trial for the accused "while ensuring that the guilty shall not escape punishment because of legal technicalities." In short, contended a member of Parliament, any attempt to gather witnesses and original documents and evidence scattered literally throughout the world and then to organize coherent trials would most likely prove unmanageable; at the least, it would delay the trials interminably.[18]

The Royal Warrant afforded additional legal safeguards to the accused. Suspected Japanese war criminals enjoyed the right to British legal counsel, as well as the right to select other legally qualified attorneys from their own or other countries. In the main, "British Service personnel, lawyers being used so far as possible for prosecution and defense," assumed these responsibilities; "though it is possible," recalled a former court president, "that Singapore [civilian] lawyers may have defended in some of the trials."[19] British military courts were open to the public "so far as accommodations permit[ted]"; the same applied to the court's presentation of verdict and sentence. All guilty verdicts and subsequent sentences were subject, should the accused so request, to further review by a confirming officer. This officer either agreed with the finding or referred the case to the judge advocate general or his deputy for further consideration and final disposition. All acquittals were final.[20] Punishments for convicted war criminals consisted of death (either by hanging or shooting), imprisonment for life or any lesser term, confiscation or a fine.[21]

British military courts did not, as a practice, deliver reasoned judgments, explaining how and why they reached a verdict and awarded sentence. Their behavior here accorded with United States procedure and differed from that of Dutch, French and Chinese military courts. Alone among Allied nations, the latter three countries provided "in various degrees of fullness, the reasons for decisions arrived at." Unlike the United States system, however, British military courts often benefited from the judge advocate's final "reading of the facts and law to the court," thus furnishing "some clue" to the reasons for the decision.[22]

British and Commonwealth trials frequently "relied heavily" upon municipal laws for their legal terminology and for their definitions of punishable war crimes. For example, as will be demonstrated, British courts repeatedly found Japanese guilty of "murder" or "manslaughter."[23] Courts and judge advocates at Commonwealth war crimes trials, also distinctively, imparted obvious importance to treatises by such renowned international jurists as Oppenheim, Hall and Lauterpacht, and governmental publications such as the *British Manual of Military Law*. Many courts accepted these works as "authoritative" or "persuasive" statements of law; such works, while not binding, often markedly influenced their decisions.[24] Finally, the British made certain that "a complete record of every word" said at every Japanese war crimes trials would be "available in London" shortly after their conclusion. For this monumental task they employed large numbers of shorthand writers, who diligently copied verbatim daily trial records.[25]

Having set down operable and equitable war crimes regulations, British authorities proceeded to cooperate with their Allies in creating a capable and effective machinery for locating, apprehending and prosecuting Japanese war criminals. Britain joined in May 1944 in the establishment of a UNWCC-founded Far Eastern Sub-Committee, based at Chungking. Chief among the Sub-Committee's duties stood the collection of evidence of war crimes committed by Japanese in China and nearby theaters.[26]

The Sub-Committee's focus of activity, almost exclusively China, soon proved too narrow. Under UNWCC auspices, two types of war crimes agencies subsequently emerged to meet the exigencies of the situation. One type, created by the national governments whose territories witnessed actual war crimes, applied to nations such as China, the Dutch East Indies and, later, the Philippines. Other Allied nations, whose troops fought against Japanese forces outside their own national boundaries and China, created another type of agency.

To British and American military authorities fell the major responsibility for investigating Japanese atrocities committed during the war throughout Japanese territory and all other parts of the East. Singapore and Tokyo, from the start, became the principal headquarters for identifying, locating and apprehending Japanese suspects for the whole of Southeast Asia and for the entire Southwest Pacific area, respectively. While each center gave first priority to investigation of war crimes perpetrated against its own nationals, each nonetheless placed its machinery at its Allies' disposal. British and Americans maintained liaison teams, exchanged investigative sections and generally accommodated and attached to their headquarters similar teams from the other prosecuting nations.[27]

Shortly after Japan's surrender in September 1945, public pressure mounted in England calling for swift adjudication of war crimes trials and swift punishment of those found guilty.[28] Stories of brutal atrocities committed by Japanese forces against helpless British nationals overseas, military and civilian, reached ever-widening audiences as large numbers of former POWs returned from their captivity. Nearly all of the ex-POWs had gruesome experiences to relate.

Despite these pressures, British officials stood firm. The secretary of state for war, Jack Lawson, assured the public that trials would proceed "as expeditiously as possible." More important, he purposefully added, was Britain's great responsibility to see that justice prevailed at all the trials. As if to underscore this attitude, Lord Mountbatten, the supreme Allied commander, publicly chastised a British officer who had permitted men in his command to humiliate Japanese commanders in custody in Singapore as war criminal suspects. No guilty Japanese, Mountbatten promised, "shall escape justice, but this justice must follow upon their conviction and must conform to the accepted civilized code."[29]

By October 1945 Britain's war crimes operation was well under way. Overseas commanders had by then received instructions to "apprehend and detain" all Japanese suspects. Investigators collected statements from all British Commonwealth POWs, civilian internees and others "in order to obtain evidence and permit the preparation of cases for trial."[30] In November the British operation expanded; arrests of Japanese suspects multiplied. Responsibility for the investigation and trial of Japanese war criminals passed to General Headquarters, Allied Land Forces, Southeast Asia, commonly known as Southeast Asian Command (SEAC). It dealt with war crimes committed throughout a vast area: Burma, Siam (Thailand), Malaya, Andaman Islands, French Indochina, the Netherlands East Indies, Hong Kong, Shanghai, Tientsin, British North Borneo, the Nicobars and Singapore.[31]

A War Crimes Branch in Singapore coordinated the entire operation. It included seventeen war crimes investigation teams, a Registry Section, a Coordinating Section and a Legal Section. Administrative duties, such as investigation and registration of cases, rested with the Judge Adjutant General's Branch; legal matters, with the Judge Advocate General's Branch.[32]

British authorities built up and handled cases in the following manner. Investigation teams "scoured" wide areas, even hundreds of miles of jungle, to round up any suspects who might have escaped capture after Japan's surrender. Meanwhile, as mentioned, officials distributed thousands of "war crimes questionnaires," for reporting of cruelties, to returning Allied POWs and soldiers. The photographing and fingerprinting of all captured Japanese enabled many ex-POWs who had made statements or given affidavits to identify the persons named in statements from a selection of approximately six nameless photographs. If the ex-POWs correctly identified assailants from the small photographic "identification parade," the original statements or affidavits were forwarded, with attached photos, to the War Crimes Registry Section at Singapore.

This section then registered the information. Additional investigation efforts reinforced the case with other affidavits and evidence from local inhabitants and from voluntary statements offered by the accused. The complete case was then returned to the Registry for last-minute scrutinization and collation, before being sent to the Legal Section. Responsibility for prosecution of the case, and for producing "live witnesses" at the trials, devolved upon the Legal Section.[33]

Due to the enormity of the undertaking, British investigation teams experienced throughout the war crimes operation great difficulty in obtaining evidence and locating suspects. Officials, in an attempt to ease their burden, frequently solicited public assistance and early in 1946 established a War Crimes Complaint Bureau in Singapore to facilitate the reporting of wartime atrocities.[34]

SEAC's headquarters maintained close liaison with the Allied governments. American, Australian, Dutch and French war crimes sections and investigation teams established offices in Singapore and worked closely with the British. Likewise, SEAC's War Crimes Branch dispatched its own war crimes teams to Tokyo (liaison section), Tientsin and Shanghai (investigation teams), and Saigon (a liaison officer).[35]

Predictably, Britain acted in closest harmony in war crimes matters with its two chief Allies, the United States and Australia. Only American assistance enabled British authorities to obtain permission from the Chungking government to apprehend (and eventually extradite) Japanese suspects on Chinese territory. Without this cooperation, believed a high-ranking British officer, British war crimes teams operating in Hong Kong "would not have been able to do more than one tenth of what they have actually done." Australians went one step further. Australia and Britain not only welcomed substantial mutual participation in each other's war crimes program; in truth, each requested it of the other. Australian and British military and legal authorities from the beginning freely exchanged relevant suggestions and opinions, although British influence on Australia's war crimes operation is more evident than vice versa.[36]

Japanese accused of committing war crimes against British nationals were tried before British, Australian, Dutch, French or American courts. Britain constituted a total of twelve military courts in Singapore, Rangoon, Hong Kong, Malaya and British North Borneo. Any trials that could not be held elsewhere, for whatever reasons, were transferred to Singapore. Courts in Malaya and British North Borneo traveled the circuit. The Australians, Dutch and French conducted their own cases in their own courts, while British military courts, the prosecution assisted by an American officer, tried American cases.[37]

The Trials

Even prior to setting up headquarters at Singapore in October 1945, Lord Mountbatten had forcefully clarified Britain's war crimes trials policy. Military authorities, he announced at that time, would "have nothing to do with trials of a purely political nature." Japanese would be brought to trial "on criminal charges only"—for example, for brutality or murder. Only where virtually "irrefutable" *prima facie* evidence existed would charges be preferred against an individual. For "nothing would diminish" more certainly Britain's prestige, he concluded, than the appearance of "instigating vindictive trials" against a former enemy.[38]

Furthermore, as early as December 1945 London advised its Australian Allies "that no opportunity should be missed for satisfying" the Japanese people "as to the fair hearing and just trial accorded to all accused of war crimes." Toward that end it urged "wide and careful publicity" of trials; wherever possible, trial reports should be sent to relatives of war criminals.[39] Perhaps no policy statement better underscored Britain's confidence in its, and its Allies', ability and steadfast determination to conduct fair hearings.

The first trial held in Southeast Asia opened in Singapore on January 21, 1946, and lasted eleven days. On trial stood a former captain, Sadaichi Gozawa, and nine subordinates. Charges against them included, in varying degrees of complicity, the brutal maltreatment of Indian POWs and the murder by illegal execution of one POW between April 1943 and September 1945.[40] Several factors determined Britain's decision to commence with this particular trial, but chiefly it was London's desire to demonstrate the "absolute equality" and impartiality of British justice by redressing first the injustices done to non-British, even non-white, victims. Not all have accepted this view.[41]

Concern over maintaining the highest standards of justice manifested itself throughout the proceedings. "Vengeance and retaliation in kind find no place here," stated the president of the court in his opening remarks. Only if and when allegations are proved "without a reasonable doubt as in a British Criminal Court," he added, will stern and just punishment be awarded. "If evidence falls short of this, this Court must, and will, fearlessly say so."[42]

Acutely aware of the unprecedented nature of the proceedings and of the active public interest deriving therefrom, members of the court acted and spoke accordingly.[43] The prosecutor, in his opening speech, reminded the court of its responsibility to "demonstrate to the world . . . that great distinction" between British and Japanese notions of justice: "We do not punish men without just trial." Therefore, he pressed, it was vital "that these proceedings be a model" for those to follow.[44] Counsel for the defense, a British colonel and lawyer, similarly stressed the trial's unprecedented character and its pattern-setting potential.[45] The court president went even further, acknowledging that "not only the accused persons . . . will be judged in times to come," but the entire proceedings and all participants.[46] To be sure, the British did not take this trial, or any other, lightly.

The defense based its case on several points, among them that Japan had failed to ratify the Geneva Convention of 1929 concerning proper treatment of captured POWs; that the accused had acted under superior military orders; that the Indian POWs had received as good or better food, care and medical treatment as the Japanese themselves. Principally, defense counsel contended that the Indians, shortly before commission of the alleged incidents, had voluntarily joined the Japanese forces. As collaborators, these *heiho*, as they were known to the Japanese, became subject to Japanese military discipline. This placed them outside the definition of POWs and beyond the scope of any court restricted to trying war crimes only. In its final plea, the defense stressed Japan's precipitous thrust over recent decades into the "customs and manners of occidental civilization." Japan, went this reasoning, lacked worldly sophistication, and its nationals all too often became blind "slaves to discipline" and superior orders.[47]

Under oath, the accused repeatedly swore that they believed the Indians had, indeed, joined Japanese ranks;[48] that they had treated the Indians the same as members of their own forces;[49] that they had acted under superior military orders.[50] Typical in this regard was the response of a Japanese elicited by defense counsel: "I had to obey my superiors without question. Privates must observe absolute obedience."[51]

The prosecutor effectively refuted defense's contentions. Japanese, he argued, remained bound to "observe International Law," despite Japan's refusal to ratify the Geneva Convention. Did the accused possess any documentary proof of Indian collaboration? They did not. Moreover, if the Indian POWs received such good treatment, he penetratingly inquired, what accounted for their poor condition at the time of liberation? He rejected as without foundation in law, municipal or international, the defense of superior orders.[52]

On February 4, 1946, after approximately two hours of deliberation, the court delivered its verdict. All the accused, with the exception of one, were found guilty of the respective charges. The court acquitted a sergeant major, having been convinced by defense counsel's argument that no *prima facie* case against him existed.[53] Lieutenant Nakamura, Gozawa's subordinate and the individual who actually organized and supervised the Indian victim's execution, received the death penalty. Gozawa, meanwhile, drew twelve years' imprisonment. Other sentences ranged from two to seven years' confinement. Sentences were confirmed on March 4, 1946.[54]

Unfortunately, this first British war crimes trial in the East lacked the presence of a judge advocate. Without his customary summation of the facts and clarification of the law, it would normally be extremely difficult to ascertain why the court found as it did. However, in this case the court took extraordinary action, as revealed by procedure followed in subsequent trials. Along with the verdict and sentences, the court read brief statements to the convicted, explaining, for example, its unusual action in meting out the death penalty to a subordinate, while taking a "merciful view" of his superior's behavior. Believing Gozawa had been "led to acquiescence" by his "more powerful adjutant," the court spared his life. In statements to two other accused, the court reinforced the general attitude toward the defense plea of superior orders. That is, while not constituting an absolute defense, the court may determine to treat it as a mitigating factor.[55]

This being the first British war crimes trial in Southeast Asia, Nakamura thus gained the dubious distinction of becoming the first Japanese condemned by a British court. The trial received ample press coverage and attracted wide public interest in Singapore, but not in England, where it was practically ignored.[56] Procedure at the Gozawa trial evoked criticism in some circles, but, generally, observers considered the trial fair and representative of British justice. In his closing statement, counsel for the defense thanked the court personnel for a trial "conducted throughout" with "scrupulous fairness and impartiality."[57] One final note: the British went to such extremes and took such great care to ensure a meticulously

Prosecution reads charges at first SEAC trial, that of Gozawa Sadaichi and nine subordinates (seated, lower right). Singapore, January 21–February 1, 1946. Imperial War Museum, London. Neg. no. SE 6383.

fair trial in a case of relatively minor importance that surely, the Gozawa trial became a working model for all future proceedings.

A torrent of trials followed. In 1946 British trials opened in Perak, Car Nicobar, Penang, British North Borneo, Rangoon and Singapore. Preparations for others in Hong Kong and Rabaul, New Britain, began.[58]

In the trial of a Japanese army sergeant, held at Kuala Lumpur, a British military court found the accused guilty of murdering a Malayan civilian at Kuala Lumpur in September 1946. Under oath, the accused swore that he had acted in self-defense and while under the influence of alcohol. While the court took these factors into consideration, the reviewing authority, seeing things in a different light, presently overrode its recommendation for mercy and confirmed the death penalty. The decision in this case, representative of many in British trials, exemplified "the introduction of Municipal (in this case English) Law concepts" into war crimes trials.[59]

Trials varied in length and character. Some required minimal preparation. In a Car Nicobar case, a court sentenced a Japanese

First British trial in Kuala Lumpur, January 30, 1946. Sole defendant, Corporal Hamada, stands in dock flanked by Indian guards while charges are read. Imperial War Museum, London. Neg. no. SE 6590.

officer to two years in prison for "being concerned" in the ill-treatment and killing of 152 civilian inhabitants of the Andaman Islands. The trial took one day.[60] Perak's first war crimes trial lasted less than two days. There a satisfied native population witnessed the passing of the death sentence upon a member of the notorious *Kempeitai* for his brutal maltreatment of civilian inhabitants between 1943 and 1945.[61]

Other trials demanded long, painstaking preparation, and often dragged on interminably. For example, civilian inhabitants of Penang anxiously awaited the commencement of the "biggest war crimes trial in the Malayan Union." Scheduled, in April 1946, to open shortly, the trial did not start until the final day of August. Charged with executing a veritable "reign of terror and promiscuous slaughter" against the local population were 35 former *Kempeitai*. British military authorities conducted the trial with impeccable care and fairness. On several occasions, the court president delayed the proceedings, explaining clearly to the accused their rights under British law. A month later the trial ended. Of the 35 accused, 21

Sole defendant, Mori Yoshitada, with his British counsel at the only Japanese war crimes trial held at Kajang (near Kuala Lumpur). Imperial War Museum, London. Neg. no. SE 6942.

received death penalties; 3, acquittals; and 11, prison terms ranging from five to fifteen years.[62]

As in other Allied theaters, British authorities went to great lengths to bring to justice those Japanese accused of serious crimes: of the 113 "known war criminals" and 40 suspects held in custody at Rangoon in February 1946, for instance, all stood charged with murder, rape, beating and torture. Burma's first trial, in fact, saw a Japanese major sentenced to hang for "killing" and "torturing" 637 inhabitants of the Indian village of Kalagon.[63]

Civic Hall, Rangoon, site of the first British war crimes trial conducted in Burma, the Kalagon Village Massacre Case. A Chinese pagoda stands in the background. Imperial War Museum, London. Neg. no. SE 7092.

The sheer enormity of their task led British authorities, as it did their Allies, regularly to hold "mass" trials. In addition to the Gozawa trial, already discussed, the so-called "Double Tenth Trial" of 21 *Kempeitai* and the "Outram Road Military Prison Case" of 44 Japanese stand out.

The former trial opened in Singapore on March 18, 1946. Charges against the 21 accused included the beating and torturing of British POWs in an attempt to exact information and confessions. Many POWs, the charge alleged, died as a result of this maltreatment.[64] The defense, composed of legally qualified British military personnel, based nearly its entire case on the plea of superior orders. To counter this argument, the prosecution cited the opinion of the German Supreme Court in the famous Llandovery Castle case of 1922 that "members of the armed forces are bound to obey lawful orders only." Apparently, the court agreed with the prosecution: it sentenced 8 accused to death, 6 to prison terms, and acquitted 7.[65]

The latter trial focused on the diabolical events which had taken place during the Japanese occupation of Singapore at the Outram Road Military Prison, or, as its inhabitants came to call it,

Kalagon Village Massacre Case, Rangoon. Trial participants and spectators rise for the entry of the court president. Imperial War Museum, London. Neg. no. SE 7096.

the "Eastern Belsen." The hearing began in Kuala Lumpur in August 1947. The indictment charged 44 Japanese "concerned" in the administration of the former POW camp, in varying degrees of guilt, with causing unconscionable tortures and suffering upon thousands of British Commonwealth and other POWs. Press coverage of the trial was widespread, as many witnesses, British and Chinese, testified to the ghoulish events at Outram prison.

At the close of the prosecution's case, the entire war crimes court traveled to and inspected for itself the Outram Road prison, scene of the alleged atrocities. Counsel for the defense implored the court to judge the accused by "standards they are used to." He reminded the court that not only Japanese were on trial, "but also the British system of justice." The court found 39 of the 44 Japanese guilty, meting out 5 death penalties, 5 life imprisonment terms and 29 prison terms ranging from one to eighteen years.[66]

While most trials conformed, generally, to a discernible pattern —former Japanese military personnel were charged with murder or other atrocities, received strong defenses, then were judged, the court having maintained throughout strict military discipline and judicious legal decorum—some inevitably strayed from the norm. A Kuala Lumpur courtroom, for example, witnessed a rice-cooking demonstration by the defense in order to show that 300 grams of rice, the basic daily rice ration for certain POWs, formed a substantial amount when cooked.[67] Spectator reaction, for instance clapping or voicing disapproval to trial motions, testimony or outcomes, was not uncommon in British courtrooms, despite the British preference for reserved deportment.[68] Courts experienced considerable difficulties with digressive Japanese interpreters and frequently chided them for holding sustained conversations with witnesses.[69] Occasionally courts tried Japanese civilians, usually former interpreters, for "being concerned" in the commission of war crimes.[70]

Courts sometimes meted out unusual punishments. In a unique instance, the wife of a convicted war criminal was ordered to pay a $2,000 fine to Indian and Chinese residents of Bangkok who had suffered ill-treatment at the hands of her husband. Another concerned a Japanese sergeant who had been ordered by his superior to beat a British POW. Threatened with severe punishment should he refuse, the sergeant reluctantly obeyed. Thereupon an empathetic court, taking into account the coercive elements involved, imposed "a nominal sentence of one day's imprisonment."[71]

One characteristic of the trials stood unchanged throughout. Invariably, Japanese accused pleaded not guilty to charges preferred against them. An experienced reporter, for example, wrote of a "dramatic ending" to a Kuala Lumpur trial of two *Kempeitai*: suddenly, both accused "decided to plead guilty to the charges against them." To his knowledge, this was the "first occasion" on which Japanese on trial in Malaya "admitted the ill-treatment of Malayan residents."[72] Perhaps this was not the only instance of its kind. Nevertheless Japanese rarely admitted their guilt.

British courts cooperated closely with Allied war crimes teams and often sat as mixed inter-Allied tribunals. An American prosecutor, acting on behalf of American victims, first appeared in a British court in April 1947. His conscientious performance later won the congratulations of the court's president.[73] Courts composed exclusively of British personnel frequently prosecuted Japanese accused of violations against American, or French, POWs.[74] Chinese legal representatives assisted British prosecutors on occasion and the Chinese consul attended several trials involving Chinese victims. A British war crimes team sent to Ipoh, Northern Malaya, worked closely with official and private Chinese in building cases against Japanese.[75] British prosecutors assisted Americans in cases at Yokohama. And more than once, British courts relied on legal principles established by Allied courts—most notably, the Yamashita precedent of "command responsibility."[76]

Certain trials immediately became a *cause célèbre*. Those related to the infamous Burma–Siam "death railway," or "Bridge on the River Kwai" if one is a Hollywood fan, attracted widespread interest. Such cases involved the deaths and suffering of literally thousands of British Commonwealth POWs. Bringing to justice all those responsible thus required several separate trials. The first ended, rather quietly, in June 1946 with the condemnation of a Japanese major found guilty of "brutalities resulting in the deaths of 570 of 2,000 POWs under him in 1943."[77]

Claims that the "Ishida 'Death Railway' Trial" would eventually rank "second only to the Tokyo trial" in importance fell short. Still the trial of Lieutenant General Ishida and four of his senior officers created a sensation in Singapore. Charges against the Japanese included, *inter alia*, the "inhuman treatment of POWs resulting in many deaths and much physical suffering"; employment of POW labor in connection with operations of war; employment of POWs in excessive work; and internment of POWs in unhygienic and unhealthy conditions.

The British prosecutor took care pointedly to describe POW life under Japanese captivity and to explain why the appropriate label "death railway" had been given. Employment of POWs in work of this kind, he asserted, constituted in itself "a monstrous international crime." Astutely, the British defense attorney countered this argument. As Allied lawyers before the IMTFE were currently debating the issue whether employment of POWs on a railway violated any existing law, he reasoned, the court should defer its finding until that tribunal rendered a decision.

Daily, ex-POWs testified to the horrible, often unbearable, conditions under which they had toiled and lived for so long. One, now a Singapore lawyer, compared Japanese treatment of POWs to slave labor in times of the pyramids or galley slaves. Witnesses commonly and coldly described Japanese guards as "sadistic." The trial lasted nearly six weeks. In the end all five accused were found guilty, with two sentenced to hang, one sentenced to twenty years' imprisonment, and the remaining two, Ishida included, drawing ten years' confinement.[78]

A trial involving atrocities perpetrated at the Sime Road Internment Camp during the Japanese occupation of Singapore attracted remarkably extensive press coverage and quickly became the most celebrated and controversial trial in Southeast Asia. Excitement surrounding the trial flowed from the personages involved: British, Australian, Dutch and American civilians and government officials, men and women, who had been wartime "guests" of the Japanese at the Sime Road camp. Anxiously, the public awaited their dramatic testimony.

British military authorities set up a special war crimes court in Victoria Memorial Hall in Singapore to hear the case. The indictment charged five Japanese, former personnel at the camp, with "being concerned" in the ill-treatment of said internees as well as in the death of one, a former Malayan government official. Two Japanese lawyers, assisted by a British captain, defended the accused, who pleaded not guilty.

One after another, former internees of Sime Road—government figures, judges, lawyers, doctors and distinguished citizens— marched to the witness stand and repeated stories of "incredibly bad" conditions in the camp. Widespread sickness, nutritional deficiencies, beatings by cruel Japanese guards, they testified, had all been common. Eleven days later, on September 12, 1946, the court, after a mere forty minutes of deliberation, rendered its verdicts and sentences. A packed, and somewhat shocked, audience heard the court sentence three of the accused to death, one to life imprisonment and one to seven years' imprisonment.[79] In relation to sentences pronounced in other trials—often involving far more abhorrent crimes—punishments meted out in the Sime Road Prison Case seemed unusually harsh. Controversy surrounded the trial for some time to come, but more on this matter will be said shortly.

Not all British war crimes trials, of course, resulted in convictions. In numerous cases British courts refused to find Japanese guilty on the grounds that charges against them had not been proven "beyond a reasonable doubt." One extraordinary case involved a British woman who had fallen 100 feet to her death from a window in Kuala Lumpur in 1943. The crux of the case centered on whether the woman had fallen from the window accidently, jumped voluntarily or been pushed or chased out by the Japanese officer who, alone with her in the room, had beaten and sexually abused her. Counsel for the defense argued that the woman had leaped voluntarily from the window in order to "refrain" from giving her assailant, Second Lieutenant Murakami, information; perhaps moral responsibility for the woman's death rested with the accused, but certainly not legal responsibility. A thoroughly surprised audience heard the court acquit Murakami on grounds of insufficient proof.[80]

Japanese also drew acquittals in cases where "doubt in the identification" or "discrepancies in the evidence" materialized.[81] A court sitting in Rabaul, New Britain, freed an accused upon his immediate superior's full acceptance of responsibility for the crimes charged.[82] Certainly strict adherence to legal principles did not always come easily to British military judges. One case witnessed four *Kempeitai* accused of torturing three Chinese to death. Conclusive evidence led to the outright conviction of three of the accused, but witnesses experienced difficulty identifying the fourth with absolute certainty. "Though there is no doubt that you were a member of this devils' gang," a rueful court president addressed the fourth accused, "there is no [concrctc] evidence to justify a conviction in your case." He went free.[83] Many other similar examples may be found.[84]

British courts occasionally "amended charges" upon the introduction of additional evidence. Leniency was shown for a variety of reasons, including the youthful age or distinguished former record of the accused, or for other "extraordinary" reasons.[85]

The British, as the preceding discussion has indicated, commissioned an exceptionally high caliber of people to serve as defense lawyers at Eastern trials. These individuals put forth conscientious, energetic and often enterprising efforts in nearly every case. Their pleas and arguments covered an almost boundless spectrum of rhetoric, emotion and legal reasoning. One defense attorney urged the court to inter the hatreds of the recent war and to assure that "the next war"—a race war . . . is not started in this room right in front of the blindfolded figure of Justice." Another British officer, himself a former POW on the Burma–Siam railway, argued that it was "illogical" to prosecute military men for crimes against civilians in an era of "total war," citing the atomic bombing of Hiroshima by Americans as an example of the latter.[86] The peculiar traditions of the Japanese military system, with their emphasis on strict discipline and Spartan values, frequently arose as mitigating factors. Lawyers sometimes stressed in their defense arguments Japanese ignorance of international law.[87] As elsewhere, the defense plea of "superior orders" dominated British trials in the East.[88]

On the whole, it appears, British legal officers assigned to defend Japanese performed admirably, evincing a generally high standard of competence and dedication. A former British court president praised, too, the efforts of Japanese defense teams. On at least one occasion, noteworthily, the latter included former Japanese judges.[89]

Apparently British defense lawyers did not complain publicly about the treatment afforded them or their clients at war crimes trials, if press silence in this regard is any indication. On the other hand, examples of defense counsel thanking the court "for affording a most impartial and considerate trial to the accused"—following a conviction, no less—may be found.[90] Even convicted Japanese occasionally acknowledged their appreciation to the court for granting them a fair hearing.[91]

Much has already been said of the British preoccupation with maintaining the highest principles of justice at Eastern trials. Perhaps no better proof of Britain's strict adherence to such principles exists than the actual behavior of the courts themselves—partially examined, above—and, more specifically, that of their chief spokespersons, the court presidents. When they chose to issue public statements, presidents frequently reaffirmed the court's intention to secure the highest standards of British justice. Typical in this regard, a British colonel asserted during a trial that "it is one of the fundamental principles of British justice that the accused person be afforded a fair trial." Situations sometimes arose, however, which necessitated action, not words. At a Singapore trial the president brought to the court's attention a local newspaper's incorrect reference to the accused as "chief" of a wartime POW camp; actually the accused had merely been a guard. Acknowledging the importance of press reports of trials, he nevertheless admonished that they "should be careful, accurate and free from tendentious content." He had the error rectified. In another instance, the president shifted the location of a trial that had been constantly interfered with by "extraneous noises," such as passing traffic. "An atmosphere of quiet and calm," he said, "is an integral part of a British Court of justice. . . ." All subsequent trials were similarly relocated.[92] Court presidents, then, not only spoke in behalf of justice, but acted in kind.

Though conducted with admirable seriousness and care, British war crimes trials in the East were not flawless. Given the innumerable complex operational components, as well as the highly emotion-filled character, of so vast a human endeavor, any expectations of perfection would have been unreal. And, moreover, while the trials received "very little publicity . . . in the home Press," they engendered considerable controversy and criticism throughout Southeast Asia.[93]

A major dispute, for example, centered about the treatment afforded Japanese war criminals. Shortly after the trials' commence-

ment some people—newspaper editors, former POWs, local residents—charged British officials with treating Japanese war criminals
"too leniently—in fact almost indulgently." Under the control of
such "softies," went the accusations, Japanese suspects awaiting
trial had "regained their swagger."[94] Reports describing the release
of two notorious Japanese war criminals without trial or punishment for lack of sufficient evidence caused prolonged and sharply
worded debate in Parliament, resulting in the reopening of the case.[95]
One respected journal, the *Singapore Malay Tribune*, denounced
the entire system of war crimes trials in Southeast Asia. Due to
inexcusable "inefficiency," it charged, some 90% of war criminal
suspects escaped punishment; unable to cope with the sizable task
at hand, British authorities were prosecuting only major criminals.[96]
And later, in April 1948, London revealed its intentions shortly to
end trials in Hong Kong under a cloud of controversy. Rumor had
it, said a member of Parliament, that the phasing out of trials and
premature release of suspects in Hong Kong was the direct conse-
quence of "an economy measure," whereby the government had
"fixed a time limit," now "expired," for the disposition of all trials.
Government officials denied the allegations.[97]

Some critics, on the other hand, argued against "too harsh"
British treatment of Japanese war criminals and called for its amendment. This group espoused, for the most part, arguments predicated
on philosophical or moral reasoning—that the "time had come for
a general amnesty" for all war-connected "political crimes," or that
to treat Japanese as harshly as they had treated Allied POWs would
be "to lower ourselves to their beastly levels."[98] Lord Hankey's
notable public dissent concentrated mainly on the IMTFE, but could
fairly be interpreted as an attack against "all Japanese war crimes
trials."[99]

By far the most intensive controversy focused on the issue of
sentencing of convicted Japanese. No set rules or pattern for sentencing existed or evolved at any Eastern war crimes trials. Military
courts therefore wielded sole discretion over the handing out of
punishments. With myriad factors influencing each case, sentences
inevitably manifested wide disparities from time to time. No better
example of this may be found than the Sime Road camp trial, previously discussed.

Public protests against the inordinately severe punishments
meted out in that case inundated the editorial desk of a leading
Singapore newspaper, the *Straits Times*. The *Straits Times* itself
had questioned the wisdom and fairness of the sentences, finding

them disproportionate to the charges proved. "A British civil court does not sentence the most brutal of hooligans to death unless he actually kills someone," wrote the *Straits Times*. Why, then, it asked—in a case where no accused had been proven, specifically, guilty of murder—"should a British military court do so?"[100] Incoming mail, most of it from former internees at Sime Road camp, overwhelmingly supported the newspaper's position. While certainly no one who wrote held a "single grain of sympathy for the Nips," nearly all expressed "the strongest disapproval over the severity of the sentences." One feared that such action would be "looked upon by many as a retrograde step in the administration of British justice."[101]

To some the court's behavior in the Sime Road camp trial typified but part of a larger, more disturbing, matrix of problems. Were Japanese, probed several English people, of the "humblest" rank—for example, POW camp guards with little education and "primitive" backgrounds who, in most instances, acted under orders—receiving the most severe punishments?[102] Some skeptics doubted the correctness of all convictions.[103]

Allegations that British courts had taken a different, more serious, view toward trials involving all white, European or Allied victims, and that "only a few adequately severe sentences had been passed in cases of atrocities committed on Asiatics" loomed most significant. To be sure, questionable discrepancies in sentences occasionally surfaced.[104] In a Car Nicobar case, for example, a Japanese received a sentence of two years' imprisonment for "being concerned" in the ill-treatment and killing of over 150 natives. One need only compare this with sentences awarded in the Sime Road camp trial. Also, why the press dubbed certain trials, say, "one of the more important war crimes trials in Hong Kong," remains unanswered. Might it have been due to the victims concerned in the case—all white, and influential representatives of three different European countries?[105]

Any comprehensive examination of sentencing trends in British war crimes trials would require much time and space. Still for now two general, though not insignificant, conclusions may be offered. The first applies to nearly all Eastern war crimes trials operations, regardless of the supervising nation. Sentences meted out in earlier trials evidenced greater and more regular severity than those in later ones. With the passage of time, wartime memories "recede[d] farther and farther"; in accordance, later courts exhibited "markedly more" moderation in their sentences.[106] Secondly, one has merely to take into account the remarkable demonstration by ex-POWs in relation to the Sime Road camp trial to understand the pervasiveness of British concern for justice and fair play. Unfair sentences may occasionally have occurred, but British public opinion would never have tolerated them as the norm. Also, London's policy of encouraging widespread publicity of Eastern trials, in Japan and elsewhere, spoke exceptionally well of British determination to assure Japanese suspects equitable treatment.

London found no difficulty in concurring with the FEC's (but United States–sponsored) "recommendations" that no new class "A" or "B" and "C" trials be initiated after February 24 and June 30, 1949, respectively. Actually, British authorities heard their final Eastern war crimes trial in December 1948, well before the FEC deadlines. London even went so far as to encourage Australian officials, in June 1948, to wrap up their trial operations within one year's time.[107]

British objectives here harmonized well with the shift in American East Asian policy, which after autumn 1948 promoted Japanese economic recovery—and winding down war crimes trials—instead of reform, for several reasons. World War II cost Britain dearly, leaving it severely weakened militarily and financially. The emergence of a hostile Soviet Union as well as of strong nationalist movements in many of its former Southeast Asian colonies forced London increasingly to rely for support on "United States political and military leadership." Not surprisingly, Britain therefore aligned itself closely with its traditional ally and, in many respects, conformed its Eastern war crimes policy to that of the United States.[108]

Besides this, British authorities correctly discerned a decided lack of interest in Eastern trials among the English. Whether war weariness, the wish to bury past hatreds and all-too-recent memories or the need to concentrate on national reconstruction accounted for this attitude, it is difficult to say. But surely a general apathy toward the subject existed. The *London Times* covered scantily trials conducted in Southeast Asia and only moderately the IMTFE in Tokyo. Even in Southeast Asia, though, British public interest in the trials waned by 1947. In February of that year a major Singapore newspaper could write that many English people "are conscious of a growing longing for the day when it will be possible to have done with the whole business" of war crimes trials. Such attitudes were not lost on British officials.[109] By 1948 London began to wind down its war crimes operation.[110]

Finally, historically a great seafaring and trading nation, Britain sought in its postwar policy energetically to resuscitate its commercial past. Evincing a strong desire to develop and expand its commercial ties with a reformed Japan, Britain deemed in its own interest, and thus encouraged, a rapid Japanese postwar economic recovery. London therefore had no desire to keep alive an issue—such as war crimes trials—which could only serve to strain and weaken Anglo-Japanese relations.[111] British officials believed, moreover, that their original aim of bringing to justice as many guilty Japanese as possible had been fulfilled by late 1948; the time had now come to concentrate seriously on effecting Japan's re-entry into the family of nations.

Precise and final statistics on British Eastern war crimes trials are as follows: cases tried, 306; accused involved, 920; accuseed convicted, 811 (88.1%); accused acquitted, 107 (11.6%); death sentences awarded, 279 (34.4% of total number convicted); death sentences executed, 265 (32.7% of total number convicted); life sentences, 55; unaccounted for or not tried, 3. Results of 2 trials went unreported. Of the 3 accused not tried, 2 were determined mentally incompetent. Over 17% of all Japanese accused eventually "either had their sentences reduced or were released failing confirmations of sentences."[112]

7. Australia and Other Commonwealth Trials (Canada, New Zealand)

Australia: Machinery and Procedure

After that of the United States and Britain, the third heaviest burden for handling and disposing of Eastern war crimes trials fell upon Australia. As with their Allies, the haunting issue of Japanese atrocities profoundly disturbed Australian officials during the Pacific War. Australia therefore participated in the founding of the UNWCC in October 1943 and, in November 1944, extended its war crimes investigations by joining the Far Eastern Sub-Committee of the UNWCC.[1]

Australians, predictably, harbored a deep enmity toward the Japanese immediately after the war. By then increasingly explicit reports of inhumane Japanese wartime treatment of Australian soldiers and civilians had filtered into the homeland, causing public indignation to mount.[2] Beyond this, in an effort to unearth all possible evidence of mistreatment against Australians, Canberra established in June 1944 (and enlarged in September 1945) its own War Crimes Commission. Headed by Sir William Webb, later designated president of the IMTFE, the Commission conducted numerous investigations throughout Southeast Asia in order "to obtain first-hand accounts of Japanese war crimes."[3]

Publication of parts of the Webb Report in fall 1945 heightened emotions in Australia. As the first judicial investigation into alleged Japanese war crimes, the Report served to confirm stories by returning war veterans describing the horrible sufferings of Australians at the hands of Japanese. Enraged, many Australians considered the Japanese their most detestable foes ever. Concerned citizens, former POWs and families of war crimes victims consequently importuned government authorities, demanding the "immediate and effective" apprehension and punishment of Japanese war criminals.[4]

Officials responded, manifesting here a determination perhaps unequaled in other Allied nations, with steadfast assurances that no war crime would go unanswered. "All those" found responsible for atrocities and criminal conduct, declared the minister of external affairs, Herbert V. Evatt, in autumn 1945, would be called "to full account"; there would be no exceptions, no immunity granted. Such "outrages," members of Parliament asserted, shook the very foundations of civilization; their redress was necessary lest "the grossest defeat of justice and a travesty of principles for which the war was fought" be the result. Accordingly, General Thomas Blamey, commander-in-chief of Australian military forces, received orders in September 1945 to use every means at his disposal to locate and detain suspects. "Any Australian authority, military or otherwise," could assist him.[5]

Australians, however, never wavered in their demand that the retribution meted out to culpable Japanese be flawlessly just. Certainly, insisted Evatt, the "Potsdam principle of punishing war criminals should be rigorously applied"; nevertheless accused persons should be brought to trial in a "spirit of justice," not revenge. Members of Parliament held that all arrests and trials must be accomplished through appropriate "channels" and take place before "properly constituted tribunals." To be sure, the government would not brook "kid-glove treatment of the Japanese," Australia's "most ruthless and barbarous enemy" ever; they "should be treated with the utmost severity," but "justly" nonetheless.[6] Before long a chorus of parliamentary demands arose, triggered largely by constituent pressure, calling for the expeditious and stern disposition of war criminals.[7]

Other factors, beyond an understandable desire to redress injustices, contributed to the shaping of Australia's war crimes policy. "Australia's basic interest in the postwar as in the prewar Pacific," observed an Australian historian, fastened firmly on "security." Britain's reduction of its overseas commitments, particularly in the Pacific, produced a mounting sense of isolation and of "additional responsibility" in Canberra.[8] Australia's fear of a resurgent Japan accentuated these feelings. Australians remembered all too well the cruel treatment afforded them by their Japanese foes. And they recalled vividly that, but for a signal American victory at Midway Island in June 1942, Australia might have become the next invasion target of the Japanese Imperial Army. Doubtless Canberra's apprehensions toward Japan at that time far surpassed any fears of a Russian threat.[9]

Government officials therefore unhesitatingly announced an overriding objective of Australian foreign policy: from their point of view, "the problem of a European settlement [could] never be regarded as so important or immediate as that of the settlement with Japan." Its "constant concern," explained Evatt, was that Japan would "not a second time rise as an aggressor. . . . We must strive for security against further aggression."[10]

While Australians supported FEC proposals that stressed the "importance of bringing about the establishment of a truly democratic and peaceful government in Japan," doubts invariably cropped up. "I am not moved at all by the statements made about the democratization of Japan," revealed one Australian legislator. Defeat had "not changed the Japanese character one iota," warned another, and he urged his compatriots not to "be misled by the present apparent submission of the Japanese," who might very well be masking hopes for a future revival of national power.[11]

Guided by such deep-rooted suspicion and enmity, Australian authorities thus became convinced that "the terms of the peace settlement with Japan must be carried out with firmness." They insisted on the destruction of the economic bases of Japan's military strength. A "firm" policy could only be achieved, reasoned Evatt, "if due account is taken of the atrocious conduct of the enemy."[12] Moreover, certain officials, including Sir William Webb, believed that major war crimes trials (the IMTFE) would do more than merely "bring Japanese war criminals to justice": they would serve to "eradicate the militarist spirit in Japan."[13] In other words, Australia's war crimes policy—to administer stern justice to all guilty Japanese—formed an integral part of its overall foreign policy objectives.

Furthermore, if Australians learned anything from their war experience it was, as one put it, "that the greater the interest of the United States in the Southwest Pacific the better it will be for us."[14] Accordingly, Australian officials acknowledged, even encouraged, American predominance in the Pacific.[15]

For its assumption of much of the Pacific defense burden, however, Washington expected Allied recognition of its political leadership in the region. Australia's relations with the United States, then, proceeded smoothly providing its major objectives coincided with those of America. Hence Australia's foreign policy, like that of Britain and other Allied nations, occasionally hewed to lines drawn or suggested by the United States.[16] Sometimes, significantly, conflicting American and Australian war crimes policies precluded total agreement.

Few nations, in a notable example, demanded more persistently and urgently than Australia that the Japanese emperor be tried as a war criminal. Shortly after the war's end Canberra named Hirohito as its "number one war criminal." Calls for "Hirohito's scalp" sprang from all over Australia and grew in intensity.[17] But American policymakers, for decidedly political reasons recounted elsewhere in this study, chose to grant immunity to Emperor Hirohito.[18] Their policy to try every guilty Japanese notwithstanding, Australians conceded, said Justice Webb, that the emperor's "immunity was, no doubt, decided upon in the best interests of all the Allied Powers."[19]

And, for reasons explained in the following section, Canberra and Washington eventually became embroiled in a heated dispute, destined to have significant consequences, over the proposed termination date of Eastern war crimes trials.

Australians based their jurisdiction on, and outlined regulations for the governing of war crimes trials according to, the Commonwealth of Australia War Crimes Act of 1945. Validated by "royal Assent" on October 11 of that year, the bill followed "generally the lines" drawn by Britain's Royal Warrant of June 14, 1945.[20] Yet distinctions between the two documents existed.

Most notably different was creation of the Australian provisions by act of Parliament, while those of Britain emanated from a Royal Warrant issued under the Royal Prerogative. Another major difference lay in the Australian Act's definition of "war crime." Section 3 of the Act defined war crime as "a violation of the laws and usages of war" or as "any war crime" so defined by a Board of Inquiry (that is, the Australian War Crimes Commission), "committed in any place whatsoever, whether within or beyond Australia, during any war."

In a practicable attempt to deal with a variety of anticipated or novel offenses, the Board of Inquiry included in its definition of war crimes a list of thirty-five separate violations. First on the list stood "crimes against peace," expressed in words similar to those used in section 2, article 5a of the Charter of the IMTFE.[21] Violations 2 to 35 consisted of crimes enumerated specifically by Australia, but which by any general definition also fell under the rubric "violations of the laws and usages of war"—for example:

"murder and massacre" (2); "torture of civilians" (4); "rape" (6); "confiscation of property" (15); and "cannibalism" (34). No allowance was made for "crimes against humanity," excepting such crimes which also fell under the phrase "violations of the law and customs of war." Australia's War Crimes Act, then, provided a definition of war crimes broader and more flexible than the Royal Warrant, but not as broad as those of the United States or the IMTFE.[22]

The Act provided Australian military courts jurisdiction in all cases where the victim had "been either resident in Australia or a British or an allied subject."[23] Power to convene military courts, "appoint officers to constitute the courts" and award, carry out and, if need be, "mitigate or remit" sentences devolved upon the governor-general or his delegate(s).[24]

Regulations relating to the composition of an Australian military court and to the appointment of judge advocates closely adhered to those of Britain. Courts consisted therefore of "not less than two officers in addition to the President." Where practicable, the measure directed, "the Convening officer should . . . appoint as many officers as possible of equal or superior relative rank to the accused." The same general principle applied in the matter of respective service branches: where practicable, "at least one officer" of the same service branch as the accused should be appointed to the court.

Australia, like Britain, adopted the institution of mixed interAllied military courts. Hence the War Crimes Act permitted appointment to courts, "other than the President," or "one or more officers of any allied or associated Power," provided that at least half the court, including the president, consisted of Australians. Australian military courts occasionally, however, appointed as president officers from England or "any other part of his Majesty's Dominions."[25]

Convening officers decided whether or not to appoint judge advocates to military courts. Following the British precedent, Australian judge advocates' roles consisted "mainly in advising the Court on matters of substantive and procedural law." They lacked voting powers. Nor were members of the court obliged to accept their advice, although their opinions generally "carried great weight."[26]

Australian courts, again like those of the British, were not bound by the ordinary rules of evidence. Military courts took into consideration "any oral statement" or "document appearing on the face of it to be authentic." The sole factor determining the admissibility of evidence rested with its probative value: that is, whether it appeared to the court "to be of assistance in proving or disproving the charge." Military courts followed procedure as set down in the Imperial Army Acts and rules of procedure relating to field general courts-martial.[27]

Australian law guaranteed Japanese accused the right to "properly qualified" counsel, either British or from any other country, including Japan. Upon an accused's conviction, military courts awarded any of the following punishments: death (either by shooting or hanging), imprisonment for life, or any lesser term, confiscation of property or a fine of any amount, or both. Here another principal distinction between Australian and British war crimes trails procedure crops up. No death sentence could be passed, according to the War Crimes Act, "without the concurrence of all those serving on the court if the court consists" of three members, "or without the concurrence of at least two thirds of those serving on the court" if the court has more than three members. Britain's Royal Warrant contained no similar provision.[28]

Australian law permitted submission by convicted Japanese of a petition to the confirming officer against the finding or the sentence or both. Should the confirming officer agree with the decision or sentence, the case ended there. If not, he referred it to the Australian judge advocate general or his deputy for final disposition.[29]

All Commonwealth nations, Australia included, relied heavily and regularly on municipal law in war crimes trials prosecutions. Charges, accordingly, reflected this reliance and often consisted of "murder" or "manslaughter."[30] Similarly, all Commonwealth nations frequently introduced as evidence, or as "authoritative statements of law," official manuals on international or military law and treatises by distinguished jurists. In one case, for example, an Australian judge advocate "urged" the court to refer to Oppenheim, a noted authority on international law, as well as the *British Manual of Military Law* before reaching its decision.[31]

Australians wasted little time organizing and launching their war crimes operation. Through wide-scale investigations begun as early as 1942, and later accelerated by the War Crimes Commission, Australian authorities amassed a tremendous amount of evidence against Japanese war criminals. By May 1945, in fact, they had rounded up 1,481 suspects for trial.[32]

In October 1945 the governor-general in council, under the War Crimes Act, delegated the power to convene military courts to certain staff officers and field commanders of the Australian military forces. Shortly after, full responsibility for "exercising and administering" pivotal control and supervision over all war criminal investigations and prosecutions devolved upon these military authorities. The adjutant general appointed an Australian officer, in civilian life a barrister, to head the operation. Army Headquarters, Melbourne, became the coordinating center.[33]

Under the direction of this central war crimes agency, Australian military authorities established "proper organs" to conduct investigations and to apprehend suspects. These "War Crimes Sections" opened in Singapore in December 1945 and in Tokyo in February 1946.

The Australian Section worked "in the closest possible liaison" with British war crimes investigation authorities in Singapore, as well as with Dutch military personnel in Java. Australian military courts constituted in Singapore or British military courts, featuring an Australian member, conducted trials involving Australian victims.

Attached to General Headquarters, SCAP, Tokyo, was the Australian War Crimes Section (SCAP). Its duties resembled those of its Singapore counterpart, except that no Australian military court convened in Japan. This branch concentrated on investigating war crimes committed against Australian POWs while in captivity in Japan. Cases sufficiently built up by the Australian Section were turned over to American military commissions, with an Australian officer sitting as a member, for trial. Frequently Australian officers served as prosecutors in these cases.[34]

Australian military forces also "actively participated" in investigating and trying war crimes perpetrated outside the scope of the Singapore and Tokyo centers. Australians, for example, performed admirably in the Southwest Pacific Area. In the New Guinea–New Britain regions, Australian military personnel assisted in the investigation and preparation of many cases against Japanese suspects. And despite the absence of individual Australian war crimes sections in New Guinea and Rabaul, Australian military courts convened and heard a substantial number of trials at these locations.

Australian military courts assembled throughout Southeast Asia and the Southwest Pacific tried Japanese for war crimes committed against "local British and European residents, Chinese and Dutch nationals, both military and civilian, Indian soldiers . . . and Australian personnel." Accordingly, in cases involving their nationals as victims, British, Chinese and Indian officers joined Australian military courts as members.[35]

Army Headquarters, Melbourne, also maintained direct communication with Australian investigation teams on Celebes Island, the Halmahera Island group, Timor, the Ceram Islands (including Amboina), the Talaud Islands and British and Dutch Borneo. Two specific Australian divisions, one in Morotai, the other in Labuan, British North Borneo, coordinated these investigations and later conducted trials in these areas.[36]

Australian war crimes teams relied, basically, on the same methods for building up tenable cases as the British: namely, broad, pervasive, firsthand investigations; extensive interviews with large numbers of ex-POWs and other witnesses; and continuous cooperation with Allied investigation teams. Interestingly, Canberra elected to circulate among its returning POWs American-type "war crimes questionnaires," for reporting of atrocities, instead of those of the British. Most Australian war crimes trials hinged upon evidence documentary in nature, that is, sworn statements and affidavits.[37] As in other theaters, the high percentage of dead or otherwise unlocated victims, rapid repatriation of ex-POWs and the general close-mouthed behavior of Japanese suspects deprived Australian hearings of substantial live testimony. Nevertheless trials held in Labuan departed from this norm, featuring an abundance of native witnesses and, to the surprise of local authorities, a good number of Japanese troops and minor camp officials "showing unexpected eagerness to give evidence against their former superiors."[38]

Australia: The Trials

Not by chance, Australia's initial Eastern war crimes trial involved a crime hitherto unprecedented in modern international law. At Wewak, New Guinea, Australian military authorities wrestled with the problem of how to deal with a Japanese officer accused of "cannibalism" against local inhabitants during the war. Twentieth-century international law contained no provisions to accommodate such a "primitive" violation.[39]

Australians, however, had wisely anticipated the situation. In its extended definition of war crimes the Board of Inquiry included two additional violations: "cannibalism" and "mutilation of a dead body." Either charge, then, served well in this case—obviously selected by Australians as the first war crimes trial in order to establish an implementable precedent for future hearings.

At the trial the accused admitted eating part of an Australian

Eyewitness to the killing and burial of Allied personnel is questioned at Australian trial of suspected war criminal Tokio Iwasa. Morotai, November 30, 1945. Australian War Memorial. Neg. no. 124133.

POW's body. Nonetheless he pleaded innocent, explaining that his starving condition had caused temporary loss of his senses. On December 4, 1945, after deliberating two days, the court found him guilty and sentenced him to hang.[40]

Trials commenced in Morotai on November 29, 1945, and in Labuan on December 3, 1945. Australian officials, prior to the start of trials, had emphasized that primary attention would be paid to cases involving the "commission of serious crimes"—for example, mass murder, starvation, savage unprovoked attacks and the like.[41] Opening trials in both these places reflected this policy. A military court at Labuan convicted a Japanese sergeant major of the wanton massacre of fifty-one POWs at Miri, Sarawak, in June 1945 and sentenced him to be shot. At Morotai, another military court judged ten of eleven Japanese guilty of "crucifixion and murder" of one American and three Australian airmen on the Talaud Islands, near Celebes, in February 1945.[42]

Australian military courts commonly held "mass trials," a practice hardly unique; all the prosecuting nations did likewise. However, whereas the largest American or British trial comprised thirty or forty accused—in itself, a considerable and unwieldy task—Aus-

An Australian military tribunal pronounces the accused, Tokio Iwasa, guilty as charged. Morotai, November 30, 1945. Australian War Memorial. Neg. no. 124134.

tralian courts occasionally ballooned to more than twice that number. One, "the biggest mass trial so far held in the Pacific area," the *London Times* called it, opened in Labuan in December 1945. There seventy Japanese stood "jointly" charged with ill-treatment of hundreds of civilian internees at Kuching, Sarawak.[43] Even more remarkable, another mass trial, held in Amboina, saw ninety-three Japanese officers and POW camp guards "charged collectively" with "calculated cruelty" and other ill-treatment of Australian, Dutch and American POWs.[44]

Trials conducted at Labuan and Morotai ended on January 31 and February 28, 1946, respectively. Between March 1 and April 29, 1946, trials took place at Darwin, these being, along with later hearings at Manus Island, the only war crimes trials held on Australian soil.[45] The center of activity then shifted to Rabaul, New Britain, where from March 1946 to December 1947 some of the most interesting trials occurred.

Denial of a fair trial during a war constituted a war crime, so ruled an Australian military court at Rabaul in a case heard on March 28 and 29, 1946. Early in the trial, the accused admitted having beheaded a Chinese prisoner in 1944. While "no court-

Two Japanese servicemen accused of war crimes against Australian airmen at Talaud Island, with their Australian defense interpreter, hear prosecution argument. Morotai, December 3, 1945. Australian War Memorial. Neg. no. 124167.

martial or other formal trial" had taken place, defense counsel argued nonetheless that the Chinese victim had been adequately investigated beforehand and proved guilty of war crimes. Furthermore, he averred, the "serious" war situation "justified" his client's act: under such circumstances, the execution constituted a "summary trial," a proceeding legal under Japanese military law. Nevertheless, the court rejected defense's plea and sentenced the accused to death. Not in vain, apparently, was the superb defense effort put forth. A higher military authority, obviously somewhat convinced by the defense's reasoning, later commuted the punishment to seven years' imprisonment.[46]

Despite its immediate results, the court's ruling in the preceding case left the central issue—denial of a fair trial—open to further deliberation. Variations subsequently arose in defense claims that victims of wartime executions had, indeed, received fair trials from Japanese, thereby preventing courts from establishing any set rule.[47]

One case involved seven Japanese charged with "unlawfully killing" eighteen natives of the Rabaul area in September 1944. Proven and self-confessed members of an underground guerrilla

Party of war criminals and witnesses on the wharf at Morotai await transportation to a POW compound. November 2, 1945. Australian War Memorial. Neg. no. 122611.

movement, the native victims had done their best over a period of years to obstruct Japanese army operations. Their functions included concealing and stealing of weapons and rations, destruction of petrol and supplies and harrassment, even killing, of Japanese soldiers—all acts defined in the Japanese military code as "war crimes."

The accused tried the natives before a summary court-martial. The trial lasted fifty minutes, four minutes being devoted to testimony, twenty minutes to deliberation over verdicts and sentences. No legal or any other representative defended the accused natives. The Japanese justified the trial's brevity "in view of the time element"; that is, Rabaul, they said, had been declared an emergency area in April 1944. Finally, counsel for the defense argued, "summary trials in the field for war criminals had been authorized by the Japanese Government. . . ."[48]

The court found the two Japanese who had served as judges at the summary trial guilty and sentenced them to life imprisonment. It acquitted the rest. The judge advocate advised the court that if the "deceased had a fair and reasonable trial"—even by Japanese standards—then the accused would be "entitled to an acquittal." But again the matter, ultimately, was left unsettled: a confirming officer, viewing the relevant facts in an essentially different light, shortly after commuted the life terms to imprisonment for two years.[49]

A good number of trials at Rabaul, and elsewhere, dealt with the legal principle of command responsibility. One typical case charged that the accused, Lt. Gen. Baba Masao, "while commander of armed forces of Japan . . . unlawfully disregarded and failed to discharge his duty as a . . . commander to control the conduct of the members of his command whereby they committed brutal atrocities and other high crimes. . . ."[50]

Evidence adduced at the hearing revealed that Masao, in late 1944 and early 1945, had ordered the evacuation of about a thousand British and American POWs from a camp at Sandakan, Borneo, so as to escape an anticipated Allied landing nearby. Though beset by widespread illness, meager rations and inadequate clothing, the POWs were nonetheless marched 165 miles "over extremely difficult country" to Ranau. The journey proved a monumental disaster: unthinkable hardships, illness, ill-treatment and outright murder of those who could not keep up by Japanese guards resulted in the deaths of hundreds. Only 183 POWs reached Ranau and of these 150 died shortly after arrival. A subordinate of Masao later ordered and supervised the execution of the 33 surviving POWs.[51]

The march to Ranau, contended the defense, became an "operational necessity" due to the exigencies of the war situation. In fact, Allied troops did land, as the Japanese expected, in Sandakan in July 1945. Moreover, the defense emphasized, Japanese soldiers had marched alongside the POWs and had suffered "the same hardships" as they. Masao testified that he "had done his best" to provide for the prisoners, that he had taken measures to secure provisions and medical supplies and that he did not learn of the murders until after their commission.[52]

Still, countered prosecutors, "the accused had an undoubted duty to ensure that prisoners of war were treated in accordance with the requirements of international law." Masao's failure to control the excesses of his troops, they alleged, whether deliberate "or through culpable negligence" made him "guilty of a violation of the laws and usages of war."[53]

Summing up the evidence and the law, the judge advocate advised the court as to "the duties of a commander" under international law. He cited, for example, the 1907 Hague Convention (armed forces "must be commanded by a person responsible for his subordinates"), the 1929 Geneva Convention (POWs "shall at all times be humanely treated and protected") and the majority judgment of the United States Supreme Court *In re Yamashita* (the "law of war presupposes that its violations are to be avoided through the control of the operations of war by commanders who are to some extent responsible for their subordinates").[54]

On June 2, 1947, the court judged Masao guilty and sentenced him to be hanged. The execution took place as scheduled. Without a reasoned judgment, there is no way of knowing exactly why the court ruled as it did. Nevertheless in light of the prosecution's argument and the passages quoted by the judge advocate in his summation, it appears that the conclusion reached by the UNWCC was sound. In this case, it wrote, "as in other cases before Australian courts, the existence of the duty of a commander as outlined in *In re Yamashita* was looked upon as well established in international law, and the failure to discharge this duty as a war crime."[55]

Australian courts, it is true, almost always convicted Japanese charged with violating the principle of command responsibility. Yet as "no hard and fast rule" existed with regard to the "extent" of a commander's duty, unique circumstances rendered each case substantially different. Sentences hence varied, ranging from death, as in the Masao case, to as little as five years' confinement.[56]

No defense plea, as previously pointed out, appeared more often at Eastern war crimes trials than that of superior orders. Indeed, Japanese on trial and their counsel frequently underscored in their defense arguments the nearly sacred quality of the twin virtues of "inflexible discipline" and obedience to orders as defined in the Japanese military code.

In one instance, a Japanese major accepted total responsibility for having ordered the bayoneting of three Australian airmen. He said that his order for the execution "was regarded [by his subordinates] as an order from the Emperor" and that the soldiers' manual declared that no matter what the nature of such an order, it must be obeyed. Japanese on trial commonly responded affirmatively to such questions as, "If you were ordered by your General to shoot your Colonel, would you carry out the order without question?"[57]

Australian military courts, in a considerable number of cases, demonstrated a merciful view toward accused who pleaded superior orders. Lenient sentences or recommendations for mercy were not uncommon.[58] Nor were acquittals. One such Singapore case caused a furor with reverberations reaching all the way back to Canberra. It involved six Java *Kempeitai* who pleaded "obedience to superior orders" in answer to charges of "being concerned" in the unlawful killing of three Allied POWs and a Dutch woman. Upon acquittal of the accused, representatives of the Australian War Crimes Section in Singapore signaled the judge advocate general in Melbourne, asking for a ruling on the judgment. While the decision remained unchanged, war crimes legal circles in Singapore decided to treat the case as extraordinary and agreed unanimously that this judgment not be considered "binding on all future cases where" the defense pleaded "obedience to superior orders."[59] Still it did not deter Japanese accused in "almost every" subsequent trial from basing their defense on these same grounds.[60]

Press coverage of Australian trials stressed the uniqueness and cogency of prosecution arguments and efforts, rather than those of the defense.[61] Newspaper reports described how, in a celebrated Labuan case, an Australian prosecutor cleverly elicited admissions from an ex-POW camp commander—yes, accused had tortured POWs; yes, he had "gouged" their eyes; and so on—devastating to the defense. And by dubbing the accused the "beast of Belsen" in his closing remarks, the prosecutor provided the public—and the court—with a pointed reminder of the subject's sadistic past.[62]

Australian prosecutors often devised novel, enterprising methods of winning convictions. One, at a Singapore trial, asked an accused to show the court how hard a *Kempeitai* officer could strike a person with a belt. The accused's "enthusiastic demonstration" helped to convict him on charges of beating a sick Australian POW.[63] Another case saw a Japanese corporal sentenced to five years' "rigorous imprisonment" for beating and kicking an Australian POW, after the prosecutor had requested a demonstration of "how he kicked." The accused insisted on the harmlessness of his kicks, but the deep dents in the wooden table legs following his courtroom demonstration indicated otherwise.[64]

Since early 1946 Australian military authorities had tried Japanese for war crimes at Singapore. In November 1947 they transferred this war crimes court to Hong Kong, where thirteen trials, covering "happenings in many parts of Southeast Asia and South-West Pacific areas," subsequently took place. War crimes teams prepared the substance of most of the cases slated for trial in Hong Kong in Tokyo, although local personnel assisted in building up about a dozen.[65] Hong Kong trials witnessed the same, now hackneyed, stories of inhumane Japanese treatment of Allied POWs and civilians which had resulted in the deaths of hundreds and suffering of countless more. Trials ended in Hong Kong in December 1948.[66] The closing of Hong Kong trials, however, portended major difficulties for Australian war crimes and foreign policy spokespersons.

Australians, it has been shown, began to "wind down" Eastern war crimes trials by summer 1948. Indeed, while investigations continued, no trials were held in 1949. Such inactivity, though, did not go uncontested. While Australian military courts had tried close to 800 Japanese war criminals as of March 1948, several hundred still awaited trial.[67] Members of the Australian government, once again, expressed loud and persistent protests insisting that "all" Japanese suspects be tried. "Appeasement" of war criminals, for whatever reasons, shouted the political opposition, would not be tolerated.[68]

About the same time, autumn 1948, the United States initiated a shift—from reform to recovery—in its occupation policy. With this shift, a somewhat altered war crimes trials policy surfaced. Keeping in mind its ultimate goal of an early, non-punitive peace treaty with Japan, SCAP pressed for the expedition of Eastern war crimes trials.[69] Concurrently, London notified Canberra of its desire that Australians complete all Japanese trials within one year's time. And in February and June 1949 the FEC recommended that all remaining trials be concluded by September 30 of that year.[70]

Through SCAP, London authorities and the FEC, then the United States strongly "suggested" to Australia and other Allied nations that they wrap up their war crimes operations before the start of 1950. This placed Australian officials in a dilemma. Granted, some Australians had grown "impatient" with war crimes trials and had called for their termination by mid-1948.[71] Most, though, still demanded prosecution of "all" culpable Japanese. No Australian government could realistically have been expected to release prematurely or rush through the hearings of Japanese still awaiting trial without suffering severe domestic political consequences.

No incident involving Australian war crimes trials generated more controversy and friction, at home and abroad, than this one. The details are as follows: Australian officials "promised" General MacArthur, in 1948, that they would complete all trials by September 1949. With the closing down of the war crimes court in Hong

Kong in December 1948, however, Australians lacked a suitable location in which to hold the remaining trials. MacArthur "absolutely refused" to allow them to be conducted in Hong Kong or Japan, even after "repeated entreaties." Australia's war crimes operation consequently stalled completely: despite SCAP's threat to release all Japanese suspects then being held in Tokyo, Canberra conducted no trials in 1949. Government spokespersons claimed lack of "proper accommodations and other essentials" needed for the trials. "Dilly-dallying," rejoined the opposition.[72]

When, in late 1949, the government expressed its concern that a good number of Japanese had been detained for four years without trial, thereby violating a standard of British justice, parliamentary opposition fulminated. In no way, asserted these individuals, would American pressure, "international politics" or "political expediency" be permitted as an excuse not to finish the trials.[73] Of course all trials would be held, just speeded up, insisted the government. Meanwhile it underlined the fundamental correctness of SCAP's position: "suspects could not be held without trial forever."[74]

In the end, the Australian government succeeded in reaching a compromise solution which reconciled its position with those of parliamentary opposition and SCAP. Canberra announced that it would prosecute only Japanese accused who faced capital charges— that is, where the crimes alleged carried a penalty of death upon conviction. Trials would be held at Manus Island, the Australian territory "nearest to Japan . . . available" for the purpose, and with all due "speed and decision."[75] In fact, Australians eventually tried 113 Japanese at Manus Island between June 1950 and May 1951, the last of all Japanese war crimes trials in the East.[76]

This matter, however, significantly influenced other important political developments in the Far East. Soon after the war, Australian authorities declared strong support for negotiation of "an early peace treaty with Japan."[77] They never wavered from this position.[78] American officials, though, believed that the termination of all Eastern war crimes trials must precede any truly lasting, nonpunitive peace treaty with Japan. Japan's leaders, it appears, agreed. During treaty negotiations held in January 1951 between John Foster Dulles and Prime Minister Yoshida, the United States and Japan reached "a basic agreement," *inter alia*, "that there should be no further additions to the list of war criminals."[79] Doubtless other factors contributed to the delay in the conclusion of a peace treaty— Russia's refusal to participate, for one.[80] Yet it seems hardly a coincidence that not until July 1951 was the final draft of the treaty prepared and not until September was it signed:[81] Australian war crimes trials at Manus Island ended in May 1951.

Australian legislators commonly responded to various aspects of official war crimes policy in a demonstrative and skeptical fashion. Indeed, public interest in and concern for factual information on the trials, from start to finish, emerged as a keynote of Australia's war crimes operation. Throughout the operation, for instance, members of Parliament complained that they were receiving too little information on war crimes trials. Was such "secrecy," they asked, by government design?[82] Often they registered strong protests against the "outrageous" judgments and sentences awarded by military courts, charging the latter with excessive leniency, or accusing them of permitting guilty Japanese to go free without justification, perhaps for reasons of "political expediency."[83]

Concern over whether such allegations, invariably denied by the government, contained any truth misses the fundamental point: that is, Australian public and official interest in the trials, that they be properly, sternly and justly administered, remained intact from 1945 to 1951. Australians, then, refused to relegate Eastern war crimes trials to a level of minor importance.[84]

As early as September 1945 Minister of External Affairs Evatt declared the purpose of war crimes trials to be the attaining of justice, not the exacting of vengeance. Official policy never, and actual execution of the trials rarely, departed from this admirable position. Australia's "conduct in victory," asserted Prime Minister Robert Menzies in 1950, "should be marked by an adherence to those great principles . . . which have characterized the whole development of what we call, in simple but proud terms, British justice." Even those whose profound hatred of the Japanese gravitated to the most vicious and deplorable level—racial—conceded that Australians, "as British people," must mete out to enemies "the same measure of justice" that they granted their own people; in this way they would "maintain" their "standards of justice."[85]

One particular incident stands out in this regard. In June 1950 rumors circulated in Canberra alleging that the government had appointed a "hangman" and had authorized construction of a gallows at Manus Island before scheduled trials even began. A barrage of scathing parliamentary attacks descended on the government. Would the premature appointment of an executioner, inquired a critic, serve to "gain the respect of the peoples of Asia for our ideas of justice?" Such rumors were unfounded, replied the minister for external territories, further reassuring all concerned of Canberra's steadfast intention to "ensure" all Japanese suspects "even-handed justice."[86]

In short, Australia's Eastern war crimes trials operation, though sternly administered, nonetheless steered clear of any "attempt to exact an eye for an eye. . . ."[87] A Japanese colonel, for example, who served as a defense counsel at Labuan, called a trial which ended in his client's conviction and sentencing to death "very fair," and thanked the court for its impartiality.[88] And while Australia's conducting of trials drew some criticism, most of this censure focused on the legal procedure applied at the trials—specifically, on the relaxation of customary rules of evidence, thereby permitting the admission as evidence of affidavits, statements, documents and the like.[89] To these critics, one might offer the same admonition offered to critics of the legal procedure applied at the Yamashita trial (see chapter 4): they "seemed to confuse the difference between domestic civil courts and military commissions." Even critics of Australian trials admitted, however, that all courts admirably featured "fair and able jurists" as presidents.[90]

Final trial statistics for Australia are summarized in the following table:

Place	No. of trials	No. of acc'd	Acquitted	Convictions
Singapore	23	62	11	51
Morotai	25	148	67	81
Labuan	16	145	17	128
Wewak	2	2	1	1
Rabaul	188	390	124	266
Darwin	3	22	12	10
Hong Kong	13	42	4	38
Manus	26	113	44	69
Total	296	924	280	644

Of the 644 (69.5% of total number accused) prisoners convicted, 148 (23%) were sentenced to death and executed; 496 (77%) were sentenced to imprisonment. The prison terms consisted of: life, 39; 25 years, 2; 11–24 years, 152; 10 years, 82; under 10 years, 22.[91]

Canada

Canada based its jurisdiction for military courts for the trials of war criminals on the Act Respecting War Crimes of August 31, 1946.[92] Canadian regulations closely resembled those contained in Britain's Royal Warrant of June 14, 1945. For example, they defined war crimes narrowly, as "a violation of the laws or usages of war" committed during any war engaged in by Canada after September 9, 1939.[93] Additional provisions permitted the convening of military courts, both Canadian and mixed inter-Allied.[94] The duties of a Canadian judge advocate consisted "mainly in advising the Court on matters of substantive and procedural law." Military courts followed procedure applicable to field general courts-martial; accordingly, they allowed for "a certain relaxation in the rules regarding the admissibility of evidence."[95]

Canadian regulations included certain features not found in the Royal Warrant. Most notable here was a provision disallowing Canadian military courts from passing any death sentences "without the concurrence of all those serving on the court" if it consisted of three members, or without the concurrence "of at least two-thirds of those serving on the court" if it exceeded three members. In this respect Canadian regulations coincided with those of Australia.[96]

During the war Canadians expressed their intentions to participate in postwar efforts to demilitarize and democratize Japan.[97] As a member of the FEC, Canada, after arranging matters with Washington in November 1945, dispatched representatives to the IMTFE in Tokyo. There Justice E. S. McDougall on the bench, and Brigadier H. G. Nolan on the prosecution staff, ably represented Canada throughout the proceedings.[98]

Contrary to some misconceptions, Canada did not restrict its Eastern war crimes operations solely to the "trial of major Japanese war criminals."[99] As early as January 1946 the Canadian embassy had informed the state department of its desire to participate in the trials of minor Japanese war criminals.[100] Canada, however, ran into trouble here. Canadian war crimes regulations, explained W. L. MacKenzie King, secretary of state for external affairs, permitted the convening of military courts for minor trials only "by states" then "in occupation of areas formerly dominated by Japan." Moreover, he added, only "senior officers in command of 'Canadian Forces'" could convene Canadian military courts. As Canada had deployed no occupation forces in the Far East, it could not convene courts in that area.[101]

Canadian war criminal prosecutions in the East therefore required British and American cooperation. Toward this end, eight Canadian officers, all possessing legal experience, arrived in Tokyo and Hong Kong in 1946. The officers, including two former Hong Kong POWs, assisted "in the collection and collation of further evidence of atrocities against Canadians" and in the prosecution of cases involving Canadian victims. Furthermore, they acted in "general liaison" with British and American war crimes teams, and occasionally provided them with evidence available from Canadian sources.[102]

A War Crimes Section at Canadian National Defense headquarters furnished these officers and their Allies with substantial evidence of atrocities committed against Canadians in Hong Kong and Japan proper. Beyond this, at the request of United States authorities Canada commissioned an officer "to sit as judge on any joint military court" for the trials of lesser war criminals, regardless of the victims' nationalities.[103]

Canada's contribution to the Allied Eastern war crimes operation, while not extensive, proved efficient. A Canadian sub-detachment in Hong Kong obtained eleven convictions for crimes directed against Canadian POWs, while its counterpart in Tokyo took part in the prosecution of eleven cases involving twenty-three defendants accused of war crimes against Canadian and Allied POWs. Canadian overseas war crimes operations closed in May 1947.[104]

New Zealand

New Zealander POWs, like their Commonwealth counterparts, suffered greatly under Japanese activity. For this reason, New Zealanders retained a deep hostility toward and fear of Japan for many years after the war.[105]

New Zealand, a member of both the UNWCC and FEC, also participated in the proceedings of the IMTFE in Tokyo. Its representatives, Mr. Justice Northcroft on the bench and Mr. R. H. Quilliam on the prosecution staff, symbolized Wellington's "special interest in the settlement in Japan and in the maintenance of peace and security in the Pacific." To be sure, its IMTFE representation, reported the *Dominion*, "identified" the government "in a special way with the punishment of war criminals."[106]

Elsewhere New Zealand's role in Eastern war crimes operations became that of "a passive observer."[107] Indeed, records of the *Parliamentary Debates* for the years 1945 to 1947 are conspicuously deficient as regards discussions of Eastern war crimes trials. One parliamentary critic decried the lack of coverage, noting that "some information about . . . [these] trials . . . would remind the people that New Zealand still had responsibilities and duties in Japan."[108]

Considering New Zealanders' wartime and postwar enmity toward the Japanese, nearly akin to that of Australians, their failure to take more assertive action in minor war criminal prosecutions seems surprising. However, their inactivity may be attributed to three factors. First, New Zealanders, like other Allied populations, experienced a growing impatience by 1947 with the length and immensity of the war crimes operation.[109] Second, as with Australia, security matters overwhelmingly dominated Wellington's interests in the early postwar years.[110] Third, and in response to the preceding factor, New Zealand willingly accepted unquestioned American predominance in the Pacific, as well as American, British and Australian supervision over Eastern war crimes trials.[111]

8. Russia

Procedure and Machinery

The Soviet Union's approach and contribution to the Allied war crimes operation in the East differed totally from that of the other Allied nations. Nearly every act planned or undertaken by Russia during and after World War II reflected, to some degree, political considerations. Japanese war crimes trials proved to be no exception.

Russia suffered horribly during World War II; millions of its people perished. Yet, for the most part, that suffering was not caused, directly at least, by Japan, but by Germany. Russia, in fact, did not enter the war in the East until August 9, 1945.[1] This reality, then, determined the Soviets' assumption of a relatively minor role in the disposition of Japanese war crimes trials.

Early in the war Russia associated itself with Allied war crimes policy. A Soviet representative sat as a guest at the signing in London, on January 13, 1942, of an inter-Allied Declaration on *Punishment for War Crimes*.[2] On December 17, 1942, London, Washington and Moscow simultaneously promulgated declarations reaffirming "their solemn resolution that those responsible [for wartime atrocities] should not escape retribution."[3] November 1943 witnessed the joint signing and issuing of the Moscow Declaration by Premier Stalin, President Roosevelt and Prime Minister Churchill. The UNWCC called this the "most important pronouncement made by Allied statesmen on the subject of war crimes, and one which set the pattern for the trial, not only of minor criminals, but also of those responsible for atrocities in occupied countries."[4] Like the preceding statements, however, the Moscow Declaration referred exclusively to German war criminals.

Such verbal cooperation notwithstanding, all major Soviet decisions hinged on political realities. Undoubtedly the most significant Allied organization, as concerned war crimes and war criminals, was the UNWCC. Creation of this multinational body stemmed from an Anglo-American understanding and joint statement of October 7, 1942.[5] At that time Allied spokespersons recognized the importance of Russian participation in the organization's many functions and urged the Soviets to join.

But Moscow insisted that the seven Soviet republics (the Ukraine, Byelorussia, Moldavia, Lithuania, Latvia, Estonia and Karelo-Finland), "on whose territory the war had actually been fought," be represented individually in the UNWCC. The members of the Commission believed otherwise: Soviet representation, they felt, should be the same as that in the United Nations; that is, the Russian government and those of Byelorussia and the Ukraine.[6]

Thus, observed a legal correspondent for the *London Times* at the end of 1946, "unfortunately, the USSR did not take part in the inaugural meeting and has not joined the Commission since." Indeed, Russia never joined and never wavered in its insistence on its terms of representation.[7] Instead the Soviet Union established its own organization, the Russian Extraordinary War Crimes Commission. With its help, a Soviet military tribunal tried and convicted German war criminals as early as December 1943.[8] Lord Robert Anderson Wright, chairman of the UNWCC, stressed in an interview in 1945 the strong desire for "close cooperation between the two commissions," as well as the compatibility of "their approaches to the common problem."[9] Such wishful thinking aside, Russia's refusal to participate in the UNWCC for strictly political reasons served as a model for future Soviet intransigent behavior.

Having entered the Pacific war in August 1945, the Soviet Union presently subscribed—in word, at least—to Allied policy regarding the surrender and postwar settlement of Japan. Russia therefore agreed to the provisions set forth in the Potsdam Declaration of July 26, 1945. Issued jointly by the leaders of the United States, Britain and the Republic of China, the document contained the Allies' offer of surrender terms to Japan. Most germane was article 10, which provided that "stern justice shall be meted out to all war criminals. . . ."[10] A Soviet representative accepted and signed, along with his Allied counterparts, the Instrument of Surrender (Japan) of September 2, 1945. Also, Moscow joined London, Washington and other Allies in the creation of the FEC in late 1945–early 1946.[11] Finally, two Russians, Maj. Gen. I. M. Zaryanov on the bench and A. N. Vasilyev on the prosecution staff, participated in the proceedings of the IMTFE in Tokyo.

Explicit materials relative to Soviet war crimes trials regulations are currently unavailable. Nevertheless examination of an actual trial proceeding, which follows, provides adequate insight into the rules which prevailed at Soviet-conducted Eastern war crimes trials.

The Trials: The IMTFE

It would be impossible to extricate Japanese war crimes trials—how the Russians viewed them, what the Russians conceived to be their objectives and their outcomes—from the entire matrix of Soviet postwar international politics. For this reason, the Russian experience vis-à-vis the IMTFE will receive considerable attention.

Though labeled "Allied," the occupation of Japan early assumed the characteristics of an "American show." Russia even refused to put troops under the command of SCAP. Doubtless "the Soviet Union well understood" America's dominant interest in postwar Japan. And "while it made feeble protests from time to time against America's monopoly of power" there, wrote historian Akira Iriye, "it did little to obstruct MacArthur's policy." [12]

Hence, when it came to organizing and prosecuting trials of major Japanese war criminals, the Russians, like everyone else, took a back seat to the United States. In fact, in January 1946 the state department instructed its chargé in the Soviet Union, George F. Kennan, to "reiterate to the Foreign Office this Government's hope that the Soviet Government will participate" in the IMTFE. [13] Up to that point, the Russians had adopted a policy of "official silence" regarding their postwar intentions in the Far East. [14] Moscow's response to Kennan's invitation revealed the surprising extent to which the Soviets had accepted American supervision over major Japanese war crimes trials.

"The Soviet Government was not adequately informed about this trial," a Russian representative told Kennan. Would the Americans, he inquired, provide them with "a copy of the indictment and also a list of leading war criminals"? Other questions followed. "Who, exactly," was Joseph Keenan? What functions were included in his role as chief of the International Section of Prosecuting Attorneys? "What body was this?" [15] Would the Charter of the tribunal be "identical with that of the Nuremberg trial? If not, in what respects would it differ?"[16]

The Russians, despite their unfamiliarity with the IMTFE, assured the Soviet representative, were not taking the matter lightly; their "interest was more than formal," and they wanted to know much more about Russia's role in the proposed trial.[17] Certainly, Moscow did not view the IMTFE and related affairs aloofly. Stalin had revealed early his desire to "participate in the occupation of Japan proper." Moscow's relatively subdued behavior was, rather, attributable to expressed American resolution to control the occupation of Japan and implied American determination to exclude Russia from all but a minimal role there.[18]

Still the Russians distrusted American motives vis-à-vis postwar Japan. Why, they asked, had the United States failed to "liquidate" entirely the Japanese general staff and armed forces immediately upon surrender? For what purposes would Japan need military officers? These sentiments, and others like them, must of course be viewed in light of burgeoning Russo-American Cold War strains and divisions. That the Soviets genuinely feared a possible future re-militarization of Japan cannot be denied.[19]

Nor can it be denied that the Russians sought to portray the Allied war crimes trial in Tokyo as being, in general, detrimental to world peace and, specifically, as anti-Soviet. Through a persistent campaign of political propaganda and polemics, the Soviet Union attempted to undermine that which it could not control: the IMTFE.

From the very beginning of the Allied war crimes operation, the Soviets challenged its effectiveness. Initially these doubts focused upon "the Japanese ruling circles" who, declared the Soviet newspaper *Red Star*, refused "to carry out the provisions of the Potsdam Declaration." The present Shidehara government, it charged, "obstructed," not assisted, Allied efforts to apprehend Japanese war criminals.[20] But soon Soviet barbs found additional, broader targets.

Many in Japan, contended M. Markov in the Russian foreign affairs weekly, *New Times*, sought to exonerate or mitigate the guilt of Japanese. Certain Japanese newspapers, he wrote, insisted that since the war "Japan has changed and cleansed herself." The Shidehara government, Markov charged, "has displayed extraordinary zeal" in its efforts "to save . . . war criminals from responsibility." Furthermore—and here lay the gist of the Russian attack—"the occupation authorities permitted the Japanese reactionaries to develop an open campaign in defense of these criminals."

Also, "carelessness" on the part of occupation authorities, went the allegations, had resulted in the escape of some guilty Japanese and the destruction of much evidentiary material. Above all, Markov argued, the list of major war criminals slated for trial at the IMTFE was "far from complete": it conspicuously and unjustifiably excluded Japan's leading industrialists, the *zaibatsu*. These "greedy capitalists" had worked hand in hand with Japanese militarists and had furnished them the means to effect their imperialistic plans. Absent, too, was Emperor Hirohito. Here Markov cited demands that the emperor be tried as a war criminal emanating from official circles in Australia, New Zealand, China, the Philippines and Japan itself. "World opinion," he concluded, "insists that Hirohito be brought to trial."

Only in this manner, Markov asserted, could "the demand of the nations for the just and speedy punishment of the war criminals be heeded." The Tokyo Trial, beyond this, "is destined to play an important role in strengthening the position of the progressive forces." Always at the core of the Soviet message, however, rested political considerations: the IMTFE "must expose the connections between the *present leaders* of Japanese reaction and the top-rank militarists who are now in the dock. . . ."[21]

Markov's article may be regarded as expressive of the official Kremlin view. Consider here the words of an East European Communist diplomat to an American journalist in re all publications within Soviet controlled countries: "It must be the official line, because otherwise it could not be published."[22]

Similar publications, equally representative of the official line, steadily revealed the true target of Russia's attacks: United States occupation policy in Japan, and those who formulated, supervised and executed it. "Organized on substantially different lines from the Nuremberg Trial," wrote S. Golunsky, the IMTFE did not emanate from "international agreement, but [from] orders of General MacArthur." MacArthur's appointments and policies, insisted Golunsky, dominated the whole proceedings. Other publications reiterated these accusations.[23]

"Staged by the Americans," the Tokyo Trial, declared one propagandist, "virtually abandoned" the "struggle against war criminals" and adhered to the "imperialist policy" currently espoused by Washington and London.[24] A constant theme in the assaults centered about America's "protection of Japanese reactionaries," especially important industrialists.[25] The "leaders of the giant Japanese monopolies . . . known as the *Zaibatsu*," who favored and "were the real instigators" of "predatory war," had escaped trial. This was "no accident," alleged the Communist Party daily, *Pravda*, but the results of a carefully calculated plot engineered by the *zaibatsu's* capitalist counterparts on "Wall Street." [26]

The Russians found it inconceivable that "American lawyers acting as defense counsel" could depict Japan "as a victim" of global circumstances. These Americans, said the Soviets, repeated "hackneyed arguments of Japanese wartime propaganda and [were] lavish in libellous attacks on the Soviet Union." Often, *Pravda* asserted, American lawyers in Tokyo "abandoned professional ethics" and used "shyster methods"; and American witnesses sometimes "lied." [27]

By far the most significant aspects of the Soviet propaganda attack focused on what Russians described as the motives behind American behavior at the IMTFE. By saving "from merited punishment arrant Japanese militarists" guilty of heinous crimes, occupation authorities were merely following the orders of their government in Washington. In this, went Russian accusations, "They are doing their utmost to whitewash and justify the aggressive policy of the Japanese imperialists. Wall Street and its agents, who direct U.S. policy, are resurrecting militarism in Japan and converting the country into a base for the promotion of their insensate plans of world domination." [28]

"Falsification of history at the Tokyo Trial," declared another critic, constituted the means by which the United States sought "to perpetuate the MacArthur policy in Japan." And "that policy . . . is [one] . . . of reviving Japanese imperialism and making it a satellite of the American expansionists." [29]

In short, the Russians perceived—or so they said—the IMTFE as an American attempt to cover up the guilt of those Japanese whom they believed to be most responsible for the war—namely, the emperor, major industrialists and capitalists, and militarists. And they openly accused the United States of obstructing the process of democratization, while encouraging re-militarization, in Japan. [30]

Despite their negligible part in creating the IMTFE's Charter and indictment, the Soviets demonstrated marked sway in the selection of one or two defendants. Allied prosecutors had narrowed to twenty-six the number of Japanese leaders to be indicted by the time the Russian associate counsel first joined them in late April 1946.

"Upon his arrival," recounted former American prosecutor Solis Horwitz, "he [the Soviet prosecutor] approved the selection of the defendants already chosen, but requested that the defendants Shigemitsu and Umezu, who had not previously been considered as principal offenders, be added and this was done upon his assurance that there was sufficient evidence to establish their guilt."

Critics, among them Noboru Kojima and Richard Minear, argued that the Soviets went beyond merely "requesting" inclusion of Shigemitsu and Umezu; rather, "Keenan and MacArthur consented only under the threat of a Soviet walkout."[31] Considering the widespread and pronounced Allied discontent with diplomat Shigemitsu's indictment and ultimate conviction, the critics' view may at first glance appear credible.[32] Yet we must bear in mind former United States prosecutor Donihi's steadfast assertion that all major IPS decisions required unanimous concurrence by participating prosecutors. Nor did the Soviets alone favor Umezu's indictment: on January 2, 1946—six days before the United States even extended its invitation to the Soviet Union to join the IMTFE—the British embassy suggested to Washington that the Allies include Umezu among the list of major war criminals.[33]

In April 1946, less than a fortnight before the opening of the IMTFE, Chief Prosecutor Keenan offered his perception of how the Soviets viewed the forthcoming trial. They saw it, he suggested, "as far more important than the Nuremberg proceedings" since it involved the participation and close cooperation of more nations. As such, he concluded, the Russians deemed the trial "a landmark in international relations and international justice."[34]

A decade later Keenan's immediate assistant in the prosecution at the IMTFE, Brendan F. Brown, drew essentially different conclusions. The "Russian attitude" toward that tribunal, said Brown, had become "obvious" in the revealing light of retrospect: "the Soviet Union regarded" the IMTFE "merely as a means for furthering political objectives"; specifically, "to advance the hegemony of the Communist party" in Asia (particularly in China) and the world. Keenan, in a work published jointly with Brown in 1950, voiced nearly the same opinion.[35]

In any event, in this international political milieu, the curtain rose, in December 1949, on the first and only exclusively Russian-held Japanese war crimes trial made public.[36]

The Trials: Khabarovsk

By late 1949 the United States had made known its willingness to sign a peace treaty with Japan without the Soviet Union. "Russian intransigence," as displayed in negotiations up to then, discerned Secretary of State Dean Acheson, "would tie up a Japanese treaty" indefinitely if permitted to continue.[37] That such unilateral action portended an even wider role for the United States in East Asia did not go unnoticed by the Russians.

In normally hostile terms a Moscow Radio commentator castigated "the American instigators of a new world war" who, in their boundless ignorance, speeded "revival of Japan's industrial [and other] war potential." The Americans hoped, continued the declaration, to forge a Pacific military alliance with Japan as the military and economic foundation, eventually planning to use Japan in their "war for United States domination."[38]

Another significant matter, left simmering up to 1949, neared the explosion point. Almost four years after the war's end, the Soviets still retained in captivity several hundred thousand Japanese POWs. While figures varied, most estimates hovered between 400,000 and 500,000 POWs. Throughout 1949 a spate of demands that these POWs be repatriated—coming from Allied Headquarters, the Japanese government, people and Communist Party and others—descended upon the Kremlin.[39] The Soviets, thought observers, had initially hoped to "indoctrinate" the POWs and to convert them to communism before releasing them. When these plans aborted, it was contended, the Russians clamped down, refusing to repatriate the Japanese. Those still in retention, countered Soviet spokespersons, were "war criminals."[40]

Apparently, believed *The New York Times* and *London Times*, *inter alia*, the Russians discerned the need, in late 1949, for a major political issue which would divert world interest from the repatriation question, cast infamy on growing Japanese-American ties and "strengthen anti-American feeling in China." For these reasons they completely disregarded FEC "recommendations" that all minor Eastern war crimes trials be terminated by September 30, 1949.[41] Instead they instituted war crimes trials proceedings at Khabarovsk, in southeastern Siberia, from December 25–30 of that year.

At Khabarovsk twelve former members of the Japanese armed forces stood charged with "manufacturing and employing bacteriological weapons. I.e., with a crime punishable under Article 1 of the Decree of the Presidium of the Supreme Soviet of the U.S.S.R. of April 19, 1943."[42] Included among the accused were General Otozoo Yamada, formerly commander-in-chief of the Japanese Kwantung Army, and several high-ranking officers in the medical services.

The military tribunal of the Primorye Military Area, reported the Soviets, heard the case before "open court sessions." Yet Western press coverage was barred.[43] On the bench sat high-ranking military officers of jurisprudence. A major general of jurisprudence, D. D. Chertov, served as court president. A state counsellor of jurisprudence had "upheld" the indictment.

Members of the Moscow Bar Association, the Khabarovsk Territory Bar Association and the president of the Primorye Territory Bar Association defended the accused. All findings on matters of bacteriology and medicine had been previously "submitted to the Court by a commission of experts" comprised of members of prestigious institutions, such as the Academy of Medical Sciences of the USSR, Department of Microbiology in the Khabarovsk Medical Institute and the like.[44]

As the court president explained, accused persons enjoyed the "right during the Court proccedings to put questions to witnesses, experts, and to each other, and to make explanatory statements on the substance of the case." Also, he added, they could call further witnesses and experts or call for other "proofs and documents."[45] Translation responsibilities fell to five Russian interpreters, provided by the court. President Chertov warned them of their "duties" and "of their liability to criminal prosecution for deliberately false interpretation."[46] Similarly, he cautioned the sixteen witnesses (all Japanese) summoned to appear on their responsibilities under the Russian criminal code to testify and to do so "truthfully."[47]

Besides the specific charge of "manufacturing and employing bacteriological weapons," the Soviet indictment virtually repeated the charges recently aired and decided upon at the IMTFE: Japan had "entered into a criminal conspiracy with Hitler Germany and fascist Italy"; it had "planned, launched and waged aggressive wars against peaceable nations"; it had undertaken "aggression against the Soviet Union"; and so on.

Moreover, read the indictment, "acting upon secret instructions from Emperor Hirohito, the Japanese General Staff and Ministry for War already in 1935 and 1936 formed in Manchuria two top-secret units for preparing and conducting bacteriological warfare."[48] In subsequent years, continued the allegations, Japanese built special laboratories and "carried on systematic biological research." They intended thereby to ascertain "which types of germs" were most pernicious and lethal, and best suited to "breeding on a mass scale." Then the Japanese planned "to exterminate large masses of people and cause economic damage by infecting cattle and crops. . . ."[49] Finally, the Soviets charged, in their "criminal" bacteriological experiments, the Japanese "monsters" conducted "inhuman" tests on living people.[50]

Soviet "medicolegal experts" completely supported these allegations. The Japanese, they found, had established in Manchuria three germ warfare "detachments," code-named 731, 100 and 1644. There they "devised methods for mass breeding of fleas, for their subsequent infection with plague and utilization for war purposes"; for producing "bacterial aerial bombs, artillery shells and contrivances for spreading bacteria from aircraft"; for contaminating food, water sources, fodder and soil; and for "infecting cattle and agricultural plants." Not the slightest doubt existed, concluded Soviet medical experts, that the defendants had freely conducted germ war experiments on living subjects; or, moreover, that Japan had employed germ warfare in certain "districts in Central China in 1940, 1941 and 1942."[51]

The decidedly political and opportunistic essence of the Khabarovsk trial soon shone clearly through the facade. Defense counsel, typically, "while not defending" an accused's crimes, stressed the Japanese soldier's "social and political environment": that is, "the influence which social, state-political and ideological factors played in forming his will and character."[52] These benighted individuals, ran the Soviet "defense" arguments, failed to develop properly, unlike those fortunates "under the Sun of the Stalin Constitution."[53] Taught to obey blindly, Japanese soldiers unquestioningly followed those, the *zaibatsu*, who "hatched" and "waged" World War II. Tojo and others convicted at Tokyo, pressed Soviet lawyers, "were merely . . . ideological brothers" of the true instigators of the war, namely, those capitalists who "shipped guns, shells, bombs and planes to battlefields" and who "willed" the preparation and use of bacteriological warfare.[54]

And why, asked the Soviet defense counsel—as if it had even the remotest connection to the trial then being heard—did the IMTFE exclude from trial any representative of the *zaibatsu*, as well as "their head, Emperor Hirohito"? Because, he answered, "ties that bound, and bind, the American monopolists with their Japanese colleagues are too strong." That explained why the American prosecutor (Joseph Keenan) barred the role of the "industrial and financial magnates in planning and organizing the second world war."[55]

But more followed. A state prosecutor, pointing to evidence adduced from testimony of the accused and witnesses, from captured Japanese documents and from Soviet medical experts, suggested that the charge of preparing bacteriological warfare had been proven beyond doubt. Why then, he pressed, had not similar revelations surfaced at the IMTFE? Actually, he said, mention of preparation of bacteriological warfare by Japan had been introduced to the Tokyo Tribunal, and by an American prosecutor no less. President Webb, however, not knowing what to do with the "entirely new" evidence, left disposition of the matter in the hands of the American-dominated prosecution staff. There, alleged the Soviet prosecutor, the issue was squashed by "certain influential persons . . . who were evidently interested in preventing the exposure of the monstrous crimes of the Japanese militarists."[56]

Often, as in the preceding instance, Soviet prosecutors seemed to be prosecuting anyone but those in the dock at Khabarovsk. "In condemning aggressive war in general" and having always fought "undeviatingly and consistently for lasting, democratic peace," the USSR, declared the state prosecutor, "emphatically repudiates the employment of inhuman means of mass extermination." For these reasons, he explained, "despite all the efforts of the instigators of a new war in the Anglo-American bloc," the Soviet Union consistently strove in the United Nations "to secure the absolute prohibition of atomic weapons."[57]

Soviet lawyers frequently noted that the Japanese planned to use bacteriological warfare as "part of a general conspiracy of aggression against the peaceful nations." In other words, "only the crushing blow of the Soviet armed forces" against the Kwantung Army in Manchuria "saved mankind from the horrors of bacteriological warfare."[58]

Another principal indication of the political nature of the Khabarovsk trial revealed itself in the docility, repentance and, ultimately, conversion of the accused. Not once during the entire proceeding did any of the defendants object to any aspect of court procedure—although they supposedly enjoyed the right to do so. And the defense offered no rebuttal to the medicolegal experts' conclusions. In truth, counsel informed the court that, "our clients, having acquainted themselves during the preliminary investigation with the findings of the medicolegal experts, fully agree with them. No unclarity or questions have arisen in their minds. . . ."[59] Ostensibly, these were the most cooperative and contented Japanese accused of all those tried after World War II.

Even more remarkably, all the accused pleaded guilty to charges preferred against them. This contrasted starkly with behavior at war crimes trials held by other nations throughout the East, where Japanese rarely admitted their culpability.[60] Beyond this, their behavior on the witness stand was by rote, almost robot-like: they made no attempt to explain, excuse or mitigate their guilt; rather, they mechanically and factually detailed their hideous wrongdoing.[61]

All the accused repented. Before the court rendered judgment, defense counsel asked each Japanese, "How do you look upon your actions now?" A typical response went: "I repent having taken part in these inhuman experiments on living people, in bacteriological sabotage and in the preparation for bacteriological warfare against the Soviet Union."[62]

Next came the accused's "Final Pleas." Eleven of the twelve confessed, again, to their guilt, concurrently expressing their repentance. Seven thanked the court for having provided them competent counsel. Several disclosed their radically revised views of the Soviet Union and its people: ". . . the Soviet Union is a democratic country which cares for the welfare of the people and stands on guard for peace." One accused waxed philosophical: "Stern punishment of us . . . will be a warning and a lesson for those criminals who are now trying to prepare to conduct a second bacteriological war."[63]

The court, not surprisingly, found all accused guilty as charged. Curiously, though, it awarded these "Japanese monsters" relatively lenient sentences: four received twenty-five years' "confinement in a labour correction camp"; two received twenty years' confinement; and the rest got eighteen, fifteen, twelve, ten, three and two years, respectively.[64] Considering the enormity and wickedness of the accused's wrongdoing, as depicted by Soviet prosecutors, one might have expected harsher penalties. Of eight Russians convicted of "spying" for the Japanese in 1946, for example, five were executed.[65]

Before long it became obvious that the Khabarovsk trial, and the ideas espoused there, represented but part of a renewed propaganda assault against United States policy in East Asia. The Khabarovsk trial, the Soviets asserted confidently, bared "conclusive and incontrovertible evidence" of "monstrous" atrocities perpetrated and planned by "Japanese militarists." Yet only a few of the guilty had been punished. Today, charged M. Raginsky, "the real initiators and organizers of bacteriological warfare flourish under the wing of U.S. General Douglas MacArthur." MacArthur, he continued, nurtured and reared these felons "with a view to using them in another world war." By denying ever having encountered evidence of germ warfare at the IMTFE, Americans hoped to "camouflage their own brigand plans."[66]

Americans not only intended to develop further their bacteriological warfare potential for future use, according to V. Mayevsky; they also aimed at restoring to power in Japan "people belonging to the same camp as the war criminals" convicted at Khabarovsk.[67] One Soviet "Observer" labeled Joseph Keenan an "advocate of plague" for his recent defense of Emperor Hirohito against Communist attacks.[68] Again, the Russians demanded that Hirohito and other "guilty" Japanese stand trial as war criminals before a special International Military Court.[69]

Soviet verbal assaults particularly zeroed in on "American plans for a separate peace with Japan." They envisaged in such designs, more than any other, "intimate associat[ion]" with the project to convert Japan "into the chief operational base for aggressive war against the Soviet Union and the Chinese People's Republic. . . ."[70] Not surprisingly, Chinese Communists repeated nearly all the charges against the "American imperialists," and in equally vitriolic terms.[71]

Obviously the Soviet conception of a trial differed substantially from that of the West. Said one British authority on international law, Viscount Maugham: ". . . the U.S.S.R. regards a trial as one of the organs of Government power, a weapon in the hands of the rulers of the State for safeguarding its interests." In contrast, added another Englishman, Lord Hankey, "the British and American systems treat a Court as an independent agency responsible only before the law."[72]

The "fatal mistake" of the IMTFE, insisted the Soviet prosecutor, A. N. Vasilyev, revolved about the tribunal's "mechanical" adoption of "Anglo-American court procedure." He had no use for the Anglo-American legal "fetish" of reading aloud in court every word of every document or piece of evidence, thereby prolonging trials interminably. And Western defense lawyers enjoyed too much leeway. Here Vasilyev cited Engels' view of the English court system: "the clever lawyer can always find a loophole in favor of the accused." Other Russians agreed with him.[73]

Indeed, the Russian trial at Khabarovsk and Allied trials elsewhere seemed to apply similarly only one legal principle: that in regard to the defense plea of superior orders. Generally, as indicated by procedure applied at Khabarovsk, Soviet military tribunals rejected it. "No pleading with reference to orders from superiors or to the status of servicemen," averred the state prosecutor at Khabarovsk, "can serve as justification" for criminal acts.[74]

Aside from official Soviet statements, little has been written on the Khabarovsk trial. Whatever comments may be found, however, are negative in their appraisal. Consider, for instance, the following: "An example of the sinister purposes a Government may have with a judicial proceeding can be found in the Khabarovsk Trial," wrote Justice Bernard V. A. Röling, the Dutch representative on the bench at the IMTFE. "No question of the use of bacteriological weapons," he assured, ever came before the Tokyo Tribunal. Furthermore, Röling concluded, the charge against the twelve Japanese at Khabarovsk remained unproved and unsubstantiated, as not "a grain of evidence [has appeared] to support it."[75]

Another noted scholar, Peter Calvocoressi, examined carefully the scope and gravity of the charges, as well as the "momentous revelations" unveiled at Khabarovsk. "Why all this had only just come to light," he reasoned, "over four years after the accused had been taken prisoner, and more than three years since the Russian troops had left Manchuria, was not explained."[76] His thoughts are well taken. Other criticism, concentrating on Soviet motives behind the trial, was leveled by a Japanese newspaper, the *Tokyo Shimbun*.[77]

Finally, certain elements of Russia's war crimes operations in the East had, and have had, long-range significance in the unfolding of international relations in that part of the world. Two notable examples stand out.

First, Soviet charges that its adversaries—"Japan and its American allies," at Khabarovsk—planned to use bacteriological warfare against Russia and other peace-loving nations have proven a useful and convenient Communist propaganda weapon since 1949. The Soviets and their Communist allies, most notably the Chinese and North Koreans, for instance, "revealed" to the world that American fighting forces in Korea were employing bacteriological weapons against military and civilian populations. "These bandits in generals' uniforms, the butchers in white gloves," alleged *Pravda*, "have unleashed the most inhuman carnage in history, warfare with the assistance of microbes, fleas, lice and spiders. . . ."[78] At the time of the 1956 Hungarian uprising, the Soviet satirical magazine *Krokodil* lumped together American generals in charge of nuclear weapons, bacteriological warfare agents and Radio Free Europe as three forms of "Western aggression against the People's Democracies." Peking explained away responsibility for a cholera epidemic in South China in August 1961 by conveniently blaming it on "agents of the American bacteriological warfare bureau." [79] And the most recent bacteriological warfare charges appeared in a "little-publicized television documentary" aired by the Tokyo Broadcasting System in 1976. As reported by the *Washington Post*'s Tokyo correspondent, John Saar, information and accusations contained in the documentary "dovetailed" closely with accounts at Khabarovsk. [80]

Second, Moscow's adamant refusal to repatriate upwards of 400,000 Japanese POWs after World War II created quite a stir in international circles. The Soviet action generated sharp protests from a wide and disparate spectrum of sources: the Japanese Communist Party, the Japanese public and government, the United Nations, SCAP Headquarters and the Australian government. [81] In October 1951, responding to a United Nations' questionnaire on the repatriation of POWs, Moscow announced the completion of the process. Only those "persons who have been sentenced or are being prosecuted for war crimes" would not be returned, said the Soviets. [82] Several days later the Voice of America reported that Russia had failed to account for some 370,000 Japanese captives. [83]

This reality could not help but serve as an obstacle, in the succeeding years, to improved Russo-Japanese relations. Indeed, attempts to achieve a normalization of relations with Moscow in October 1956 proved that much more difficult because, as Edwin Reischauer put it, "there were real bones of contention between the two countries, and Japanese resentment against the Russians ran high." "For one thing," continued Reischauer, "large numbers of war prisoners have never returned from Siberia and had to be considered the victims of conditions in Soviet prison camps." [84]

Nor have Japanese and Russian attitudes changed much of late. A recent American ambassador to Japan, Armin H. Meyer, commented on the lingering distrust between Tokyo and Moscow, attributable, at least in part, to the POW repatriation issue. [85] Finally, a diplomatic correspondent for *The New York Times* reported in January 1976 that Japanese-Russian relations, *inter alia*, "are at odds over . . . the continuing detention of 400 Japanese prisoners of war in the Soviet Union." [86]

9. China

Procedure and Machinery

No nation sustained more victims of Japanese war crimes than China. Sino-Japanese hostilities began in July 1937—Chinese and some others said September 1931—and lasted, technically, until the Japanese surrender in September 1945. Actually, large heavily armed Japanese contingents remained active in parts of China up until at least November 1946.[1] There, on Chinese soil, Japanese forces perpetrated some of the most heinous and massive violations of the entire war. Property damage and loss to human life were incalculable.

Not surprising then, given China's terrible suffering, the Chinese government expressed at an early date its firm determination to assist actively in the prosecution of Japanese war criminals. The surprise, however, rested in its ability at this time, amidst virtually nationwide chaos and consternation, to take action commensurate with its intentions.

A Chinese minister attended the signing of the Allied Declaration of St. James, concerned with the future disposition of war criminals, in London in January 1942, and subscribed to its principles. All perpetrators and "authors" of war crimes, said the minister, would "be held accountable" and "equally dealt with according to law."[2] China joined in the establishment of the UNWCC in October 1943, and spearheaded the creation of an additional "branch," a Far Eastern Sub-Committee, in May 1944. Based in Chungking, the Sub-Committee's investigative scope fastened firmly on war crimes committed in the China theater. Chinese representatives sat on the FEAC and, later, on the FEC. In fact, a Chinese presided over the latter's committee No. 5, "War Criminals," throughout its existence.[3] Also, a Chinese judge sat on the bench and a Chinese lawyer assisted Allied prosecutors at the IMTFE in Tokyo, while a fact-finding group scoured China for evidence and witnesses for use at the tribunal.[4]

Under UNWCC auspices, China founded in late 1943 a war crimes agency suited to its particular situation and needs. Unlike, say, the cases of the United States or Britain, Chinese territory had actually witnessed Japanese war crimes. Therefore China created a National Office, "charged with the duties of investigating the crimes which fell within its sphere, apprehending the accused . . . and conducting the trials in its own courts."[5]

Chinese law concerning war crimes differed fundamentally from that of most of its Allies. A Law Governing the Trial of War Criminals of October 24, 1946, provided Chinese courts with a very broad legal basis, as it included, "simultaneously and in a given order of precedence, international law, special war crimes rules, and provisions of Chinese common penal law." In other words, Chinese courts recognized international law as the principal source for the trial of war criminals. The "special provisions" of the Law of October 24, 1946, supplemented the rules of international law. Finally, in cases left uncovered by the October 1946 Law or international law, a "subsidiary source," that is, the provisions of the Chinese Penal Code, applied.[6]

Chinese war crimes trials regulations reflected, noted the UNWCC, an acute awareness of circumstances "peculiar to China and the events she [had] gone through during the [previous] two decades."[7] Nowhere is this more clearly demonstrated than in China's definition of war crimes and war criminals.

The Law of October 24, 1946, offered a listing of four major offenses for which Chinese courts were empowered to try Japanese war criminal suspects. First on the list stood a field of offenses commonly known as crimes against peace. In language similar to that used in the Nuremberg and Tokyo charters, Chinese law defined as a war crime the "planning, conspiring or preparing" of an aggressive and therefore unlawful war or "doing the same" in "an aggression against the Republic of China."[8]

Category 2 covered the field of war crimes in the more conventional sense—that is, as violations of the laws and customs of war. Adopting the practice of some other nations (for example, Australia and the Netherlands), the Chinese Law of 1946 supplemented its third category with an additional list of offenses constituting war crimes "in the narrower sense." Of the thirty-eight offenses enumerated, many easily fitted under the heading of conventional war crimes or even that of "crimes against humanity": for instance, "planned slaughter, murder or other terrorist action"; "killing hostages"; "starvation"; "rape"; and "enforced collective torture."

Other listed offenses, however, dealt with crimes particular to China's or, in a broader sense, the Orient's past. Special emphasis therefore was assigned to offenses involving narcotic drugs or poisons: "distributing, spreading or forcing people to consume, narcotic drugs" or "forcing people to consume or be inoculated with poison." One notable violation, "stupefying the mind and controlling the thought" of the Chinese people, apparently pertained to psychological warfare, being listed separately from drugs and poisons.[9]

Category 4 listed offenses as defined in the Chinese common penal law which had been "committed during the war . . . or a period of hostilities against China." For all practical purposes, this group included any or all crimes committed by Japanese against Chinese nationals or property left uncovered by the previous three listings. Chinese authorities, then, "adopted the concept of war crimes in a wider, non-technical sense" than did most of their Allies.[10]

Chinese legislation provided each different type of offense with a relevant time period for which Japanese could be held guilty. That is, Japanese on trial for crimes against peace must have committed the violation in the period running "prior to or during the war." This recognized the fact that "planning, conspiring or preparing" a war of aggression could precede indefinitely the start of actual war. Therefore the relevant time period varied according to the case.[11]

For conventional war crimes, the relevant time period covered that which ran "during the war or a period of hostilities against the Republic of China." Chinese authorities included reference to the "period of hostilities," as distinct from the war itself, so as to take into account all crimes committed during a state of Sino-Japanese *de facto* belligerency that existed prior to the war. According to the Chinese, this state commenced with Japan's invasion of Manchuria in September 1931. The same relevant time period applied to crimes punishable under the Chinese Penal Code.[12]

Finally, Chinese might prosecute Japanese suspected of perpetrating crimes against humanity anytime "during the war or a period of hostilities . . . or prior to the occurrence of such circumstances." The latter portion of the provision, significantly, deemed punishable crimes against humanity even when committed before the invasion of Manchuria by Japan.[13]

China tried Japanese suspects before military tribunals convened and supervised by the Chinese War Crimes Commission, following approval by the ministries of defense and justice. While the Law of October 1946 directed that military tribunals be composed of five military judges and one to three prosecutors, it allowed for the increase of both "when necessary."[14] In fact, Chinese courts rarely exceeded five judges.[15]

Chinese war crimes regulations directed that crimes committed under orders of a superior did not in themselves "relieve the perpetrator from penal liability for war crimes." In this respect, China acted in accordance with general Allied policy. But unlike its Allies, China did not specifically provide for mitigation of punishment upon the plea of superior orders if the court so deemed. Similar provisions applied, under Chinese law, to crimes committed in line with official duty, or in pursuance of the policy of the offender's government or out of political necessity. Moreover, Chinese law expressly referred to the legal principle of command responsibility: not only superiors who issued orders "but also those who tolerate[d] criminal acts of their subordinates" without taking appropriate preventative measures were held penally responsible.[16]

Chinese war crimes regulations also differed considerably from those of other Allied nations in the area of punishments. Chinese law, that is, prescribed mandatory sentences upon conviction for specific crimes. Hence crimes against peace or crimes against humanity carried automatic sentences of either death or life imprisonment upon conviction. Conviction for conventional war crimes, meanwhile, drew a variety of sentences depending on the crime itself. For example, conviction on charges of "murder" or "killing hostages" called for sentences of death or life imprisonment; "forcing women to become prostitutes" or "robbing" drew either death, life imprisonment or ten years' confinement; and "malicious insults" or "violating Red Cross regulations" resulted in life imprisonment or imprisonment for not less than seven years. Reduction of sentences was not allowed.[17]

All convictions required confirmation by the ministry of defense. In cases involving death sentences or life imprisonment, the ministry further submitted all relevant information to the president of the Republic—Chiang Kai-shek—"for a fiat of execution." If, for any reason, the ministry or the president believed the judgment to be "faulty or improper," they returned the case for re-trial. An accused could appeal a conviction within ten days of the judgment. Finally, the Chinese—ever alert to see that no guilty Japanese went unpunished—permitted the ministry of defense to refer any case back for re-trial after further examination. Here particular attention was shown to trials ending in acquittals or in instances where the case "gave rise to doubts."[18]

The Trials

Strangely enough, American officials supervised the first war crimes trials conducted on Chinese soil. Beginning in early 1946, a series of trials centering about the inhumane treatment afforded captive American airmen by Japanese took place in Shanghai. Closer examination of these trials is found in chapter 5.[19] Interestingly, despite initial and sometimes irritating (to Americans) delays by Chinese authorities, the eventual unfolding and disposition of these hearings resulted from closely coordinated Chinese, American and even British investigation and preparation.[20]

Meanwhile, as Americans organized and conducted trials in Shanghai, Chinese authorities busily apprehended Japanese suspected of committing war crimes against Chinese civilians during the occupation period. At first, most arrests occurred in the Peiping-Tientsin region, as war crimes teams and accompanying military personnel swept northward.[21] But soon investigations spread throughout China's vast spaces. After some delay, the number of atrocities reported and suspects named reached staggering proportions. On March 3, 1946, the inspection department of the Shanghai District Court announced that it had compiled 11,889 cases of war crimes. Nine days later reports disclosed that the number of cases of Japanese atrocities filed in Shanghai alone had ballooned to over 30,000.[22]

Those Japanese subsequently arrested generally consisted of army and "gendarmerie" personnel, and some civilians. Most were suspected of "murder and manslaughter," or "wilfully destroying properties"; far fewer with "torturing civilians," "plundering" and "rape." In an effort to manage this enormous task, Chungking constituted a total of thirteen military tribunals in thirteen districts, including Canton, Hankow, Northeast Hsuchow, Chuchow (Chekiang), Honan, Hunan, Shanshi, Hopei, Suiyuan, and Taiwan.[23]

For a while Chinese officials struggled with the problem. Lack of proper accommodations and the seemingly boundless demands of investigation and preparation caused several delays and postponements.[24] By the second week of April 1946, however, trials were underway. A Chinese major general and member of the military court prefaced the opening of the first war crimes trial held in the Peiping-Tientsin area by declaring his determination to try all cases "according to military law." Despite "bestial, wartime Japanese behavior," he further asserted, his court intended to dispense justice, not revenge.[25] The trial commenced on April 10, and closed eight days later. Of the five Japanese charged with "murdering Chinese civilians," all were found guilty. Four of them received the death penalty, while the fifth got five years' imprisonment at hard labor.[26] Before too long, war crimes trials began all over China.

The charge most frequently preferred by Chinese prosecutors against Japanese, as previously mentioned, was murder. And while precise figures are unavailable, it would appear accurate to conclude that, regarding this particular offense, Chinese tribunals convicted considerably more Japanese than they acquitted. Death sentences were common.[27]

Perhaps the most unique aspect of Chinese war crimes trials rested in the heavy reliance upon international law. Other nations, to be sure, applied international law at their trials. Yet none did so as frequently, broadly or assertively as the Chinese. Typical examples follow.

One celebrated Nanking case concerned the wartime behavior of the ex-governor of Japanese-occupied Hong Kong, Lieutenant General Isogai. Charges against him included, *inter alia*, "having allowed his troops in the advance on Nanking to rape, loot, murder and burn," and having "encouraged the sale of opium to destroy public morale."[28] While, as the UNWCC noted, "no rule of customary International Law providing that a court delivering judgment in a war crime trial must state the reasons for its opinion" existed, Chinese courts invariably did.[29] Accordingly, a five-man military court found Isogai guilty on all charges, particularly of "instigating and supporting imperialistic aggression." For this "crime against peace" it sentenced Isogai to life imprisonment.[30]

The trial of Lt. Gen. Hisao Tani, the "Japanese Fire Eater," also engendered much sensation in Nanking. According to the indictment, Tani had "authored" the Rape of Nanking in 1937. The "blood guilt of untold thousands," assailed the press, clung to his hands. Tani pleaded not guilty, but the overwhelming evidence adduced against him, as well as the testimonies of hundreds of eyewitnesses, indicated otherwise.[31] More than a month after the trial began, the court read its decision: "Hisao Tani, having been convicted of instigating, inspiring and encouraging during the war the men under his command to stage general massacres of prisoners of war and non-combatants and to perpetrate such crimes as rape, plunder and wanton destruction of property, is hereby sentenced to death." Following appeal and confirmation of sentence by the ministry of national defense and President Chiang Kai-shek, Tani was duly executed.[32]

For "breaking international law" a Japanese admiral, former commander-in-chief of the Imperial Fleet in China, drew fifteen years' confinement from a Chinese military court in Shanghai. The defendant, said the court, had assumed an "instrumental" part in forming the South China puppet regime during the war and had "participated in mapping out Japanese aggression against China."[33] Chinese courts regularly based convictions on similar grounds.[34]

Chinese authorities sometimes took extraordinary measures. In one instance, instead of merely confirming the verdict, the national defense ministry issued a "formal edict" demanding that the three defendants be put to death. Because they wantonly killed "Chinese combatants and non-combatants," expounded the ministry, the accused had "to be executed in accordance with the Chinese Law and the Hague War Regulations."[35] Chinese courts frequently convicted Japanese of offenses which overlapped the bounds of both conventional war crimes and crimes against peace. For example, they adjudged Japanese guilty of "conspiracy to make war" or "conspiracy to murder."[36]

A substantial number of Chinese war crimes trials dealt with the legal principle of command responsibility. Determined from the start to prevent culpable Japanese from escaping responsibility for the misdeeds of their subordinates, Chinese authorities relied heavily on the Yamashita precedent.[37] Of the trials that fit in this category, one surpassed in importance all the others, as it highlighted clearly both the principle of command responsibility and the defense plea of superior orders.

The accused, Takahashi Sakai, had served as a military commander in China during the war of 1937 to 1945. Between 1931 and 1934, evidence adduced at the trial revealed, Sakai had spearheaded the formation of terrorist organizations in Peiping and Tientsin; had threatened to attack these places by artillery and air force; and had ordered the establishment in South China of a puppet administration designed to overthrow the Chinese government.[38]

From 1939 to 1945, read the indictment, Sakai incited or permitted his subordinates to commit atrocities in Kwantung, Hainan and Hong Kong. His actions resulted, alleged Chinese prosecutors, in the massacre of some 200 people, and the torture and mutilation of many more. Sakai was subsequently charged with commission of crimes against peace, conventional war crimes and crimes against humanity.

Sakai pleaded not guilty. To charges that he had participated in a war of aggression and had instigated a war against peace, he responded that he had merely obeyed the orders of his government. Charges of atrocities he countered by arguing that he had been unaware of his subordinates' acts and therefore was not responsible for them.[39]

The Chinese military tribunal, rejecting Sakai's pleas, found him guilty on all charges. From the judgment one may discern, as did a noted author on international law, Ian Brownlie, that Sakai's "liability for crimes against peace lay only in the fact that he had conducted military operations which formed part of a war of aggression" against China. "This view of liability," perceived Brownlie, "is wider than that taken" by the tribunals at Nuremberg and Tokyo.[40]

In dismissing Sakai's plea of superior orders, the tribunal said: "Aggressive war is an act against world peace. Granted that the defendant participated in the war on the orders of his Government, a superior order cannot be held to absolve the defendant from liability for the crime."[41] In this respect, the court's behavior paralleled the generally accepted rules and practices of the other Allied nations.

Left unclear in the judgment—probably intentionally—was whether the tribunal found Sakai guilty for crimes against peace committed during the war of 1937 to 1945, or whether it encompassed the period of hostilities from 1931 to 1937.[42] The court also determined Sakai guilty of conventional war crimes and crimes against humanity in that "he had violated the Hague Convention concerning the Laws and Customs of War on Land and the Geneva Convention of 1929."

Regarding the question of Sakai's responsibility for the acts of his subordinates, the tribunal adopted a position generally recognized "by nations and their courts of law" and firmly established by the Yamashita case: ". . . a field Commander must hold himself responsible for the discipline of his subordinates." Failure effectively to prevent, or conscious toleration of, the commission of violations by subordinates, the court in effect ruled, constituted a war crime.[43] The court condemned Sakai to be shot. After ratification by Chiang Kai-shek, the execution took place, as scheduled, before a large, approving public audience.[44]

The wartime actions of General Yasutsugu Okamura dominated the most publicized, interest-provoking and, ultimately, controversial trial held in China. Former commander-in-chief of all armed forces in China during the war, Okamura, averred the *China Press*, represented the "highest" wartime Japanese authority in China "pulling strings behind the puppet Wang Ching-wei regime in Nanking." Many Chinese considered him "the Number One Japanese war criminal in China." To be sure, Okamura's name headed the Yenan Communists' list of war criminals as early as December 1945.[45]

In preparation for Okamura's trial, the ministry of national defense organized a special military tribunal in Shanghai. A large auditorium designed to accommodate many expected spectators was provided for the occasion. The China Film Company prepared energetically to capture on newsreel the historical events soon to unfold. Extensive pre-trial publicity touched upon nearly all aspects of the case.[46]

Chinese authorities, too, recognized the unusually high degree of public interest generated by the forthcoming trial. They therefore felt an urgent need for placing the trial and related events in proper perspective. No one denied the true significance of the upcoming Okamura hearing, conceded the president of the five-man military tribunal assigned to the case, Sheh Mei-yu. Beyond this, he predicted that the hearing was destined to "occupy an important page in the annals of the Chinese military commissions." Above all, however, he declared publicly his and the government's resolution to ensure Okamura a "fair trial." Neither leniency nor a "revengeful attitude," but justice according to the evidence adduced, said President Sheh, would determine Okamura's fate.[47]

Charges brought against Okamura included, *inter alia*, supporting aggression, violating article 46 of the Hague Convention (guaranteeing respect and protection for civilian lives and property in areas occupied by belligerent forces) and "tolerating the massacre of Chinese civilians and burning of houses by Japanese troops and other crimes."[48]

Responsibility for the deaths and the destruction of property of countless Chinese civilians, contended the prosecutor, rested squarely on Okamura's shoulders. A military commander, he pressed, must be responsible for all acts of his subordinates. In reasoning that sounded far more political than legal, he inquired: "If Okamura should be let go free, what would the Chinese nation think of this tribunal? What would the relatives of victims of Japanese brutalities think of this military commission?" He demanded that Okamura be put to death.

Such assertions lacked legal foundation, argued defense counsel. He insisted that the prosecution had failed to produce any "concrete evidence" of Okamura's direct guilt; his client should therefore be acquitted. "Supervision" over the actions of troops could only be effectuated by "immediate superiors," not by commanders— like Okamura—behind the front. Okamura, he maintained, "did send supervisory orders in the written form to the front, prohibiting soldiers from killing, committing arson, and attacking innocent people." He concluded with a pithy, basic and cogent peroration: "We are here to try Okamura with law. Since there is no evidence against him, he should be released." The court then adjourned *sine die*.[49]

For the next five months the Okamura trial remained unsettled. A "serious ailment," believed to be tuberculosis, hospitalized Okamura, resulting in indefinite postponement.[50] Not until January 1949 did the trial resume, and later that month the tribunal rendered its verdict. "Lack of evidence," declared the court, dictated only one possible decision: not guilty. But the court then proceeded to go even further, expounding in its opinion a legal reasoning which seemingly undermined much of the validity of the doctrine of command responsibility.

Okamura's appointment to the commander's post in China, stated the tribunal, preceded V-J Day by only eight months. Merely being the nominal head of the Japanese army, it decided, could not in itself constitute a war crime, nor could he be held accountable exclusively for violations perpetrated by subordinates. Furthermore, the court added, Okamura had acted commendably in ordering his men to surrender their arms and cease hostilities after V-J Day.[51]

Okamura's acquittal drew immediate and strident criticism from the Chinese Communists. A Peiping broadcast mocked the Nationalist government for its weakness, and demanded the re-arrest and re-trial of Okamura and other "unjustly" released Japanese war criminals.[52] Particularly irritating to the Chinese Communists—and perplexing to students, no doubt—were reports that Okamura, along with 259 "other Japanese war criminals," had been turned over to the custody of SCAP in February 1949.[53]

Japanese suspects, it would appear, enjoyed adequate treatment from their Chinese captors. On several occasions unsolicited press reports described the rather comfortable conditions of incarceration afforded war criminal suspects: "housed in rooms, furnished Japanese-style; rooms are heated and they get generous rations; they can read and play games." According to another journalist, Japanese suspects awaiting trial in Canton led "a comparatively easy life."[54] Treatment of this type is all the more remarkable when one recalls the intense animosity felt by Chinese toward Japanese circa 1945. By no means is this meant to suggest that Chinese authorities treated Japanese war criminals indulgently during the years 1945 to 1949. It is meant, however, to indicate Chinese humane behavior toward suspects not yet proven guilty. In fact, Chinese sometimes felt the need to remind themselves and their compatriots of the recent brutality of the Japanese. "We cannot afford to be over-lenient in our attitude towards the Japanese," cautioned one official statement issued in late 1947.[55]

Chinese justice, too, noted officials, set sternness, not vengeance, as its goal.[56] And while Chinese military tribunals convicted many Japanese and awarded harsh—often the harshest—penalties, they also acquitted a good number of suspects. In the early stages of China's war crimes operation, Chinese authorities found not guilty and subsequently released 180 Japanese suspects after a full preliminary investigation.[57] A tribunal in Tsingtao acquitted a Japanese colonel and 13 subordinates, despite the seriousness of the charges leveled against them.[58] A Hankow court acquitted a Japanese "for lack of evidence."[59] Not to be overlooked, of course, is the exculpatory decision delivered in the Okamura trial, already discussed.

Chinese trials sometimes, not always, took place before public audiences. Celebrated cases received wider publicity. Chinese authorities ordered at least one trial broadcast live, others, like Okamura's, filmed.[60] Chinese officials exerted every effort to present direct eyewitness testimony at trials. In this manner, they hoped, "concrete evidence" would either prove or disprove the charges against an accused. Unlike trials conducted by other nations, in fact, at Chinese trials civilians, "acting as representatives of the people," could (and were encouraged to) "present their opinion to the court."[61]

Chinese authorities, as previously mentioned, cooperated closely with Allied war crimes teams in China. Such cooperation, however, worked both ways. Chinese prosecutors, for example, first appeared before a United States military commission in Yokohama in September 1946. There they assisted an American prosecutor in the initial case involving a Japanese accused of war crimes against Chinese nationals.[62] Moreover, the first Sino-American joint military commission opened in Yokohama in November 1947. On trial stood eight Japanese servicemen accused of committing acts of brutality, torture and murder against Chinese POWs. Additional joint tribunals in Japan followed.[63] On one occasion American officials agreed to transfer to Canton for re-trial by the Chinese a notorious Japanese war criminal, previously tried and sentenced to death by a United States tribunal in Shanghai.[64]

China sought and received help from Australia, too, early in its war crimes program. Reports describing the efficient and cohesive manner in which Australians had prepared their cases, based on evidence adduced in the Webb report, impressed Chinese officials. Thereupon Dr. Liang, China's representative at the UNWCC, in late 1944 contacted the Australian legation in Chungking. His request that "specimens" of the Australian cases be used by his government as a guide in preparing evidence and trials drew an affirmative response from the Australians, who shortly thereafter furnished Chinese war crimes authorities with three such specimens. Australians, conversely, did not hesitate to request assistance from Chinese, particularly in asking that the Chungking government "take the appropriate action in areas under [its] control where Australians have been imprisoned [by the Japanese]."[65]

China's entire war crimes operation must be viewed and assessed against the backdrop of those internal convulsions which dominated its policy, national and international, from 1945 to 1949. Barely had Japan capitulated in September 1945 when another major crisis loomed. Bitter disagreement over whose forces should accept the surrender of Japanese troops, seize enemy equipment and occupy enemy territory erupted into "increasingly frequent" and ever-widening armed clashes between Nationalist and Communist Chinese.[66] By 1946 full-scale civil war exploded and soon raged across wide areas of China until Communist forces eventually secured control over the mainland in October 1949.

Moreover, as far as trials went, center stage in China was reserved for those of local "puppets"—that is, Chinese who, during Japan's prolonged occupation, collaborated in the Japanese design. Chinese on trial usually included well-known judges, politicians, governors, business leaders, civilians and mistresses of Japanese authorities and Chinese collaborators. For years the local population had awaited longingly the day when these culprits would receive their just deserts. Only the trials of the most notorious Japanese war criminals attracted as great or greater attention than these "puppet" trials.[67] Similar situations, it will be shown, developed in the Philippines and France regarding trials of nationals accused of collaborating with the enemy (see chapters 11 and 12).

Seen in this light, the Nationalist government's success in locating and apprehending Japanese suspects, and in organizing and conducting an effective war crimes operation in general, appears quite a remarkable achievement. Chinese, however, had suffered immeasurably under the cruel hand of their Japanese invaders. Never did they waver in their determination to obtain just retribution.

For that reason Chinese war crimes trials continued into 1949, the steadily deteriorating Nationalist military position notwithstanding. But pressure engendered and exacerbated by the civil war eventually took its toll. Communist forces scored telling victories all through the latter part of 1947 and after.[68] War crimes courts consequently closed in Canton, Hankow and Peiping in early 1948. Authorities transferred all unfinished cases to Shanghai for completion.[69]

Conditions in China, meanwhile, worsened. In August reports disclosed use by both Nationalist and Communist Chinese of large Japanese forces to fight one another.[70] By November the *New York Herald Tribune* could forecast gloomily that word out of China "clearly indicate[d]" the grave possibility "that the entire country will be lost to the Communists." Chinese authorities thereupon accelerated further the "tempo" of their war crimes operation in a desperate attempt to wind up all trials before the situation no longer allowed for it.[71]

Here the matter becomes even more complex. Significantly, it would appear, internal events determined to a considerable degree the termination date of war crimes trials in China. Most other Allied nations tried, while not all succeeded, to phase out their trials in accordance with time limits set by Washington, SCAP or the FEC. Chinese authorities, on the other hand, did not—could not—wait for these American-sponsored directives. They took initial steps toward winding down war crimes trials in late 1947 and persisted in these efforts all through 1948 and into early 1949—months before the issuance of relevant "recommendations" by SCAP or the FEC.[72] Indeed, in February 1949, the Nationalist government transferred 260 convicted Japanese war criminals to Tokyo to serve out their terms of imprisonment. Apparently, war-torn China could not at that time accommodate the prisoners.[73]

However an alternative or, more accurately, a supplementary thesis exists. Perhaps, that is, Chiang Kai-shek's view of Japan and Japanese war criminals became, by 1949, somewhat altered by his assessment—cold and sobering, as it must have been—of waning Nationalist fortunes on the mainland. With Communist takeover imminent and deepening Russo-American Cold War strains and divisions already clearly evident, surely Chiang must have discerned the need for closer association with United States policy in the East. And that policy, after autumn 1948, stressed the economic recovery and political stabilization of Japan, in order to transform the archipelago into a Pacific democratic bastion against Communist regional advances.

Perhaps this explains the virtual cessation of trials in China after March 1949 as well as the surprising decision in the Okamura case. Continued prosecutions and convictions of Japanese war criminals, Chiang may have thought, would not lend themselves very well to accommodating American policy. Nor would Chinese insistence, later on, upon heavy Japanese reparations payments or the imposing of undue obstacles to repatriation of Japanese citizens in Taiwan. Accordingly, the Republic of China "magnanimously abandoned" its reparations claims (Peking did not) and facilitated Japanese repatriation.[74]

In any event, and for whatever reasons, China basically determined its own war crimes policy. This held true despite the Nationalist government's acceptance of enormous amounts of United States military, economic and other aid between V-J Day and 1949. It applied, too, to American-conducted trials on Chinese territory. "Primary responsibility" for war crimes trials, stated a Joint Chiefs of Staff directive in 1946, "rests with the Chinese Central Government"; any American action in China required "the acquiescence of the Chinese Government."[75]

Different reasoning dictated China's role in international affairs, specifically, that is, at the IMTFE. Like Australia and New Zealand, China shortly after the war promulgated a "politically explosive list" of Japanese war criminals headed by Emperor Hirohito. The list so embarrassed American officials, reported correspondent Frank Kelley of the *New York Herald Tribune*, that for a while they tried to deny its existence.[76]

Yet there can be no gainsaying that Chinese authorities "knew the score" as it applied to the IMTFE. It had "been obvious from the beginning," observed the *China Press*, "that Americans would run the Tokyo Trial." Allied policy in the Far East, wrote a correspondent for *The New York Times* in 1945, actually "means American policy in the Far East."[77]

Nevertheless, even in later years, Chinese officials questioned the decision to grant immunity to the emperor, insisting on his guilt. Mei Ju-ao, China's representative on the bench at the Tokyo Tribunal, expressed immediately after the trial his belief that the IMTFE possessed "plenty of evidence" which proved Hirohito had been "an abettor or participator" in crimes against peace.[78] Still, one senses that, partly at least, these declamations were intended to appease the popular demand in China for Hirohito's head. For the issue itself, it seems, had been resolved much earlier. On March 25, 1946, Joseph Keenan, chief prosecutor at Tokyo, arrived in Chungking to confer with President Chiang Kai-shek in re China's forthcoming role at the IMTFE. Chiang, it later became known, opposed deposing of the emperor, fearing that such action might precipitate political instability in postwar Japan. Whether he disclosed such views at the conference, however, is unclear. Be that as it may, on that same day, Judge Mei Ju-ao announced in Tokyo that he had brought from China a list of prominent war criminal suspects. While he refused to name those on the list, he revealed the emperor's exclusion.[79]

A word on the role of the Chinese Communists vis-à-vis China's war crimes operation is warranted. As with the Russians, their intentions were strictly political. Certainly the Chinese Communists registered some legitimate grievances against, and claims to try, Japanese war criminal suspects. A few reported instances even disclosed Chinese Communist trials and executions of guilty Japanese. But, for the most part, political overtones dominated all their actions. From the beginning Yenan demanded that members of the Nationalist government stand trial as war criminals.[80] American soldiers (aiding in the transfer of Nationalist forces to Northern China), alleged the Yenan Communists in 1947, had committed "atrocities" against Chinese in the Peiping area.[81] Chinese Communists incessantly mocked the Nationalist government's premature releasing or acquitting of "guilty" Japanese.[82] Further along these lines, they ordered that all war criminals be turned over to them. And SCAP, they charged, in accepting the transfer of 260 Japanese war criminals from Shanghai to Tokyo, interfered "in the internal affairs of China."[83]

Communist political propaganda gradually picked up momentum. A renewed barrage of rhetoric followed the establishment of the People's Republic of China in October 1949. Americans, particularly General MacArthur, now emerged as the new target. Chou En-lai, Peking broadcasts, the Hsinhua News Agency and local Chinese newspapers scathingly denounced "the premature liberation of the Japanese war criminals by MacArthur."[84]

Especially strident criticism was leveled at SCAP's early parole, in November 1950, of a major Japanese war criminal convicted by the IMTFE, Mamoru Shigemitsu. "Under no circumstances," declared Chou, would the Chinese people "let MacArthur, the representative of American imperialism, encourage Japanese fascism for the purpose of renewing aggression."[85] Chinese Communists, predictably, aligned themselves in this matter with their Soviet "comrades." Similarly, they supported wholeheartedly the findings of the Russian-held Japanese war crimes trial in Khabarovsk (see chapter 8). They, too, insisted that all "the top Japanese war criminals, headed by Hirohito," stand trial before an "International War Crimes Tribunal" for the crime of "preparing bacteriological warfare" for use against the Allies in World War II.[86]

Finally, in August 1952 the governments of Japan and Taiwan, the new Nationalist stronghold, ratified a treaty of peace and normalized relations between their nations. Ozaki, Japan's foreign minister, emphasized at that time Tokyo's "delight" with the treaty, wherein the Republic of China "waived the benefit of the services required to be made available by Japan under the San Francisco Treaty, and . . . opened the way for the release of Japanese war criminals convicted by Chinese Courts." Eighty-eight of the Japanese war criminals in question were released forthwith.[87]

Final and total Chinese war crimes trials statistics are as follows: cases tried, 605; accused tried, 883; accused convicted, 504 (56.0%); acquitted, 350 (39.6%); death sentences, 149 (29.7% of total accused convicted); life sentences, 83; unaccounted for, escaped, not apprehended or indictment withdrawn, 29 (3.3%).[88]

10. The Netherlands

Procedure and Machinery

Mainly British and American military authorities, preceding chapters have shown, handled the principal burden of identifying, locating and apprehending Japanese war criminals in the East. Australia then rendered the next most significant contribution to the overall Allied war crimes effort. Not to be underestimated, though, was the role played by Dutch authorities operating in the Netherlands East Indies. There Dutch military courts tried 448 cases involving more Japanese accused (1,038) than any other nation save the United States.

Dutch authorities demonstrated their desire to join in an Allied war crimes operation as early as January 1942. At that time they actively participated in the founding of the International Commission on the Punishment of War Crimes, and subscribed to the inter-Allied Declaration of St. James, emanating therefrom. The Netherlands entered the UNWCC in October 1943. In 1944 it accepted an invitation to join an additional branch of that organization, the Far Eastern Sub-Committee on War Crimes, based in Chungking.[1]

Dutch representatives subsequently sat on the FEAC and its more permanent offspring, the FEC. August 1945 brought a stern warning from Dr. H. J. Van Mook, lieutenant governor-general of the Netherlands East Indies (NEI), to Japanese commanders in the Islands that those who mistreated the civilian population or POWs in prison camps "would be treated as war criminals."[2] Also, the Hague sent to Tokyo for service at the IMTFE two jurists, Justice Bernard V. A. Röling and assistant prosecutor Justice W. G. F. Borgerhoff-Muller.

The Netherlands in time created two sets of regulations governing war crimes trials in the East and in Europe. Metropolitan Dutch courts in Holland, to wit, relied "mainly on existing provisions of

Dutch common penal law." They treated war crimes as offenses against the municipal law, not as violations of the laws and customs of war.[3]

Dutch authorities in the NEI, however, took a considerably different legal approach to war crimes. Enacted in 1946 by the lieutenant governor-general, several special decrees regulated war crimes trials in the NEI. These regulations, wrote the UNWCC, relied "on novel provisions introducing in the sphere of war crimes numerous exceptions to the N.E.I. Penal Code." Put simply, they approached war crimes trials independently of municipal law. Primary reliance was placed on international law, albeit in the narrow sense—Dutch regulations, that is, excluded specific reference to "crimes against peace" or "crimes against humanity." Furthermore, NEI penal law applied only in those instances where its "general principles and rules" coincided with the special war crimes legislation.[4] In their legal approach to Eastern war crimes trials, then, the Dutch basically followed lines similar to Britain, Australia and Canada.

Article 1 of the NEI Statute Book Decree No. 44 of 1946 defined war crimes as "acts which constitute a violation of the laws and usages of war committed in time of war by subjects of an enemy power or by foreigners in the service of the enemy."[5] The Dutch, similar to procedure employed by Australians and Chinese, supplemented this definition with a list of thirty-nine specific offenses. Numbers 1 to 34 included acts which might appropriately appear in any general definition of conventional war crimes or crimes against humanity: for example, "murder and massacres" (1); "torture of civilians" (4); "confiscation of property" (15); and "poisoning of wells" (33).

Farseeing NEI legislators also listed five additional crimes so as to deal "with types of offenses committed by Japanese war criminals repeatedly and on a large scale." These included, *inter alia*, "ill-treatment of interned civilians or prisoners" (35); "carrying out or causing execution to be carried out in an inhuman way" (36); and "intentional withholding of medical supplies from civilians" (38).[6]

Jurisdiction over war crimes trials in the NEI devolved upon military authorities. Japanese accused stood before temporary courts-martial, appointed by the governor-general "where a state of seige [had] been declared." One president (a civilian lawyer) and two members, all officers and at least twenty-five years of age, composed temporary courts-martial. Beyond this Dutch courts, by virtue of a special NEI statute, exercised jurisdiction over offenses perpetrated outside Dutch territory. All relevant provisions, it held, "with regard to war crimes are applicable irrespective of the place where the crime is committed."[7]

Dutch war crimes courts therefore adhered to procedure applicable in military courts, following common law rules of evidence, with certain exceptions. Like their Allied counterparts, Dutch military courts departed from the normally strict rules of evidence in their practicable attempt to prosecute as many Eastern war criminals as expeditiously as possible. A Dutch judge, for example, recognized as legal evidence "all documents produced at the sitting and all statements wherever made." Whereupon he could "ascribe to them such conclusive strength as he thinks they may possess," depending on whether he believed such material constituted the best or most reasonably accessible evidence under the circumstances.

Under the NEI statute, Japanese on trial had the right "to be represented and choose counsel for defense." Those refusing to designate counsel had one assigned by the court president. Japanese accused also enjoyed the right to rebut "in person or through counsel" the prosecution argument. More important, Dutch courts in every case granted final argument to the accused. The prosecution, on the other hand, could at any time during the hearing alter the charges "as it finds necessary in face of the facts and evidence produced." Specifically, this enabled an enterprising prosecutor to introduce additional or more serious charges while a trial was pending.[8]

Several notable features distinguished NEI war crimes regulations from those of many, if not all, of its Allies. For one, NEI legislation explicitly recognized the concept of "conspiracy." "Any attempt at or complicity and conspiracy in a war crime," it read, "are equally punishable with the crime itself."[9] In this respect Dutch law embraced a much broader application than that of its Allies. Chinese and American regulations, it is true, referred to "conspiracy." Yet both restricted its application, and only theoretically, at that, in the case of the United States, exclusively to the sphere of crimes against peace.[10] Dutch law contained no such exclusionary provision; conspiracy might be charged in the commission of any type of war crime.

NEI law also prescribed penalties to be awarded upon conviction: "He who has been guilty of a war crime shall be punished with the death penalty, or imprisonment for life, or imprisonment for not less than one day, and not more than twenty years." In each case the court decided which sentence to mete out. Of the Allied nations, only China similarly handed down pre-set penalties.[11]

As regarded the defense plea of superior orders, NEI legislation followed "the generally accepted rule in contemporary international law": that is, commission of a war crime upon superior orders did not in itself relieve the perpetrator of criminal responsibility. Likewise Dutch statutes acknowledged the legal principle of command responsibility: a commander who "tolerated" or failed to take reasonable action to prevent the commission of war crimes by his subordinates was "equally punishable" for said offenses.[12] Here NEI law resembled that of its Allies. But, departing from Allied practice, NEI War Crimes Penal Law also contained a provision which explicitly freed from guilt "he who commits a crime under duress."[13] Allied nations, more restrictive in this respect, made little or no allowance for offenses performed under threats or strain.

Again in common with some of its Allies, the Netherlands created special provisions for war crimes committed by "criminal groups" or "organizations." The Allies, however, restricted use of this charge to European war crimes trials, specifically, to such notorious groups as the Gestapo and SS, where they felt such conspiratorial behavior could readily be proved. Dutch military courts nevertheless prosecuted Japanese criminal groups for commission of specific crimes.[14]

In yet another aspect NEI law contrasted from that of its Allies. Dutch war crimes regulations, remarkably, empowered an accused to "challenge any member of the court on the ground of lack of impartiality." Left, thereupon, to the discretion of the court was the decision whether to act upon, or ignore, the challenge. Not surprisingly, however, no other Allied nation's war crimes regulations specifically permitted Japanese on trial such leeway, although American military tribunals in rare instances acknowledged a defendant's protest, and thereby replaced a member of its bench. Nevertheless, in truth, many Allied countries explicitly precluded such practice in their own war crimes regulations.[15]

Dutch military courts, like those of China and France, delivered reasoned judgments. NEI law prescribed that such judgments provide "the reasons for the verdict and the description of the offense," as well as "the circumstances which, in accordance with the law," produced said verdict and sentence. This outstanding feature won praise in international legal circles. "It cannot be doubted," averred the UNWCC, "that the courts" which gave "reasoned judgments have tended the most *detail* to the existing store of knowledge on the international law of war crimes."[16]

Paralleling Allied regulations, NEI law allowed mixed inter-Allied courts. Beyond this, all Dutch sentences required confirmation by the commanding general of the area concerned. All judgments needed this "fiat" of execution. Death sentences were eventually referred to the governor-general, who elected to grant or forgo pardon. All accused, regardless of the sentence, were entitled to submit a petition for mercy. The Supreme Court then examined the petition, offering its advice before transmitting it to the governor-general for final disposition.[17]

Dutch authorities closely linked their war crimes machinery with that of the British. General Headquarters, SEAC, in November 1945 assumed primary responsibility for the "investigation and trial" of war crimes perpetrated by Japanese against British nationals. A War Crimes Branch in Singapore coordinated the entire operation. SEAC's scope of action covered so vast an area, however, that it soon developed into the major war crimes investigation center for the whole of Southeast Asia.

The Netherlands, along with the United States, Australia and France, established its own War Crimes Section at SEAC's Headquarters in Singapore. There it maintained "the closest liaison" with its Allies, "with the result," observed a "special correspondent," "that everyone work[ed] in complete harmony to achieve one aim." The Netherlands also formed its own team to investigate war crimes committed against Dutch nationals.[18]

As in other theaters, Allied investigation teams attached to SEAC steadily built up cases against Japanese suspects. British personnel handled much of this work, it is true. Still, liaison teams, as mentioned, freely exchanged information, and Dutch, as well as local, authorities in the NEI contributed their share in the region under their control. Furthermore, the Dutch constituted their own war crimes courts and conducted their own trials in Batavia, Java; Pontianak, (Dutch) Borneo; Medan, Sumatra; Amboina Island; and Macassar, on Celebes Island.[19]

Dutch representatives also assisted in the investigation and trial of Japanese suspected of war crimes against Americans. Soon after Japan's surrender, United States war crimes branches operating in the India-Burma theater uncovered evidence of atrocities in Java, Sumatra and the Celebes. These mainly involved "ill-treatment in prison camps and illegal executions of American airmen." Most of the POWs in the prison camps had been Australian and Dutch military personnel. United States officials, therefore, relied heavily upon the cooperation of Australian and Dutch authorities in order to locate and prosecute suspects. In the end, prosecution cases rested firmly on "joint" American, Dutch and Australian evidence.

Americans, in turn, helped the Dutch war crimes effort. In one instance, SCAP, Legal Section, transferred to the NEI for re-trial a Japanese admiral previously sentenced to life imprisonment by a United States tribunal in Guam.[20]

Australians, too, conducted wide-scale investigations of war crimes in the NEI area. Occasionally officers from the Netherlands sat as members of Australian military courts in cases concerning Dutch victims. And by January 1946 Australian military forces operating in Dutch Borneo turned over to their Dutch counterparts substantial quantities of evidence and suspects.[21]

The Trials

Already by December 1945 the War Crimes Section in Batavia had designated over 200 Japanese suspects for trial. Of these, mostly POW camp officials and guards, 43 had by then been arrested.[22] Dutch military authorities squandered little time. Nevertheless the preparing, scheduling and executing of war crimes hearings required much effort. Consequently Dutch authorities did not conclude their first trial until September 1946, when a court in Batavia sentenced a Japanese captain to death. Charges against the accused had included, *inter alia*, causing "physical and mental cruelties" upon Dutch, British and American civilian and military internees of a POW camp.[23] Despite limited coverage by *The New York Times*, the trial attracted little notice abroad: witness the report presented by Britain's secretary for war, in January 1947—some four months later—that trials by "Netherlands authorities are to begin shortly."[24]

Charged with "the war crime of enforced prostitution," a Japanese hotelkeeper in Batavia figured prominently in one noteworthy trial. "In time of war and as a subject of a hostile power," read the indictment, Washio Awochi committed "war crimes by, in violation of the laws and customs of war, recruiting women and girls" to serve as prostitutes at his establishment. "Under the direct or indirect threat" of the *Kempeitai*, continued the allegations, the women were held involuntarily and forced to serve Japanese civilians solicited by Awochi.[25]

Evidence adduced at the trial basically substantiated the charges. Some twelve women who had been forced into prostitution testified against Awochi, who admitted running the brothel, but insisted that he had done so only under orders of the Japanese authorities; he "personally" had "never" forced or threatened the women.

The court found Awochi guilty of violating the laws and usages of war. Specifically, it cited entry number 7 on the NEI's supplemental list of war crimes: "Abduction of girls and women for the purpose of forced prostitution." The threatening shadow cast by the *Kempeitai*, stated the court, was "rightly considered as being synonymous with ill-treatment, loss of liberty or worse," whereupon this amounted "to compulsion in all its possible forms."

Furthermore, reasoned the court, as "leader and head" of the hotel, Awochi "had great financial interests" in its profits. This, linked to the Dutch nationality of the women forced into prostitution, led to the court's conclusion: in view of the total Japanese control over Batavia, and with regard to the abusive and overbearing Japanese beliefs of racial superiority, "it may be taken that" Awochi was "directly responsible" for the ill-treatment imposed on these women. Awochi received a sentence of ten years' imprisonment.[26]

Japanese wartime treatment of Allied personnel and civilian populations only rarely varied. Generally speaking it was harsh, even cruel, everywhere. Therefore it should come as no surprise that many of the charges brought against Japanese in the NEI closely resembled those brought by British, Chinese, American and other Allied authorities elsewhere in the East.

A Netherlands temporary court-martial in Macassar, for instance, tried a first lieutenant of the Japanese navy "for violations of the rules of warfare concerning the treatment" of POWs in the Celebes. Specifically, the indictment charged Tanabe Koshiro with "intentionally and unnecessarily exposing [Dutch, British, American and Australian] POWs to acts of war," and with "employing POWs on war work."[27]

The court here predicated its judgment on the rules of international law. Its decision cited article 6 of the Hague Regulations respecting the Laws and Customs of War on Land, appended to the 4th Hague Convention (1907), and article 31 of the Geneva Convention (1929) relative to the treatment of POWs. Basically, these statutes provided that: captured officers could not be compelled to work; POW work should not be "excessive" and should have "no connection" with the war effort; and POWs should be moved to zones of safety as soon as possible.

Koshiro, who pleaded not guilty, was nevertheless convicted

"on the ground of circumstantial evidence." "No direct proof" of his ordering the crimes surfaced at the trial. The court, rather, "deduced" his guilt from indirect evidence. In closing argument, the Dutch prosecutor urged the members of the bench to take into account the seriousness of the charges, and to thereupon award the defendant a five year sentence. Interestingly, the court exceeded his request, imposing a punishment of seven years' confinement.[28]

A trial conducted in Amboina is particularly important, inasmuch as its indictment embraced several diverse charges and its judgment contained references to both international and municipal law. Initially Dutch prosecutors charged the accused, a first lieutenant of the Japanese Army Engineer Corps, Susuke Motosuke, with two crimes: "contrary to the laws and customs of war," ran the indictment, Motosuke had "intentionally, by abuse of the authority he enjoyed over his subordinates . . . incited the latter" to execute Indonesian natives, subjects of the NEI, while knowing that the victims "had not been tried, at any rate in a legal manner." Thus, also imputed to Motosuke was the unlawful execution of accused persons without first providing them a fair trial.[29]

Later developments further complicated the case. In his defense, Motosuke argued that one of the executed Dutch subjects, named Barends, had earlier joined the ranks of "volunteer combatants" serving with the Japanese army. Motosuke ordered a summary execution only after allegations of insubordination had been proven against Barends. The execution, Motosuke thereupon contended, "was a purely internal matter of the Japanese Army, and constituted a lawful act under Japanese laws."[30]

The problem lay in this: evidence introduced at the hearing verified that Barends "had freely joined" the Japanese army operating in the NEI. Consequently the court decided that Barends "was not a Netherlands subject at the time of his execution and therefore no longer a subject of the United Nations." The United Nations, however, had previously authorized that its member nations deal only with *"war crimes committed against subjects of the United Nations."* Having lost his nationality, reasoned the court, Barends could not be considered a war crimes victim; and therefore Motosuke could not be tried as a war criminal in this specific instance. That Japanese forces had deprived the victim, Barends, of a fair trial was irrelevant.[31]

Acquittal, nonetheless, escaped Motosuke. Circumventing the limited United Nations' definition, the court instead judged him guilty of the common law crime of "intentional incitement to murder by abuse of authority," as prescribed in the NEI Penal Code.[32] In doing so, the court underscored its (and other Allied military tribunals') jurisdiction over cases "in which the victims are, technically, not nationals of the State whose territory is occupied but are nonetheless entitled to the same right of . . . lawful proceedings before punishment." Moreover, and of considerable significance, the court's ruling in this case, "technically, concerned an 'enemy' subject."

For the deaths of the other three victims, the court found Motosuke guilty of the "war crime" of murder. It based its judgment on the belief that the Indonesians had been deprived of a fair and legally constituted trial. Much of the prosecution case seemed to rest on the testimony of one Japanese witness, a prosecutor at the trial in question, whose testimony corroborated these allegations.[33]

Significantly, in both findings the court acknowledged the commission of "punishable offenses" by the Indonesian victims. Therefore in both cases Motosuke's "culpability consisted in that, although the victims were guilty of offenses and were liable to punishment by the occupying authorities, they were punished in an unlawful manner."[34]

Dutch military tribunals, like their Allied counterparts, directed their prosecution efforts primarily against Japanese accused of the most serious or heinous crimes. A court in Pontianak, Dutch Borneo, for example, convicted and condemned to death Japanese Vice Admiral Michiaki Kamada for ordering the decapitation in 1944 of fifteen hundred West Borneo natives. The victims allegedly had "plotted" against Japanese rule there.[35] For "murdering and terrorizing" some two thousand Dutch POWs in a prison camp on Flores Island, NEI, four Japanese received death sentences before a Batavia court. Ten other accused, found guilty to lesser and varying degrees, drew sentences ranging from three to fifteen years' imprisonment.[36] And a temporary court-martial in Medan, Sumatra, charged four Japanese with killing "through maltreatment" five thousand Indonesian slave laborers, a thousand civilian internees and five hundred Allied POWs during the Japanese occupation of Indonesia.[37] Other examples may be found.[38]

Some Dutch trials, though, manifested unique aspects or twists which set them apart from those conducted by other Allied nations. One trial, for instance, centered about the misdeeds of sixteen members of the *Tokkeitai*, Special Japanese Naval Police, in Macassar during the occupation. Charges against the men included, *inter alia*, that they, "contrary to the laws and customs of war, carried out unlawful mass arrests and/or exercised systematic terrorism [that is, torture] against persons suspected by the Japanese of punishable acts. . . ." What distinguished this trial from others was that "the defendants were tried not as individuals, but as members of a group as a whole with the commission of specific crimes."[39]

All sixteen eventually drew guilty verdicts, in varying degrees. Nine, including the two senior officers, received the death penalty, and the others got sentences ranging from one to twenty years' imprisonment. In rejecting the defense plea of superior orders of several accused, the court determined that "no subordinate may be successful with this plea if the orders were clearly criminal in themselves."[40]

In another singular case Colonel Akira Nomura, chief of the Japanese planning board in Java, confessed to stealing part of the $30-million state treasury. Unfortunately, he insisted, he could not remember where he hid it. The Netherlands prosecutor thus lodged against Nomura a "double charge, illegal possession of property and responsibility for war crimes."[41]

Perhaps two of the most remarkable trials took place in 1947. At that time two Dutch military courts convicted four Japanese of the war crime of "commission of hostilities contrary to the terms of an armistice." The accused, evidence proved, had taken part in the military operations of Indonesian rebels in the NEI after the Japanese surrender. Technically, a state of war still existed then between the Netherlands and Japan. In contravening an armistice, the court therefore ruled, the accused violated international law and committed a war crime.[42]

In March 1949 the *Stars and Stripes* reported as currently underway the "last" trial "involving Japanese" in the NEI. Yet in December of that year the *Malay Mail* disclosed that eight war criminal suspects remained to be tried by the Netherlands.[43] Dutch executions of condemned Japanese, it is certain, continued right up until the end of 1949.[44] Nevertheless the date of the last war crimes trial in the NEI remains a mystery.

Not so with final, precise Dutch war crimes trials statistics. A reputable Japanese source reported the following complete figures: cases tried, 448; accused involved, 1,038; accused convicted, 969 (93.4%); acquitted, 55 (5.3%); unaccounted for, 14 (1.3%); death sentences awarded, 236 (24.4% of total number convicted); death sentences executed, 226 (23.3% of total number convicted); life sentences, 28. As indicated, 10 death sentences were commuted, either to life imprisonment or a lesser term. Also, the fate of 14 accused is unclear, due to escape, repatriation because of illness, dismissal of charges or lack of information. One life sentence was reduced to an indefinite term.[45]

A mere glance at the above tabulation reveals that the Dutch convicted over 93% of all Japanese tried. Just over 23% of all accused convicted were executed.[46] These figures, at least as regards convictions, point to the relative harshness of Dutch justice: British military courts, in comparison, convicted 88.1% of all accused, condemned 32.7%; Australian military courts convicted 69.5%, condemned 23%; Chinese military courts convicted 56.9%, condemned 29.7%; and Philippine military courts convicted 78.7%, condemned 12.8%.[47]

Also, Dutch treatment of Japanese war criminals contrasted starkly with that afforded German war criminals in Europe. Dutch courts in Holland after World War II, to wit, sentenced only 14 Germans to death, and, of these, only 5 were executed. Only 193 Germans were convicted in all. So few Germans stood trial, explained a noted Dutch jurist, because in the "confused days" after the Nazi surrender, most war criminals escaped.[48]

In any event, as internal convulsions—a series of military campaigns fought between Dutch forces and Indonesian nationalists— overtook postwar NEI, the Dutch war crimes operation ground to a halt. Considering the profound difficulty they were experiencing in Indonesia, Dutch authorities most likely would have agreed with the FEC's prescribed termination date (September 1949) for trials. But in December 1949 the *Malay Mail* reported that Dutch trials would continue into the new year, the delay being due to the "trouble with the Indonesian nationalist movement." The Netherlands closed out its Eastern war crimes operation with the transfer, in early 1950, of all convicted Japanese to Sugamo prison in Tokyo.[49]

11. The Philippines

Procedure and Machinery

While perhaps not approving of such sentiments, few reasonable persons would deem blameworthy, or incomprehensible, pervasive Filipino hatred of Japanese after World War II. From the time they conquered the Philippines (May 1942) until the day of General Douglas MacArthur's dramatic "return" (October 1944) and after, Japanese occupation forces exercised oppressive, iron-fisted control over the archipelago. Beatings, torture, abject humiliation and murder became during that period frighteningly commonplace to a generally defenseless Filipino population. To be sure, the unconscionable atrocities bared at the Yamashita and Homma trials constituted the most pointed examples of both widespread and concentrated brutalities perpetrated by Japanese in the Philippines. But others occurred—certainly less publicized, yet equally inhumane.

Any account of Filipino contribution to Japanese war crimes trials must stress foremost that group's unique status during the period under study. Unlike other participating nations, the Philippines, up until July 4, 1946, lacked national independence; it remained a colonial possession of the United States. Accordingly, Americans influenced to a great degree, and often prescribed, Filipino activities relative to war crimes and other spheres. Want of national sovereignty also prevented inclusion of the Philippines as a member of the UNWCC, founded in October 1943.

However, the same did not apply in regard to other Allied organizations. Having previously decided to grant the Islands their independence in July 1946, Washington saw to it that Filipino representatives sat on the FEC and its progenitor, the FEAC. Beyond this, Ambassador Carlos P. Romulo doubled as "Permanent Representative of the [soon to be] Republic of the Philippines" to the

United Nations and the FEC. Of the seven working committees created at the latter's inaugural meeting of February 26, 1946, Committee No. 5, entitled "War Criminals," outlined as "subjects for consideration" the "identification, apprehension . . . trial . . . and punishment" of Japanese war criminals. Chaired by a Chinese, this important committee nonetheless throughout its existence had as its deputy chairman a Filipino: initially F. C. Rodriguez, who was succeeded by J. U. Jovellanos.[1]

Filipinos also participated in the trial of major Japanese war criminals at the IMTFE. An amendment to the original Tokyo Charter enabled each FEC member to nominate a justice and an associate prosecutor to the tribunal. Justice Delfin Jaranilla, in fact, delivered a "Concurring Opinion" complementary to, yet separate from, the majority judgment of the IMTFE.[2]

Meanwhile groundwork for the preparation and actual presentation of war crimes cases in the Philippines was being laid by American authorities there, occasionally assisted by Filipinos. SCAP Headquarters established in Manila in April 1945 the War Crimes Investigation Detachment. Assigned to this office was the task of obtaining evidence and investigating accounts of war crimes inflicted upon American and Philippine personnel. On July 1, 1946, this detachment officially became Legal Section, Manila Branch. As a territorial possession of the United States, and after, the Philippines worked in close cooperation with American war crimes teams in the Islands. However, not out of disinterest, but for reasons which will be examined in the succeeding pages, Filipino authorities often "dragged their feet" when it came to war crimes investigations and prosecutions. Prompting by Americans therefore at times proved necessary and was often fruitful: Filipino army officers, in an early example, ably assisted the Investigation Detachment in unearthing evidence later used so effectively in the prosecutions of Generals Yamashita and Homma.[3]

As in China, wartime atrocities had taken place directly on Philippine territory. Unlike the British or Americans, consequently, Filipinos had no need to create war crimes agencies abroad. Rather, adopting the model set by China, but originally prescribed by the UNWCC, they established a national office, "charged with the duties of investigating the crimes which fell into its sphere, apprehending the accused . . . and conducting the trials in its own courts."[4]

"Under United States pressure"—the American judge advocate general and other officials repeatedly "urged" President Osmena—Filipino authorities prepared in March and April 1945 a measure outlining war crimes trial procedure. Signed on August 16, 1945, executive order No. 64, as it became known, spawned the National War Crimes Office as a branch of the Philippine army. Immediately thereafter responsibility for "effecting the speedy and prompt trials and just punishment of Japanese war criminals" devolved upon this office. Or, rather, so directed executive order No. 64. Actually, primary responsibility for these duties remained in the hands of Americans until January 1, 1947.

The National War Crimes Office, read the directive, was also "to proceed with the collection of evidence of . . . atrocities committed within the Philippines against both persons and property from all available sources" extending over the period from December 1941 to the Japanese surrender. Its functions included maintenance of relevant records and the sifting, collation and analysis of evidence. Among other things, the measure underscored the signal importance of American-Filipino association. "Jointly coordinating with the United States War Crimes Office," the Philippine counterpart would effect the "speedy and prompt trial of all alleged guilty persons" apprehended and arrested by investigation teams. Specifically, executive order No. 64 prescribed that "direct liaison" between American and Filipino war crimes offices be preserved at all times. In this manner, free exchange of relevant "information and evidence," as well as "cooperation" in the "apprehension and trial" of Japanese suspects, would result.[5]

American authorities conducted all war crimes trials in the Philippines until January 1, 1947, when the United States War Crimes Branch, Manila, closed. Filipinos, as mentioned, had participated in the gathering of evidence at some of these trials. Despite the closing of their Manila office, American personnel nevertheless remained in the Islands, effectively assisting their Allies in the preparation of uninitiated or unsettled cases at least until June 1947. Such action allowed for the orderly transition of war crimes–related duties from the United States to its former colony, now the Republic of the Philippines. Responsibility for the disposition of remaining trials, involving non-American victims, from that point on rested with Filipino authorities.[6]

National independence necessitated, among a score of other things, new or supplemental war crimes regulations. Executive order No. 64, after all, left conduct of Japanese trials to American military commissions. Accordingly, on July 29, 1947, President Manuel A. Roxas signed and announced executive order No. 68, which "expressly" repealed its predecessor. Section 1 of this measure directed that Japanese war criminal suspects be tried by military commissions "to be convened by or under the oath of the President" of the Philippines.[7]

Military commissions, following the American pattern set down in SCAP war crimes regulations of December 5, 1945, required a minimum of three officers on the bench. Usually, though, Philippine commissions comprised five men. Of these, one was designated both president and "Law Member." As in Allied courts in other theaters, Filipino authorities exerted every effort to place on commissions officers of equal or superior rank relative to the accused. Philippine army generals, for instance, always presided over trials involving Japanese generals or flag officers.[8]

A panel of qualified Philippine army lawyers was assigned, under the supervision of Captain Pedro Serran, to defend Japanese accused. Filipino authorities, in most instances, permitted Japanese defendants to select their own defense counsel, usually civilian lawyers from Japan. In a similar vein, a special Philippine army division handled the prosecution of war criminals, although, on some occasions, civilian lawyers employed by the Philippine government assumed this task. Interpreters and reporters, provided by the National War Crimes Office, served each commission.[9]

"The Procedure, the Facts, the Law and the Consequences followed by the Philippine Military Commissions," noted a Philippine author on international law, paralleled those "of the Nuremberg and Far East Tribunals." In this manner Philippine military courts defined war crimes broadly as did the charters of the two international tribunals as well as United States regulations. War crimes thus constituted crimes against peace (planning and waging wars of aggression in violation of international law and agreements); crimes against humanity (generally, offenses perpetrated against non-combatants and property belonging thereto); and conventional war crimes (violations of the laws and usages of war.)[10]

Rules governing the admission of evidence, again, closely hewed to those instituted in SCAP and other Allied regulations. Actually, United States influence in this respect is beyond question. Couched in language nearly identical to that found in corresponding American provisions, executive order No. 68 ordained: "The Commission shall admit such evidence as in its opinion shall be of assistance in proving or disproving the charge, or such as in the Commission's opinion would have probative value in the mind of a reasonable man. The Commission shall apply the rules of evidence and pleading set forth herein with the greatest liberality to achieve expeditious procedure." Hence Philippine military commissions admitted as evidence, *inter alia*, "any document, irrespective of its classification, which appears to the Commission to have been signed or issued" by any member or agency of "any Government"; "any report which appears . . . to have been signed or issued by the International Red Cross"; affidavits, depositions or other signed statements; any diary, letter, sworn or unsworn statements; copies of any of the above; "facts of common knowledge"; and hearsay.

Also, Philippine military commissions adopted generally recognized procedure regarding the defense plea of superior orders. Such a plea, directed executive order No. 68, "shall not constitute a defense, but may be considered in mitigation of punishment if the Commission determines that justice so requires." A supplemental provision set the stage for trials of Japanese who occupied high governmental posts, either in the Philippines or Japan, during the war. An accused's "official position," it read, "shall not absolve him from responsibility, nor be considered in mitigation of punishment." Trials ending in convictions required further examination by a National War Crimes Review Board. Death penalties demanded confirmation by the president of the Philippines before their execution.[11]

A subsection of the Philippine War Crimes Regulations, entitled "Rights of the Accused," contained the following: the right to have well in advance of trial a "clearly worded" copy of all charges and specifications preferred against him; to testify on his own behalf, present evidence and cross-examine adverse witnesses; to have fully translated all charges, evidence and proceedings; and, of course, to be represented by himself, court-appointed attorney or counsel of his own choosing.[12] Once more in this, as in so many other respects, Philippine regulations closely resembled those of the United States; in jurisdictional, evidentiary and procedural aspects, in fact, they were nearly the same.

One final element distinguished Philippine war crimes trials from those conducted elsewhere. Filipino hearings featured an abundance of live testimony. As all alleged offenses had taken place, so to speak, "in their own backyard," Filipino military authorities experienced relatively less difficulty in locating and bringing forth eyewitnesses. Only in China, likewise the scene of actual atrocities, did a similar pattern develop. Generally, as has been shown, Allied trials instead depended heavily upon evidence of a documentary nature.[13]

The Trials

Transfer of responsibility for war crimes trials from American to Philippine authorities consumed time. This was no simple undertaking—especially in light of three national and international crises, all of monumental proportions, which squarely confronted the newly independent Republic at this time. Brief discussion of these matters follows. Here it would be useful to note one example of just how long a single case might remain unsettled in the Philippines.

In June 1947 American war crimes personnel in Manila had nearly completed preparations for the trial of thirty-one Japanese accused of cannibalism. According to the American prosecutor, S. Melville Hussey, United States forces captured the accused in February 1947 in Mindanao, in the southern Philippines. There the Japanese unit had hidden from American forces in mountain caves since Japan's surrender. Alleged offenses occurred during this hiding period, that is, after the war itself. "At least a dozen" confessions, written and signed by Japanese prisoners, were obtained by Hussey. American investigation teams also secured the testimonies of numerous eyewitnesses. The Japanese had "enjoyed eating human flesh and ate well beyond what was required to keep them from starving," these individuals attested. Hussey himself described the atrocities as "the worst of the war."

Turning over all relevant materials to Filipino authorities charged with handling this and other trials, Hussey predicted that the present hearing would "be held in Manila within three months."[14] Obviously, much of the foundation of this case had already been constructed by the time it passed to Filipino trust. Yet despite an ample head start, according to press accounts, Filipino authorities did not ultimately dispose of this trial until late September 1949. At that time, ten of the accused were sentenced to hang, four received life imprisonment terms and three were acquitted. The fate of the rest remains unclear.[15]

Eventually Philippine authorities became more organized, at least as concerned trial scheduling. After some delay, to wit, trials unfolded with increasing regularity. November 1947 saw the commencement of several Manila hearings, including the archipelago's first mass trial. Charges "ranging from looting to multiple rape and murder" in two small towns on Cebu Island during 1944 confronted thirteen Japanese officers and servicemen. Much time also passed, however, before the final settlement of this trial. Not until mid-

February 1949 did the National War Crimes Board of Review confirm the twelve death sentences meted out to the accused.[16] While this trial attracted only moderate public interest, events which unfolded at a hearing later in the month captured the lion's share of headlines.

In an abrupt and dramatic reminder to all concerned just how little time had actually elapsed since V-J Day, fisticuffs erupted in a Philippine courtroom. On trial for war crimes stood Lieutenant Junzo Matsuta, a former chief of the *Kempeitai* in a province of Luzon. A Filipino captain, chief of the Philippine army prosecution division, had offered repeated objections to frequent postponements in the arraignment and trial of the accused. Arguing on behalf of Matsuta was a Japanese civilian lawyer. Presently tempers flared; the two lawyers exchanged harsh words. Then, apparently without physical provocation, the Japanese defense attorney attacked the Filipino prosecutor and "used judo" on him.[17] A near scandal resulted. SCAP's Legal Section investigated the brawl, in which, later press reports disclosed, "the Filipino prosecutor . . . and four Japanese lawyers [had] exchanged blows frequently."[18]

In the end Filipinos replaced Japanese civilian lawyers as defense counsel for Matsuta.[19] Nevertheless, as if to underline sharply its determination to mete out justice, not vengeance, at war crimes trials, the Philippine military commission shortly after "dramatically" acquitted Matsuta. Charges preferred against him had included "responsibility for atrocities committed by men under his command." That is, they involved the legal principle of command responsibility—the same grounds upon which Generals Yamashita and Homma had been convicted and condemned. That such a decision should result in a case characterized by so disgraceful a show of mutual enmity as to embroil court personnel in fisticuffs deserved notice. And so, asserted the *China Press*, "The acquittal was hailed as a demonstration of Filipino justice and fair play based on the court's belief in the defense claim that Matsuta had been relieved of his *Kempeitai* command prior to the commission of the atrocities."[20]

As might be expected, a good number of other Filipino trials also concerned the legal principle of command responsibility. Not surprisingly, too, the memories of Yamashita and Homma—the crimes attributed to them as well as their ultimate fates—cast long shadows across the minds of Filipino prosecutors, the Philippine population and similarly accused Japanese. Generally Philippine authorities brought this charge only against the highest-ranking Japanese or those, like Matsuta, who commanded notoriously wicked posts during the occupation.

As a matter of fact the "first Japanese general to be tried by a Philippine war crimes commission" stood accused of violating this principle. Preparations for the trial of Lt. Gen. Shizuro Yokoyama, who headed the army which occupied Manila, began in September 1948. Charges brought against Yokoyama constituted a list as replete with nefarious deeds as imaginable: "direct responsibility for the destruction of the city of Manila"; deliberate destruction of churches and other public and private buildings; "murder" of President Elpidio Quirino's wife and three children during the "rape of Manila"; and allowing the commission of atrocities by troops under his command, resulting in the deaths of over 35,000 civilians in Manila's neighboring provinces. Upon the latter charge, however—violation of command responsibility—Filipino prosecutors predicated their case. To this effect, they cited testimony from the Yamashita trial to prove that the "chain of command" had passed from the Japanese commander-in-chief to Yokoyama.[21] Other high-ranking officers—for example, Maj. Gen. Kenshichi Maska, former commander of all Philippine *Kempeitai* in late 1944—faced similar charges.[22]

Probably the most celebrated case tried by a Philippine military commission examined the wartime behavior of Lt. Gen. Shigenori Kuroda. Kuroda, Yamashita's predecessor, remained the "only living former commander-in-chief of the Japanese Army of the Occupation, Philippines." A five-man commission, headed by Brig. Gen. Calixto Duque, deputy chief of the armed forces of the Philippines, heard the case, which attracted widespread publicity. Presenting argument on behalf of the accused were three Philippine Army officers, appointed by the court. As allegations against Kuroda included commission of offenses upon United States personnel, SCAP's Legal Section dispatched S. Melville Hussey to "handle the prosecution of the American phase of the case." He worked cooperatively with Filipino prosecutors.

Specifically, prosecutors charged Kuroda with command responsibility for the thousands of instances of "maltreatment, torture and murder" inflicted upon Filipino inhabitants by troops under his authority during 1943–1944. Atrocity deaths attributable to such barbarity, assailed prosecutors, exceeded 2,800. Eleven months after Kuroda's arraignment the military commission reached a verdict. Kuroda, it said, was guilty as charged. Yet in overt contrast to action taken by United States military commissions in cases involving similar legal principles, charges and circumstances—those of Yamashita and Homma, to be precise—the Philippine military commission spared the accused's life: it sentenced Kuroda to life imprisonment at hard labor.[23]

For this reason alone the Kuroda trial stands out. It is impossible to ascertain exactly why the court ruled as it did in this case: press accounts were incomplete, often insubstantial and repetitive, and the trial transcript is, as yet, inaccessible. Before delivery of judgment Kuroda addressed the court with words hauntingly reminiscent of Yamashita's. His "conscience," he began, was "clear": he had done all he could to "enhance," not envenom, "Filipino-Japanese relations." Concluding, he said simply, ". . . as a man of reason and rectitude, [I] did my best to prevent my subordinates from committing any acts that were illegal."[24]

Perhaps as wartime memories and passions gradually receded further into the past, decisions like that rendered in the Kuroda trial became possible—as they had not been at the time of Yamashita's trial. In September 1945, less than two weeks after Japan's surrender, Imperial Prince Higashikuni implored Americans to "forget Pearl Harbor" and "bury hate." *The New York Times* replied editorially that maybe sometime in the future, when Japan had been "liberated" and "democratized," this could be accomplished. As for now, it stated solemnly, "It's too soon to forget."[25]

One thing concerning the Kuroda and similar trials is certain: Philippine military commissions manifestly adjudged that command responsibility "rests on a just and sound foundation." "Historically speaking," wrote a Filipino specialist on international law, "command responsibility has been in being from the time of the existence of the armed forced of any nation. . . ." "At the bottom of the principle," he continued, "is the solemn obligation of every superior officer to maintain strict discipline among his subordinates."[26]

Philippine military commissions heard a variety of trials covering a multiplicity of charges, accused, twists and characteristics. Filipinos, for example, frequently tried Japanese for perpetrating "mass murder of unarmed non-combatant" Philippine residents. The number of victims in these cases extended anywhere from twenty into the thousands; often, they had been members of the Philippine guerrilla movement. Methods of killing varied, but commonly included bayoneting, beheading, hanging, torturing, burning and shooting.[27]

The "longest war crimes trial ever held in the Philippines" lasted 113 days. It ended with death sentences for all fourteen accused for wartime atrocities committed in the town of Infania, Quezon Province, Luzon. The defendants, former Japanese naval officers, ranged in rank from lieutenant commanders down to ensign. Specific charges brought against them included "murder, rape, ordering the deaths of Filipino and Chinese citizens" or carrying out illegal orders to commit the same.[28]

Figuring in another noteworthy trial was the man who issued the illegal orders in the preceding case, former Rear Admiral Takesue Furuse. So important did Filipino officials consider this trial that they appointed Commodore Jose V. Andrada, "the highest ranking Philippine naval officer," to head the military tribunal. Furuse, in a rare departure from customary practice in Japanese war crimes trials, pleaded guilty. So enthusiastically, in fact, did Furuse accept responsibility for ordering members of his command (the fourteen accused already discussed) to kill 152 unarmed Filipino non-combatants in Luzon that both his defense attorney and Commodore Andrada stepped in during the trial. They re-appraised him of his rights, explaining "that he could plead not guilty and place the burden of proof on the prosecution." Despite this "admonition," Furuse "insisted on pleading guilty." Subsequently the court convicted him and sentenced him to hang.[29]

The first execution of a Japanese upon sentence of a Philippine military commission took place in August 1948. Captain Chuhiro Kudo, the condemned, had been judged responsible for the slaying of more than a hundred Filipinos at Bay Laguna in February 1945.[30] In a pointed display of impartiality, a Manila military court convicted a Filipino accused of "wartime spying" for the Japanese while, at the same time, acquitting a Japanese officer on war crimes charges. Lieutenant Toru Kurasawa's acquittal, like most Philippine acquittals and case dismissals, was based on "insufficient evidence."[31]

Interestingly, some convicted Japanese afterwards experienced changes of heart. Shortly before their execution, three Japanese seamen addressed a letter to President Quirino in which they "volunteered" to fight Communist insurgents (the Hukbalahaps) in the Philippines or elsewhere. In another instance, thirteen condemned Japanese requested "admittance to the Christian faith" before their execution. These former *Kempeitai*, convicted of "torture and murder of Filipino civilians" during the war, were duly baptized in an Adventist church in Manila.[32] And Filipino President Manuel Roxas figured prominently in one extraordinary war crimes–related incident. Some time in 1946, word reached Roxas of a Japanese war criminal confined by the Nationalist Chinese at Tsinan, in north

China. Recognizing Lt. Col. Nobuhiko Jimbo as the man who, years before in the Philippines, had saved his and other Filipino lives, Roxas wrote to Chiang Kai-shek on his behalf. Chiang soon after freed Jimbo.[33]

Manila military courts delivered their final sentence on December 30, 1949. The case involved an issue frequently heard at other Allied trials, particularly Australian and American ones. Found guilty of ordering the execution of twelve civilian prisoners without first providing a fair and legally constituted trial was Maj. Gen. Kensichi Masuoka. The former *Kempeitai* commander drew ten years' confinement at hard labor.[34]

Some Filipinos decried the procedural aspect of military-supervised war crimes trials. Among such individuals, most vocal and pronounced stood Justice Gregorio Perfecto, a member of the Philippine Supreme Court which had considered (and turned down) Yamashita's initial appeal. By 1948 Perfecto's censure had grown even more strident than at the time of his previous dissent three years earlier. Yamashita and Homma, he told a university audience, "were convicted and executed substantially by the same methods through which the Japanese imperial army murdered so many of our citizens." "Under the standards of our administration of justice," he closed, "the whole thing appeared as a sanguinary farce."[35] Focused as these attacks were upon the procedural facet of the trials, they may also be regarded as attacks against Philippine-conducted war crimes trials: Filipinos, it will be recalled, followed nearly exactly American procedure and rules of evidence.

Filipino officials responded to their critics with arguments akin to those offered by other Allied trial proponents. Military tribunals, they pointed out, should be distinguished from civil courts. The unique character of the former necessitated a relaxation of the ordinarily strict rules of evidence. War crimes trials, explained a spokesperson for the Judge Advocate General's Office, presented "circumstances beyond one's control." It was "not feasible to bring before the Commission all eyewitnesses" to crimes "committed several years ago."[36]

Some individuals declared Philippine war crimes trials generally, not specifically procedurally, unfair. Criticism of this kind usually stemmed from moralistic, rather than legalistic, objections. A Presbyterian pastor in Manila, Eugene A. Hessel, exemplified this type of critic. Hessel leveled a piercing indictment, both broad and specific in its scope, against the entire Philippine war crimes operation. It was impossible, he contended, "for either the prosecution or defense witnesses accurately to recall details" relative to crimes committed three to five years ago. Moreover, as "the crimes were committed during the heat of war," who was fit, he pressed, to judge those who had acted "first of all" out of motives of "self-preservation" or under the orders of a superior? Hessel also questioned the "legal" qualifications of Philippine army officers who served on commissions. Most disquieting, he suggested that "evidence is accumulating that the prosecution tends to be vindictive": witnesses had been coerced into testifying adversely—lying—against Japanese defendants; prosecutors sometimes denied evidence, records and witnesses to the defense. To rectify such injustice, Hessel proposed a return to practices employed in Biblical times: force those who would mete out such inequitable punishments to witness their own handiwork; better still, "Let the Judges Do the Hanging!"[37]

Hessel and persons who agreed with him, it would appear, represented a minority. More important, it should be emphasized that at the heart of the pastor's message lay a moralistic condemnation of "man's greatest crime," war itself. Witnesses and Japanese accused at Philippine war crimes trials, technically and by statute at least, enjoyed protection from the type of coerced testimony or forced confessions alleged by Hessel. Executive order No. 68, that is, held that statements and confessions "procured" by questionable means should be nullified or disregarded by military commissions.[38]

Above all, there were a number of voices supporting the trials as "fair." Especially relevant here are the comments of Captain Pedro Serran, chief of the panel of Philippine army lawyers assigned to defend Japanese accused. Despite a "snowstorm" of letters from former guerrilla comrades-in-arms and neighbors of his native village beseeching him "to abandon his task of defending Japanese war criminal suspects," Serran stood firm. "Whether a Japanese indicted is convicted or acquitted" mattered not to him. "However," he stressed, "I am duty bound to see that every Japanese accused of atrocities is given a fair trial." "No right-thinking citizen," Serran confidently asserted, "would like to see the Philippines commit a historical blunder through its courts by allowing conviction of innocent people just because they were former enemies."[39]

According to the press, Philippine officials had indeed refrained from committing just such a "historical blunder." Consider, for instance, the editorial observations of the *Manila Bulletin* in re the death sentence awarded Chushiro Kido, the "Butcher of Bay Laguna": "Such were the hatreds generated by Japanese cruelties during the years of occupation that the whole orderly process of trial and conviction reflects credit upon the Philippines. It is a victory of the legal process over the kindred emotions of vengeance and reprisal. . . . The verdict was harsh but the offense was great." "The entire proceedings," added the *Bulletin*, "were marked with maturity and dignity."[40] Similar conclusions had been drawn, it will be recalled, by editors of the *China Press* in relation to the Matsuta trial. And a respected Philippine authority on international law, Adamin A. Tallow, determined that the trials heard by Philippine military commissions followed the same high standard of justice that prevailed at Nuremberg and Tokyo.[41]

Final statistics for trials held in the Philippines are as follows: cases tried, 72; defendants involved, 169; convictions, 133 (78.7%); acquittals, 11 (6.5%); cases dismissed, trials adjourned or sentences not approved, 25 (14.8%); death sentences, 17 (12.8% of total accused convicted); life sentences, 87. Filipino authorities released and repatriated 182 Japanese because of insufficient evidence against them.[42]

The Philippines confronted three grave crises in the immediate postwar period, each affecting in some manner or degree its war crimes policy.

No issue, in the first instance, proved more nationally divisive than that of collaboration. The succumbing of many of the Philippines' highest and hitherto most respected government officials and citizens to Japanese occupation rule—serving as puppets, carrying out odious policies and even persecuting their compatriots—weighed heavily upon the national conscience. After the war Filipinos faced the problem of what to do with collaborators: that is, whether to inter past hatreds and humiliations, absolve these individuals and concentrate on national rebuilding; or to seek redress for past evildoing and, in some cases, outright treason.[43]

Almost immediately after V-J Day American officials demanded the expulsion "from authority and influence" in the Islands of all collaborators. Expedite the "Quisling trials," said *The New York Times*. The political fortunes of Philippine leaders rose and fell according to their wartime records.[44]

But what has all this to do with Japanese war crimes trials? Nothing—and therein lies the significance. As long as the collaboration issue remained unsettled, as it did until at least 1948, Filipino attention—official and private—was substantially diverted from other, less searchingly intimate, matters. Indeed, a perusal of the Philippine *Congressional Record* reveals a burning interest in the question of what to do with collaborators; reference to war crimes trials and relative concerns, on the other hand, are conspicuously scant. Congressmen typically characterized the collaboration issue as "a matter of momentous importance to the Philippines"; no such phraseology appeared in talks regarding war crimes trials.[45]

A similar situation, discussed previously, developed in China, where the preponderance of public, private and press attention centered about the trials of notorious wartime puppets of the Japanese, rather than those of Japanese war criminals (see chapter 9). So, too, did the trials of Nazi collaborators and Vichy puppets dominate postwar France's political scene (see chapter 12).

"The Hukbalahaps constituted the greatest threat to law and order the postwar [Philippine] Republic had faced," concluded one scholar.[46] To be sure, shortly after the Islands became independent the Huks resumed their campaign to overthrow the government and establish in its stead a Communist, anti-American regime. Before long the degree and magnitude of violence accelerated sharply, and between 1946 and 1953 the Philippine government engaged the Huks in a guerrilla-type civil war.[47]

Therefore another major national crisis presented itself to the Filipino people and government at the same time that the collaboration issue smoldered. It also served to deflect Filipino interest from other, less critically pressing, matters—like Japanese war crimes trials.[48] Philippine measures designed to counter such threats to its security, as well as other exigencies, exerted great—overwhelming —pressure on the national treasury. Whence would these funds come?

Four years of war left the Philippines a shambles. Industry, heavy and light, and agriculture lay prostrate. Food production, like per capita production, declined precipitously, causing widespread starvation. Manila, the archipelago's key urban center, and other cities and towns lay devastated. In light of such "economic chaos," reasoned one scholar, Filipinos grew predominantly concerned with the question of "physical survival"; ". . . all other considerations had to be judged in this context."[49]

For aid in their time of desperation, Philippine authorities looked directly, and naturally, to the United States. As early as April 1945 President Truman had promised President Sergio Osmena that he "would ask Congress for generous aid to help reconstruction" in the war-blasted archipelago. American assistance was certainly forthcoming, flowing until, by early 1950, some "$2 billion worth of overall aid" had reached the Islands.[50]

How did such economic and political realities affect the Philippines war crimes operation? Doubtless the nation's desperate financial plight considerably impeded, even curtailed, war crimes trials functions. A Filipino former chief of prosecution, Legal Section, Manila, SCAP, for example, explained the Philippines' initial dilatoriness in launching its war crimes operation in economic terms. Filipino tardiness in establishing a National War Crimes Office, despite persistent American prodding, Dr. Manuel Lim believed, stemmed from President Osmena's "conscious[ness] of the financial bankruptcy of the nation."[51]

Manila also found weighty the financial drain of maintaining its representation and auxiliary personnel at the IMTFE in Tokyo. And when Allied authorities requested in December 1948 further Filipino participation in three minor war crimes trials to be held soon in Japan, it declined. "Apparently," observed the press, such action derived from "lack of funds." At the same time—as if to dispel doubts of Filipino ability to continue its trials, while simultaneously admonishing and encouraging his compatriots—the Philippine ambassador to the United Nations, Carlos P. Romulo, underscored his nation's need to evolve a "definite policy regarding further war crimes trials."[52] Put simply, the exorbitant costs of conducting an extensive war crimes operation exceeded Manila's financial ability.

Furthermore, Philippine reliance on the United States for money and defense rendered it, particularly in the immediate postwar period, inordinately susceptible to American influence in certain areas. Certainly Filipino foreign policy, as Vice-President Elpidio Quirino said in April 1947, was "tied up with that of the United States."[53] As concerned war crimes trials policy, it may fairly be said that American authorities "called the shots." Hence while some Filipinos registered dissent against procedure and/or policy adhered to at the IMTFE, most accepted it. Notably, no enduring public or official outcry demanding the trial of Emperor Hirohito as a war criminal materialized in the Philippines, as it did in Australia, China or New Zealand.[54]

As has been shown, Philippine military commissions basically followed policy and procedure as set down in SCAP regulations. Frequent delays notwithstanding, Filipino authorities adequately responded to American urgings that they initiate, conduct and expedite war crimes trials. And while Manila failed to comply with the FEC "recommendation" that all war crimes trials be completed by September 30, 1949, it did succeed in bringing all hearings to a close by December 30 of that year.[55]

Japanese war crimes trials, then, occupied a relatively minor level of importance vis-á-vis more pressing Philippine national and international priorities. Such national preoccupation explained, for instance, how newly elected President Roxas could deliver in June 1946 a lengthy "state of the nation" address, touching "on almost every problem engaging his attention in Washington and Manila," without including a single reference to the question of war crimes trials;[56] why large numbers of condemned Japanese war criminals sometimes awaited execution indefinitely—death sentences required final presidential confirmation and usually he was "too busy with pressing matters of state to attend to them";[57] and the reasoning behind a journalist's conclusion in August 1948 that "Filipinos would rather forget war atrocities. . . ." Specifically, he alluded to the paucity of public responses to a government-circulated questionnaire detailing Japanese wartime violations.[58]

In brief, in light of these three major crises and their relative aspects, it is truly remarkable that the Philippines conducted as many war crimes trials as it did; and no less so that it conducted them in such generally orderly and procedurally correct fashion.

12. France

Procedure and Machinery

Save (perhaps) for the Soviet Union, France conducted fewer Japanese war crimes trials than any other major Allied participant. This was due less to indifference than to past and concurrent events in Europe and the unique wartime and immediate postwar status of Indochina, the site of French-related war atrocities. Four years of humiliating foreign occupation left an indelible imprint on the French consciousness. When it came to war crimes, therefore, French attention primarily focused on incidents which had occurred in Europe, and the postwar trials there of Germans, members of the Vichy government and Nazi collaborators. Indeed, within the initial twelve months after the war's end some 40,000 Nazi collaborators and sympathizers had been sentenced by special French courts.

Furthermore, agreements concluded in 1940 and 1941 between Vichy and Tokyo resulted—technically at least—in Franco-Japanese collaborative rule over Indochina from 1941 to 1945.[1] Such action limited the scope but did not preclude the commission of actual wartime hostilities and war crimes on Indochinese soil. And, finally, no sooner had World War II ended when French forces in Indochina engaged in bitter guerrilla war with indigenous Communist-led nationalists. Thus did such elements unite to limit France's contribution to the investigation, apprehension and prosecution of Japanese war criminals.

Nevertheless France actively associated itself with Allied war crimes policy. Delegates of the Free French National Committee signed the Inter-Allied Declaration on *Punishment for War Crimes* in London on January 13, 1942. Along with the Soviet Union, China, the Dominions and India the "Fighting French" took a decidedly constructive step in October of that year by "jointly support[ing]" an Anglo-American proposal to establish forthwith a UNWCC. Serious Allied investigation into the perpetration of war crimes, European and Eastern, began in October 1943 with the founding of the UNWCC. Among the Commission's "distinguished lawyers and diplomatists" from sixteen nations, thus, sat representatives of the French government. The French also entered and participated in the activities of the UNWCC's Chungking Sub-Committee, set up in May 1944.[2]

Without compromise to the united effort, each Allied representative of the UNWCC understandably evinced specific concern for information relative to offenses inflicted upon his compatriots at various locations throughout the East. Most pressing to the French, for example, said François de Menthon, minister of justice, were reports of "Japanese war crimes in French Indo-China."[3]

By late autumn 1944 the Allied liberation of France neared completion. A somewhat rejuvenated nation, led by Charles De Gaulle, thereafter assumed a more assertive stance vis-à-vis the conflict in the East. "Any Japanese guilty of mistreating French or Indochinese citizens would be regarded as a war criminal and treated as such," General De Gaulle warned Tokyo in May 1945.[4] A French representative joined General Douglas MacArthur and delegates from eight other nations in the signing of the Japanese Instrument of Surrender on September 2, 1945. Later that month Chinese Nationalist military authorities invited the French commanding general to attend the Japanese formal surrender ceremonies in Hanoi. The French officer, however, declined for diplomatic reasons.[5]

The French, moreover, sought to participate, even peripherally, in the postwar settlement of Japan. French representatives therefore attended the convening of the FEAC in October 1945, and the inaugural meeting of its offspring, the FEC, on February 26, 1946. They served on the FEC throughout its existence. And France dispatched to Tokyo for service at the IMTFE two individuals, Justice Henri Bernard and assistant prosecutor Robert Oneto. Justice Bernard, in fact, delivered a dissenting opinion, separate from the majority Judgment.[6]

An ordinance of August 28, 1944, provided French military tribunals with jurisdiction to try war criminals. While French war crimes regulations were designed, primarily, to accommodate trials held in the "French Zone of Germany," certain articles rendered the rules "applicable not only to Metropolitan France but also to Algeria and the Colonies [that is, Indochina]." For instance, under article 1 persons liable to prosecution included: "Enemy nationals or agents of other than French nationality who are serving the enemy administration . . . and who are guilty of crimes or delicts committed since the beginning of hostilities; either in France or in *territories under the authority of France,* or against a French national, or a person under French protection . . . or against the property of any natural persons enumerated above, and against any French corporate bodies."[7]

Remarkably, and unlike those of any of the other Allied nations, French regulations left undefined the terms "war crime" and "war criminal." The closest thing to an official definition of war crimes was found in a statement by Minister de Menthon of July 17, 1944: "A war crime is a crime under common law which would come within the purview of French penal law, whether committed in Germany or elsewhere against French nationals." In actuality, French military tribunals deemed punishable, first, offenses which constituted violations of French municipal law; only secondarily did they consider whether such infractions were "justified by the laws and customs of war." Consequently French commissions applied either a narrower or broader definition of war crimes than, say, the British Royal Warrant, depending on what the *Code Pénal* and the *Code de Justice Militaire* interpreted as illegal. No nation, not even those of the Commonwealth, relied as heavily upon municipal law in the trials of war criminals. Such practice, assessed the UNWCC, resulted in the substantial "enrichment" of the international law of war crimes "by the importation of concepts and definitions from municipal laws."[8]

Again uniquely, the ordinance omitted any specific mention of trial procedure. Hearings, it directed simply, should be held "in accordance with the French laws in force." Thus following the *Code de Justice Militaire,* tribunals consisted of five military judges, the majority of them "selected among officers, non-commissioned officers and other ranks belonging, or having belonged, to the French Forces of the Interior or a Resistance Group." A president, invested with special powers, presided over each military tribunal. His authority in regard to rules of evidence, for example, enabled a relaxation of ordinarily strict practice, if deemed necessary: "The President shall have a discretionary power in relation to the conduct of the proceedings and the finding of truth. He shall be able . . . to cause to be produced any evidence which seems to him to be of value for the finding of truth, and to call . . . any person to whom it seems necessary that a hearing should be given."[9]

Responsibility for lodging an indictment (*Acte d'Accusation*) and presenting the case against an accused rested with a public prosecutor, usually a civilian lawyer employed by the French government. Under French regulations a Japanese on trial enjoyed the right to choose his own attorney. Upon his refusal to do so, the court "officially" appointed defense counsel for him. Prior notification of the accused as to "crimes alleged, the text of the law applicable, and the names of . . . witnesses" slated to be called by the prosecution was mandatory. French law prohibited a defendant from testifying "on oath"; still he could take the witness stand unsworn. After all testimony, witnesses and arguments had been heard, the accused and his counsel offered final words. Except where the tribunal determined as potentially dangerous "to public order or morals," war crimes trials took place in public courts. Pronouncement of judgment, in any event, had to be in open court.[10]

Military tribunals reached all decisions, including whether to acquit or convict, by majority vote.[11] Before awarding sentence, tribunals considered any possible extenuating circumstances. Thereupon the president read "in public sitting" and "in various degrees of fullness, the reasons for decisions arrived at." Adopted regularly only by French, Dutch and Chinese courts, this practice of delivering reasoned judgments won, as previously noted, the praise of the UNWCC. Undeniably, that organization concluded, the courts which provided reasoned judgments "tended the most *detail* to the existing store of knowledge on the international law of war crimes."[12]

Upon a conviction, French military tribunals awarded a wide range of punishments under municipal criminal law. Basically, tribunals meted out punishments labeled "corporal and ignominious," which included the following: death; penal servitude for life; deportation; penal servitude for a term; detention; and confinement. In reference to certain offenses the *Code Pénal* demonstrated greater specificity. To wit, it provided a penalty of death upon conviction for premeditated murder or poisoning, while voluntary homicide drew life imprisonment, except when "preceded, accompanied or followed by another crime."

Under the *Code de Justice Militaire* a convicted accused could register an appeal within twenty-four hours of the time of judgment. Review of such petitions by a Military Appeal Tribunal followed. This court concentrated exclusively on determining whether the decision pronounced "thereby constituted a correct application of the law"; "questions of fact," that is, were overlooked. Invalidation of an inferior court's decision might occur in several unusual cases —among others, upon proof of an improperly composed military tribunal; "when the rules of competence [had] been violated"; when the penalty meted out failed to conform with the appropriate provisions of the criminal code; and upon proof of "a violation or omission of the [valid] formalities." Decisions by a Military Appeal Tribunal were final.[13]

At this point it would be well to note a distinction between this and preceding chapters. The present chapter contains no separate examination of the trials. This is due to the inaccessibility of relevant materials as well as to the practical limitations of space vis-à-vis France's relatively minor role in the Allied war crimes operation.[14] Rather, an attempt is made to integrate significant information relative to the trials within the following section on France's war crimes trials machinery.

The *Code de Justice Militaire* required the establishment "in time of war" of "at least one Permanent Military Tribunal in each military region." As the "seat" of this court, the *Code* further directed, "shall, in principle, be the chief town of the military region," Saigon became the site of French war crimes tribunals in Indochina.[15]

Central throughout this entire study has been the theme of Allied cooperation. Yet in still another departure from generally accepted Allied (save for the Soviets) procedure, the ordinance of August 28, 1944, excluded any provision enabling the creation of mixed inter-Allied tribunals. Despite this conspicuous omission, French authorities nonetheless in other areas actively pursued Allied collaboration. At the Singapore headquarters of British-supervised SEAC's War Crimes Branch, to wit, France maintained its own War Crimes Section. Operations of such war crimes teams included liaison functions and the investigation of atrocities perpetrated against French nationals there and in adjacent regions. At various locations within SEAC's control, French officials constituted their own courts and heard their own cases. In turn, SEAC stationed a war crimes liaison officer at French military headquarters in Saigon.[16]

French-Allied cooperation ranged beyond exclusively British-supervised theaters. Paris dispatched a liaison officer to SCAP's War Crimes Branch at Yokohama, where he remained throughout 1947. Separately, and in close coordination with the Legal Section's Investigation Division of SCAP, this officer conducted investigations of violations concerning French nationals. SCAP sometimes arrested Japanese suspects upon request of French authorities in Indochina. As with the British, French military authorities reciprocated, extending assistance to United States war crimes teams in regions under their control. Expansion of India-Burma theater's war crimes activities shortly after Japan's surrender led to the unearthing of numerous crimes involving American victims. Most concerned ill-treatment of POWs and captured airmen throughout Southeast Asia. The incredibly difficult task of locating, identifying and apprehending Japanese suspects in these regions resulted in the successful completion of only four cases in Indochina, involving the illegal executions of eleven American airmen. Of seven Japanese tried, five were sentenced to death and two to imprisonment.[17]

While friction undoubtedly existed between French and Chinese Nationalist forces in Indochina circa autumn 1945, evidence of cooperation may also be found. In one instance, a Shanghai military tribunal in January 1948 transferred to local French authorities for trial in Indochina a notorious Japanese war criminal. Imputed to the accused, General Chijisima, was a long list of tortures and murders committed during his tenure as governor-general of Indochina and as commander-in-chief of Japanese forces in Java and other South Sea regions.[18]

Aside from its general application, French municipal law as comprised in the *Code Pénal* and the *Code de Justice Militaire* specified certain offenses which proved particularly effective in the prosecution of war crimes. These included, *inter alia*, "the illegal recruitment of armed forces"; "criminal association"—for example, organizations "engaged in systematic terrorism"; "poisoning"; "premeditated murder" and killing as a form of reprisal; "illegal restraint of civilians"; "illegal" employment of POWs on "war work"; "pillage"; "abuse of authority"; and "offenses against wounded, sick or dead soldiers."[19]

As it developed, the overall pattern of French war crimes trials did not stray far from that set down by the other prosecuting nations. Definite distinctions, it is true, manifested themselves in the formal texts of French and other Allied war crimes regulations. Nevertheless tribunals sitting in Saigon, Singapore, Yokohama, Java, Manila and elsewhere applied similar law, espoused similar principles of law and justice and experienced similar fortunes, good and bad.

French military authorities in Saigon, for instance, before too long learned the necessity of distinguishing between European and Eastern war crimes: to wit, crimes perpetrated by Japanese forces, even specially formed contingents such as the *Kempeitai*, defied strict interpretation as so-called group crimes (that is, commission of specific offenses by units, not individuals). That such conspiratorial behavior had occurred routinely in Europe, by the Gestapo, SS and other "criminal organizations," was beyond gainsaying. Not so in the East, however. And so the French, like their Allies (except for the Dutch—see chapter 10), forwent prosecution of criminal groups and in its stead regularly resorted to the holding of "joint" or "mass" trials. These hearings, previously described, featured groups of Japanese numbering anywhere from three to ninety-three charged simultaneously with committing, or participating in, the same or similar offense(s). One notable Saigon case of this kind witnessed forty-nine *Kempeitai* tried "jointly" on war crimes charges. As the alleged crimes had been charged "variously" and in various degrees of guilt, so, too, the sentences handed down reflected this diversity. Thirteen of the accused, including four *in absentia*, received the death penalty; twenty-seven received prison terms of different lengths, all at "hard labor" and several in "solitary confinement"; and nine were acquitted.[20]

French military tribunals, again like their Allied counterparts, tried Japanese on a wide variety of offenses. But whereas Allied courts in most cases alleged war crimes which might easily and simultaneously be interpreted as violations under their respective municipal laws, French tribunals invariably adhered to this practice. Thus French prosecutors accused Japanese of "mass murder" of French POWs by "outright decapitation" or prolonged torture; or "ill-treatment of POWs and having forced them to do certain work in violation of international conventions"; of "mass slaughter" or "assassination" of French POWs, civilians and men and women of the Indochinese Resistance movement.[21] French indictments commonly charged Japanese with "rape," "ordering the execution [of a French officer] without trial," and murder of literally hundreds of non-French, that is Vietnamese, POWs.[22] Again, each of these alleged offenses constituted explicit violations under French municipal law. Moreover, no Japanese stood before a Saigon court charged with "crimes against peace" or "crimes against humanity." Japanese suspects against whom tenable cases could not be built were subsequently released and returned to Japan.[23]

A recurring defense plea at Eastern war crimes trials was that of superior orders. While the *Code Pénal* held that no crime was committed "when the homicide, wounding or striking was ordered by the law or by legal authority," supplemental legislation reversed this long-established provision, adjusting it to comply more readily with generally accepted Allied practice. According to the ordinance of August 28, 1944, "Laws, decrees or regulations issued by the enemy authorities" in no way justified the commission of crimes. Only "in suitable cases" might such a defense "be pleaded as an extenuating or exculpating circumstance."[24]

Similarly, French authorities maintained a stance akin to that of their Allies in regard to the legal principle of command responsibility. Attributing the actual perpetration of an atrocity to a subordinate did not necessarily free superiors from responsibility. Rather, French law considered the latter "as accomplices in so far as they [had] organized or tolerated the criminal acts of their subordinates."[25]

The precise termination date of French-conducted Eastern war crimes trials is unclear. Press accounts indicated that as of December 1949 some fifty-three Japanese suspects still awaited trial in Saigon. As late as March 1951, it is known, French military authorities were still in the process of executing condemned Japanese war criminals.[26]

Significant procedural, statutory and interpretive discrepancies, then, existed between the French municipal codes and the Allied nations' specially created war crimes regulations. France's operation in the East nonetheless generally embraced a philosophy, if not a strict definition, of war crimes and war crimes trials similar to that of its Allies.

Final, total statistics for French war crimes trials in the East are as follows: cases tried, 39; accused, 230; convicted, 198 (86.1%); acquitted, 31 (13.5%); unaccounted for, 1; sentenced to death, 63 (31.8% of total accused convicted); death sentences carried out, 26 (13.1% of total accused convicted). Thirty-seven of those condemned, as well as four and two given life and other prison terms, respectively, were sentenced *in absentia*, having eluded capture.[27]

Epilogue: Ideals Upheld

Alas, hopes that the Nuremberg and Tokyo principles would assist in the deterrence of future wars failed to materialize. In truth, as Eugene Davidson, a noted authority on the Nuremberg Trial, has suggested, "it may be argued that the uneasy peace that has endured between the major powers since World War II has been kept not because of, but despite, Nuremberg."[1] His point is well taken: any serious attempt to apply and enforce the Nuremberg principles might have caused a world war in given situations in certain troubled areas of the globe. The majority of governmental leaders in the immediate postwar period, however, enjoyed no such perception.

As concerned the Pacific War, one undeniable factor surely impressed Allied leaders. During the conflict Japanese military and civilian personnel perpetrated countless atrocities against countless Allied POWs, civilian captives and local populations. While perhaps not the result of an organized governmental plan—a conspiracy—these crimes were not "stray incidents" either, as Justice Pal submitted.[2] True, Japan was not Germany, and Tojo was not Hitler. Nevertheless 27% of Anglo-American POWs held by Japanese forces had died while in captivity compared to only 4% of those held by German forces. Repeated warnings and protests against such crimes had been lodged by Allied and neutral officials with the Japanese foreign ministry throughout the war. Not surprisingly, consequently, Allied leaders expected cessation of such incidents. Yet they continued.

Certain of the defendants at the IMTFE admitted having learned of Allied and neutral protests during the war. Unable, they swore, to effect any change by themselves, they had subsequently forwarded these remonstrances to "competent authorities." One wonders, though, why these defendants, the military men among the accused and the "competent authorities" utterly failed to halt or reduce Japanese atrocities in the field—particularly in light of the Japanese people's profound veneration for discipline; the Imperial Rescript of 1882 whereby every Japanese serviceman vowed to regard all superior orders as emanating directly from the emperor himself; and the fact that, despite diehard determination to fight to the bitter end, Japanese armed forces unquestioningly obeyed Hirohito's surrender proclamation of August 14, 1945. Put simply, might not the issuance and enforcement of high-level orders to Japanese army and navy field commanders demanding, not indulgent, but civilized, treatment of opposing captives and civilians have proved partially effective? This assumes, of course, that those responsible for issuing such orders cared enough to pursue satisfactorily the matter at hand.

By and large, the underlying point is this: had the Tokyo defendants been tried on conventional war crimes charges only—as lesser Japanese suspects were—most likely no substantial controversy or criticism of the IMTFE would have arisen. But the Allies chose another course.

By autumn 1945 Allied leaders breathed easily. The most destructive war in all history had been fought and won; those who had gravely threatened the peace-loving and democratic nations, peoples and institutions of the world lay prostrate. Never again, these leaders soberly discerned, could the world afford to become embroiled in total conflict, especially with the advent of atomic power. Even limited wars posed great menace in a world of mounting interdependence: indeed, the potential for expansion of local discords and clashes into global wars, manifested twice in the past quarter century, was alarmingly high. Some attempt—no matter how minute its chance of success—had to be offered to deter war. Toward fashioning an improved and secure international order, free from aggression, the Allies thereafter directed their full attention. What better way to begin, they reasoned, than to hold for trial before the bar of international justice those individual leaders they believed responsible for recent aggressions?

Still, as political philosopher Hannah Arendt so effectively underscored, the purpose of a trial is to pursue and attain justice, nothing else.[3] Whether the IMTFE deviated from that righteous path, and whether victorious Allies unjustly subjected vanquished Japanese leaders to unprecedented trial and charges for political purposes, is—and will continue to be until some modern day Solomon provides definitive answers—a matter of feverish controversy. "Victors' justice" to one reasonable person is a sincere attempt to expand the scope and application of international law and justice to another. To be sure, the legal/historical debate surrounding this question remains as heated today as at the time of the Nuremberg and Tokyo tribunals.[4] Actually, one might posit such contentious matters alongside the many fiercely disputed, yet presently unsettled and seemingly irresolvable elements of international law and order: for example, the stubborn undefinability of the term "aggression"; or, as regards the function of superpowers in the United Nations, the question "Who will control the controllers if they should fight among each other?"[5]

With this in mind, several brief observations may be offered.

First, for those who believe, and in 1945 believed, in the absolute necessity of establishing an international legal order aimed at deterring war, the Nuremberg and Tokyo principles—in spite of their shortcomings—contributed substantially to this goal. While "deeply flawed as moral education," suggested international law expert Richard A. Falk, "however there is more to Nuremberg than its Judgment. Certainly the Nuremberg trial contributed to an international learning experience on world order...." To historian Arthur M. Schlesinger, Jr., the Nuremberg principles constituted, "along with other treaties, rudiments of an international consensus" worthy of enforcement. "Such documents," he added, "outlaw actions that the world has placed beyond the limits of permissible behavior."[6] If they achieved nothing else, the International Military Tribunals put hitherto unclearly defined and unapplied laws and legal principles firmly on record for future reference.

Second, given this reasoning, few tenable alternatives to conducting such trials existed in 1945. Indisputably some high-level Japanese and German government and military officials were responsible, directly or indirectly, for the commission of frequent and widespread conventional and other war crimes. Realistically speaking, could the Allies have been expected to let these persons go unpunished or untried? Such a course, Chief Prosecutors Keenan and Robert Jackson tellingly pleaded, would serve as a "mockery of justice." Nor did the prospect of "executing forthwith" major war criminals upon capture, favored by such notables as George F. Kennan, Henry Morgenthau and some Englishmen, augur well for securing the "fundamental principles of justice."[7]

Third, the IMTFE prosecution and majority notion of an all-inclusive seventeen-year criminal conspiracy involving all the accused strained credibility. Their contention that "from 1928–1941 each change in [the Japanese] government was brought about either to further the common plan or to meet a situation created by some act furthering the plan" betrayed an underlying inability to grasp the dynamics of Japanese politics or a misplaced determination to force, after the fact, unrelated and fortuitous events into a preconceived thesis. The conspiracy charge should have been excluded from the indictment.

Fourth, creators of the Nuremberg and Tokyo tribunals conceived the idea of postwar trials of leading war criminals with Allied unity as their foundation. Indeed, characterizing the thoughts of Allied leaders were visions—however misguided they may now appear—of "one world." Was it so unreasonable, though—in 1945–1946—to accept the argument that the eleven nations which had fought Japan and comprised the IMTFE spoke for the remainder of the peace-loving world? They included the bulk of humanity in numerical terms. Nothing in life is absolute; it would have proved impossible to win the approval of *all* the world's nations. And, moreover, if the trials were political in nature, they lucidly reflected political realities then existing and accepted: witness the United Nations General Assembly's unanimous adoption in December 1946 of a resolution affirming "the principles of international law recognized" by the Nuremberg Charter and Judgment.[8]

Perhaps the Allies would have been better advised to try major war criminals before regularly constituted courts-martial—in this case, mixed inter-Allied ones—as they did so proficiently in their own theaters in trials of lesser suspects. Here the emphasis would have been *more clearly* on military justice; conceivably, then, application of military law and procedure at the International Military Tribunals (IMTs) might have engendered less criticism and controversy in legal and academic circles.

Or, moreover, the Allies might have charged Japanese and German leaders with responsibility, *principally*, for commission or allowance of conventional war crimes. That is, count 1 in the Tokyo and Nuremberg indictments could have addressed this universally recognized crime, while subsequent counts could have referred to "crimes against peace," "crimes against humanity" and so forth. By thus shifting the emphasis of allegations, the fact that no Japanese or German at the IMTs lost his life for committing an unprecedented crime would have been more sharply underscored. Also, crimes against peace and crimes against humanity could have been treated by prosecutors and the IMTs as auxiliary to principal allegations contained in count 1. In this manner, the desired legal precedents would have been set and the scope of international law expanded—albeit certainly less dramatically—with contemporary and future observers given at the same time a clearer perspective into the conventional and proven, as compared to the novel and debatable, offenses of the accused.

Finally, that the Nuremberg principles, as Davidson rightly indicated, have since proven incapable of enforcement cannot be denied. Nevertheless the question perforce arises: does their inapplicability stem exclusively from inherent impracticality or have decisive—and perhaps indiscernible in 1945—adjustments in the postwar international order mainly accounted for their desuetude? Hasn't the entrenchment of the nuclear age, that is, virtually precluded the Nuremberg and Tokyo type of war crimes trials where superpowers' interest (or those of client states) are concerned?

We must keep in mind that upon the concept of total victory— "Germany's *debellatio* and the *co-imperium* exercised by the Occupying Powers over Germany," and "Japan's unconditional surrender, that is, the consent of the defeated enemy Power"—the Allies based the jurisdictions of the IMTs.[9] Without a total Allied victory there would have been no jurisdictional basis for major war crimes trials. Yet in the nuclear age it is extremely doubtful that such a war could be fought, and such a peace won, without destroying human civilization as we know it. The infeasibility of total war and victory in the atomic era, then, far more than the pervasive idealism of the tribunals' creators, explains the inapplicability of Nuremberg principles since World War II.

A final aspect, whose importance cannot be overestimated, remains. It would be egregiously unfair and inaccurate to assess the entire Allied war crimes trials operation in the East exclusively on the basis of the IMTFE. It is hoped that the present study has gone far in elucidating the small part assumed by the Tokyo Trial in relation to the overall Allied effort. Some 2,200 trials, involving 5,700 accused, it would seem, constitute a far better instrument of evaluation than one trial involving 28 accused.[10] Noteworthily, a good number of authorities who have criticized the IMTs have praised the conduct of minor trials throughout the East for their fairness and justness. George F. Kennan is a notable example.[11]

Beyond this, as recounted elsewhere but nonetheless worthy of repetition, lesser Allied tribunals applied fundamentally different —narrower—legal reasoning than the IMTFE. With rare exceptions, only Japanese accused of actually committing, ordering or allowing atrocities—that is, conventional war crimes—stood before Allied military commissions outside of Tokyo.

Furthermore, minor trials featured, with admirable consistency in the various theaters, excellent and devoted defense counsel; sufficient procedural safeguards, subject, of course, to military law; fair-minded judges; extraordinarily thorough and impartial review procedures in all theaters (save perhaps the Russian); adequate translation facilities;[12] generally (with some exceptions) public hearings; and accessible, complete records of the proceedings. A considerable percentage of the accused, too, were acquitted; perhaps not as many as might have been expected received death sentences. Commutation of sentences was not uncommon.

Occasional departures from the ideals of justice and "fair play," to be sure, may be found. The death sentence awarded General Yamashita springs quickly to mind. But the Yamashita decision, issuing from the first of all Eastern war crimes trials, thereby assumed a *sui generis* character; it must be considered the rare exception, not the norm. Far more often, for example, American, Australian, British or Filipino court presidents interrupted trial proceedings on behalf of an accused, carefully explaining a complicated legal point or re-clarifying his rights under the respective national or international law; or Allied leaders, military personnel and court members proclaimed before and during a trial their own, and their government's deepest resolution to secure and maintain the highest standards of justice.

Outstanding instances of Allied concern for impartiality and fair play at the trials abound. British citizens, all former POWs in the East, protested vehemently against the unduly "harsh" sentences given former guards at a Singapore camp—despite their admitted personal abhorrence for the accused. Sentences meted out were so "lenient" and acquittals so plentiful at Port Darwin trials that Australian citizens and parliamentary officials registered bitter complaints against the government. A Philippine military commission acquitted a former *Kempeitai* officer after a trial in which several Japanese attorneys unprovokedly attacked a Filipino prosecutor; in another case, it dropped charges against a Japanese suspect, while finding his co-accused, a Filipino, guilty of spying. Chinese military authorities, having failed to adduce sufficient evidence after a preliminary investigation, released without trial and repatriated 180 Japanese suspects. American reviewers at Yokohama confirmed only 51 of 124 death penalties awarded, and reduced sentences in 48 additional cases. Such demonstrations of evenhandedness and compassion by far outnumber recorded instances of palpable injustice.

Equally important, the Allied Eastern war crimes operation constituted what, for all practical purposes, may be considered the final manifestation of genuine Allied wartime cooperation. Save for the Soviets (who nevertheless participated in the IMTFE up to November 1948), Allied forces effectively assisted and worked with one another to a remarkable degree and with remarkable consistency throughout 1945 (and earlier—witness the UNWCC, for example) to 1951. The scope of this cooperative activity, it will be recalled, stretched across East, Southeast and parts of Central Asia, as well as the South and Southwest Pacific Ocean—in itself, a monumental achievement.

In his penetrating dissent in the Yamashita case, United States Supreme Court Justice Frank Murphy cautioned his compatriots never to allow the pursuit of retribution to "justify the abandonment of our devotion to justice." "To conclude otherwise," he said, "is to admit that the enemy has lost the battle but has destroyed our ideals."[13] If anything, the IMTFE and other Eastern war crimes trials sought to institutionalize ideals—so vital to a peaceful and prosperous world, their creators believed—not destroy them.

The Allied war crimes operation in the East, certainly, was imperfect, as one would reasonably expect of any human endeavor of such formidable magnitude and complexity. Nevertheless it is doubtful whether any better solution to the problem of how to deal with Japanese war criminals in 1945 could have been devised, given the identical circumstances which confronted Allied leaders. On the whole it may be concluded that, while flawed, the Allied war crimes operation in the East successfully upheld those cherished ideals exalted by Justice Murphy.

Notes

Introduction

1. Richard H. Minear, *Victors' Justice: The Tokyo War Crimes Trial* (Princeton, N.J., 1971).

1. Warning and Occupation

1. *Punishment for War Crimes*: The Inter-Allied Declaration Signed at St. James' Palace, London, on January 13, 1942, and Relative Documents (London, 1942), p. 15; Great Britain, *Parliamentary Debates*, House of Commons, March 10, 1942, v. 378, p. 930.
2. International Military Tribunal for the Far East, *Judgment*, Tokyo, November 1948, vol. 2, p. 1099.
3. *Punishment for War Crimes*, p. 15.
4. United Nations Information Organization, *Information Paper No. 1*, 1946, pp. 7–8 (emphasis added); Solis Horwitz, "The Tokyo Trial," *International Conciliation*, v. 465, 1950, pp. 477–478.
5. Supreme Commander for the Allied Powers, *Trials of Class "B" and "C" War Criminals. History of the Non-Military Activities of the Occupation of Japan* (Tokyo, 1952), Monograph 5, pp. 38–39; *New York Times*, May 13, 1945.
6. SCAP, *Trials of Class "B" and "C" War Criminals*, p. 38; IMTFE, vol. 2, 1117–1126.
7. Horwitz, "Tokyo Trial," p. 479; Potsdam Declaration, July 26, 1945.
8. U.S. Department of the Navy, *Final Report of Navy War Crimes Program in the Pacific*, Submitted by the Director of War Crimes, U.S. Pacific Fleet to the Secretary of the Navy, 1 December 1949, vol. 1, p. 122.
9. Lord Robert A. Wright, *The History of the United Nations War Crimes Commission and the Development of the Laws of War* (London, 1948), pp. 2, 120, 127–131; M. E. Bathurst, "The United Nations War Crimes Commission," *American Journal of International Law*, v. 39, 1945, pp. 566–570.
10. Harry S. Truman, *Year of Decisions* (New York, 1955), p. 412.
11. Ibid.; Edwin O. Reischauer, *The United States and Japan*, 3rd ed.

(New York, 1965), p. 47; U.S. Department of State, "United States Initial Post-Surrender Policy for Japan," August 29, 1945, part 2, art. 1.

12. Reischauer, *United States and Japan*, p. 47; Far Eastern Commission, "Activities: Report by the Secretary General, February 26, 1946–July 10, 1947," Publication 2888 (Washington, D.C., 1947), pp. 2–3; *The Far Eastern Commission: A Study in International Cooperation, 1945–1952*. Dr. George H. Blakeslee (Washington, D.C., 1953), p. 237.

13. Joseph B. Keenan and Brendan F. Brown, *Crimes against International Law* (Washington, D.C., 1950), pp. 176–177; *China* (Shanghai) *Press*, September 5, 1948; Papers of General Thomas Blamey, letter from Sir William Webb to J. D. L. Hood, Department of External Affairs, June 26, 1945, CRS A1066, Item H45/580/6/2, Australian War Memorial.

14. See reference in Potsdam Declaration, arts. 6 and 10, and "United States Initial Post-Surrender Policy for Japan," parts 1 and 2; also see Reischauer, *United States and Japan*, pp. 286–288; Kazuo Kawai, *Japan's American Interlude* (Chicago, 1960), p. 22. Among MacArthur's immediate occupation aims were: "First destroy the military power. Punish war criminals. Build the structure of representative government. Modernize the constitution. Hold free elections. . . ." Douglas MacArthur, *Reminiscences* (New York, 1964), pp. 282–283.

15. SCAP, *Trials of Class "B" and "C" Criminals*, pp. 3–4.

16. Winston Churchill, *The Grand Alliance* (Boston, 1950), p. 605.

17. Wendell Willkie, *One World* (New York, 1943), pp. 202–206.

18. Robert E. Sherwood, *Roosevelt and Hopkins* (New York, 1948), p. 870; Cordell Hull, *The Memoirs of Cordell Hull* (New York, 1948), vol. 2, pp. 1314–1315.

19. Franz Schurmann, *The Logic of World Power* (New York, 1974), pp. 13–17.

20. C. A. Pompe, *Aggressive War: An International Crime* (The Hague, 1953), Introduction, pp. xii–xiii; for contemporary criticism of the trials, see statements by Robert Taft, *New York Times*, October 6, 1946; also see *Stars and Stripes* (Tokyo), August 9, 1946.

21. Robert H. Jackson, *The Case against the Nazi War Criminals* (New York, 1946), p. 3; U.S. Department of State, *Occupation of Japan: Policy and Progress*, Publication 2671 (Washington, D.C., 1947), p. 28; Keenan and Brown, *Crimes against International Law*, p. 155.

2. The International Military Tribunal for the Far East: Trial and Judgment

1. United Nations Information Organization, *Information Paper No. 1*, 1946, p. 10. On initial Allied disagreement, consider that some Americans (Treasury Secretary Henry Morgenthau, notably) and many British people objected to the notion of international trials, favoring instead summary executions of major Nazi war criminals. See James F. Byrnes, *Speaking Frankly* (New York, 1947), p. 182; Henry Stimson

and MacGeorge Bundy, *On Active Service* (New York, 1948), pp. 584–588.

2. On comparisons between the Tokyo and Nuremberg tribunals, see, for example, Solis Horwitz, "The Tokyo Trial," *International Conciliation*, v. 465, 1950, pp. 475, 486; Robert K. Woetzel, *The Nuremberg Trials in International Law* (New York, 1960), pp. 226–232.

3. Horwitz, "Tokyo Trial," p. 475; Dorothy Borg and Shumpei Okamoto, eds., *Pearl Harbor as History* (New York, 1973), p. xii; A. Frederick Mignone, "After Nuremberg, Tokyo," *Texas Law Review*, v. 25, 1947, p. 483.

4. Wright, Lord Robert A. *The History of the United Nations War Crimes Commission and the Development of the Laws of War* (London, 1948), p. 383.

5. See, for example, *New York Times*, September 6, 9, 12, 13, 22, 1945.

6. On the destruction of documents and evidence by Japanese, see *New York Herald Tribune*, December 12, 26, 1946.

7. Horwitz, "Tokyo Trial," p. 482. For MacArthur's "special proclamation," see General Orders No. 1, GHQ, SCAP, January 19, 1946, U.S. Department of State, "International Military Tribunal for the Far East, Established at Tokyo January 19, 1946, Publication 2675, pp. 5–10. Background information on Keenan contained in a letter from former American prosecutor at the IMTFE, Robert Donihi, to author, May 31, 1977, and letter from Donihi to a third party, May 30, 1977.

8. Wright, *History of UNWCC*, p. 383; FEC, "Activities," p. 2, appendix 39, pp. 97–100; FEC, "Third Report by the Secretary General, Dec. 24, 1948–June 30, 1950" (Washington, D.C., 1950), pp. 4–5.

9. Horwitz, "Tokyo Trial," p. 483. For the original and amended charters see U.S. Department of State, "International Military Tribunal for the Far East," Publication 2675 (Washington, D.C., 1947), pp. 5–16; U.S. Department of State, "Trial of Japanese War Criminals," Publication 2613 (Washington, D.C., 1946), pp. 39–46.

10. IMTFE Charter, articles 1–3.

11. Ibid., article 4.

12. Unlike the Nuremberg Charter, which included reference to crimes perpetrated against the German population, the Tokyo Charter was "restricted to offenses committed against persons other than Japanese *nationals*." See Wright, History of UNWCC, p. 205. Also see Walter L. Riley, "The International Military Tribunal for the Far East and the Law of the Tribunal as Revealed by the Judgment and the Concurring and Dissenting Opinions," Ph.D. dissertation, University of Washington, 1957, p. 40; Horwitz, "Tokyo Trial," p. 487.

13. IMTFE Charter, section 3, articles 9a–e.

14. Ibid., articles 13a–d.

15. See *Law Reports of the Trials of War Criminals*, 15 vols., selected and prepared by the UNWCC (London, 1947–1949), v. 1, annex 2, p. 117.

16. Great Britain, *Parliamentary Debates*, House of Lords, 5th Series, (Hansard), vol. 142, 1945–1946, pp. 663, 678. Also, war crimes trials presented "circumstances beyond one's control"; it was "not feasible" to bring forward "all eyewitnesses" to crimes committed years before, concluded the Philippine Judge Advocate General's Office. See Adamin A. Tallow, *Command Responsibility: Its Legal Aspect* (Manila, 1965), pp. 200–201. See also comments by an American trial reviewer, Paul E. Spurlock, "The Yokohama War Crimes Trials: The Truth about a Misunderstood Subject," *American Bar Association Journal*, v. 36, 1950, pp. 388–389.

17. IMTFE Charter, section 5, articles 16, 17.

18. Horwitz, "Tokyo Trial," pp. 489–490; David N. Sutton, "The Trial of Tojo: The Most Important Trial in All History?" *American Bar Association Journal*, v. 36, 1950, p. 94.

19. Horwitz, "Tokyo Trial," pp. 490–492; *New York Times*, April 11, 1946; *Stars and Stripes* (Tokyo), June 18, 1946.

20. For the indictment, see U.S. Department of State, "Trial of Japanese War Criminals," pp. 45–63. Also, *New York Times*, April 29, 1946.

21. Horwitz, "Tokyo Trial," p. 498; Walter I. McKenzie, "The Japanese War Trials," *Journal of the National Association of Referees in Bankruptcy*, v. 21, 1947, p. 104.

22. Letter from Donihi to author, May 31, 1977, and Donihi to a third party, May 30, 1977. Still another prosecutor wrote that the chief counsel at Tokyo (Keenan) had the right of final decision and final responsibility. See Sutton, "Trial of Tojo," p. 94.

23. U.S. Department of State, "Trial of Far Eastern War Criminals," *Bulletin*, 14, May 19, 1946, pp. 847–848, 853. For brief biographical sketches of each accused, see Horwitz, "Tokyo Trial," pp. 578–583.

24. See, for example, Potsdam Declaration, article 10; Australia, Department of External Affairs, *Current Notes on International Affairs*, Sydney, January 1946, v. 17, no. 1, pp. 19, 23; March 1946, v. 17, no. 3, pp. 134, 136. On the Allied emphasis on expediting war crimes trials operations, see, for example, *New York Times*, November 16, December 1, 1945; *New York Herald Tribune*, November 8, 24, 1945. Indeed, no one originally expected the IMTFE to last beyond six months, in H. A. Hauxhurst et al., "Forum on War Crimes Trials (Addresses)," *American Bar Association*, Comparative and International Section, 1948, p. 31.

25. Joseph B. Keenan and Brendan F. Brown, *Crimes against International Law* (Washington, D.C., 1950), p. 155; *New York Times*, January 22, 1946.

26. Said President Webb: "There has been no more important trial in all history," in Keenan and Brown, *Crimes against International Law*, p. 7. On the IMTFE's deterrent potential, see prosecutors' views, ibid., pp. 5–7; McKenzie, "Japanese War Trials," p. 105; Hauxhurst et al., "Forum," pp. 33–34.

27. As quoted in the *China* (Shanghai) *Press*, November 25, 1945. See *New York Times*, September 6, 15, 1945; *London Times*, September 18, 1945.

28. *London Times*, editorial, February 5, 1946; *New York Times*, editorial, April 30, 1946.

29. Horwitz, "Tokyo Trial," pp. 495–496.

30. See, for example, Richard H. Minear, *Victors' Justice: The Tokyo War Crimes Trial* (Princeton, N.J., 1971), pp. 18, 37; *New York Times*, December 6, 1945.

31. "The indictment of an industrialist" could "not be undertaken unless his conviction was almost a certainty" lest an acquittal be regarded in Japan "as a blanket approval of all Japanese industry and industrialists," said Horwitz, "Tokyo Trial," pp. 497–498.

32. *New York Times*, June 18, 1946.

33. Moscow Radio Broadcast, in *New York Times*, May 5, 1946; for the "politically explosive" war criminal list naming Hirohito the "No. 1 war criminal" submitted by Australia, New Zealand and China, see *New York Herald Tribune*, November 6, 11, 1945; January 17, 1946; for Filipino response, see *Stars and Stripes* (Shanghai), October 23, 1945; Senator Richard Russell introduced legislation calling for the emperor's trial—see *Straits Times* (Singapore), September 20, 1945.

34. See editorials, *New York Times*, September 13, 20, 1945; *Straits Times*, October 22, 1945; *Stars and Stripes* (Shanghai), November 1, 2, 1945.

35. *London Times*, January 12, 1945; *China Press*, October 15, 1945; *New York Herald Tribune*, November 13, 1945.

36. Keenan statement in *London Times*, September 26, 1947; Horwitz, "Tokyo Trial," p. 497.

37. "Joseph Keenan Meets the Press," *American Mercury*, v. 70, 1950, p. 459.

38. *New York Times*, January 14, 15, 1949.

39. MacArthur to Chief of Staff, U.S. Army (Eisenhower), U.S. Department of State, *Foreign Relations of the United States, 1946* (Washington, D.C., 1971), pp. 395–397.

40. Ibid.; *New York Times*, January 15, 1949.

41. U.S. Department of State, "United States Initial Post-Surrender Policy for Japan," August 29, 1945, part 2, provision 2; Edwin O. Reischauer, *Japan: The Story of a Nation* (New York, 1970), p. 265.

42. *London Times*, November 13, 1948.

43. *New York Times*, January 15, 1949.

44. See the remarks of Prime Minister Yoshida in Shigeru Yoshida, *The Yoshida Memoirs*, translated by Kenichi Yoshida (Boston, 1962), p. 51; also, the Allied attitude toward the emperor won "applause" in the Japanese House of Representatives—see *New York Times*, June 25, 1946. Winston Churchill later praised MacArthur's "wisdom" and foresight in this matter—see *New York Times*, August 16, 1951.

45. Arthur S. Comyns-Carr, "The Judgment of the International Military Tribunal for the Far East," *Transactions of the Grotius Society*, v. 34, 1948, p. 145; *London Times*, April 30, 1946.

46. International Military Tribunal for the Far East, *Proceedings*, Tokyo, May 3, 1946–April 16, 1948, pp. 21–22; also, see Lafe Franklin Allen, "Japan's Militarists Face the Music," *American Foreign Service Journal*, v. 24, 1947, p. 15; *New York Times*, May 3, 1946.

47. *New York Times*, editorial, May 14, 1946.

48. *London Times*, editorial, February 5, 1946; *China Press*, editorial, June 6, 1946.

49. Horwitz, "Tokyo Trial," pp. 503–504.

50. Australia, *Current Notes*, May 1948, p. 235; Sutton, "Trial of Tojo," p. 95; Horwitz, "Tokyo Trial," pp. 494, 535.

51. Horwitz, "Tokyo Trial," pp. 538–539; Australia, *Current Notes*, May 1948, p. 235; *New York Herald Tribune*, January 17, 1946.

52. For examples of how cross-examination was limited, see IMTFE, *Proceedings*, pp. 886; 38,480; 38,487.

53. Ibid., pp. 384–386.

54. Horwitz, "Tokyo Trial," pp. 507–508.

55. Ibid., pp. 505–519; Australia, *Current Notes*, May 1948, pp. 234–239.

56. Keenan and Brown, *Crimes against International Law*, p. 15. Hereafter, extended reliance will be placed upon this work in presenting the prosecution argument. The work "constitutes . . . the position taken" by the U.S. at the IMTFE, and is "based on statements" by the authors who served as chief prosecutor and his immediate assistant, respectively. See p.v. See Kenzo Takayanagi, "The Tokio Trials and International Law. Answer to the Prosecution's Argument Delivered at IMTFE on 3 and 4 March 1948" (Tokyo, 1948), p. 81.

57. IMTFE, *Proceedings*, pp. 459–461, 463–464; also, Keenan and Brown, *Crimes against International Law*, pp. 123–125.

58. IMTFE, *Proceedings*, p. 391. "The world had to get on with justice," said a contemporary, Robert B. Walkinshaw, in "The Nuremberg and Tokyo Trials: Another Step toward International Justice," *American Bar Association Journal*, v. 35, 1949, p. 363.

59. Keenan and Brown, *Crimes against International Law*, pp. 73, 75, 120.

60. U.S. Department of State, "Trial of Far Eastern War Criminals," pp. 846–847.

61. Keenan and Brown, *Crimes against International Law*, pp. 22, 18–19; IMTFE, *Proceedings*, pp. 139–140.

62. Horwitz, "Tokyo Trial," pp. 521–525.

63. IMTFE, "Summation of the Prosecution," *Proceedings*, A–F, pp. 21, 24ff.; see, too, remarks of prosecutor Tavenner, IMTFE, *Proceedings*, pp. 48,339–48,348, 48,355; 48,400–48,401; *New York Times*, February 11, 1948; *Stars and Stripes* (Tokyo), June 28, 1946; April 10, 1947.

64. Horwitz, "Tokyo Trial," p. 525.
65. The assessment of Takayanagi is that of James T. C. Liu, "The Tokyo Trial," *China Monthly*, v. 8, 1947, pp. 242, 245; Takayanagi, "Tokio Trials," pp. 42, 50, 73–74.
66. Takayanagi, "Tokio Trials," pp. 59, 65, 4–5; IMTFE, *Proceedings*, pp. 187, 221–222.
67. IMTFE, *Proceedings*, pp. 188; 17,034–17,037; Takayanagi, "Tokio Trials," pp. 12, 14, 72, 79–80, 87–89.
68. IMTFE, *Proceedings*, p. 186; also, *Stars and Stripes* (Tokyo), May 3, 1946.
69. Takayanagi, "Tokio Trials," pp. 8, 78–81.
70. For Kiyose's actual arguments, see IMTFE, *Proceedings*, pp. 17,060–17,086, *passim*.
71. Ibid., pp. 17,085; 17,091; 17,094–17,095; 17,097–17,102.
72. For Tojo's testimony, see *New York Times*, December 26, 1947. For his written statement, see Hideki Tojo, "Affidavit of Hideki Tojo, Individual Defense," Tokyo, IMTFE, December 19, 1948.
73. *New York Times*, April 1, 1947; Takayanagi, "Tokio Trials," p. 36.
74. IMTFE, *Proceedings*, p. 231. Argued Kiyose: "The method of selecting the head of the Cabinets since 1928 was largely a matter of chance." And the Manchurian Incident, China Incident and Pacific War "were separate events having separate causes." See ibid., pp. 17,038; 17,041.
75. Takayanagi, "Tokio Trials," pp. 96–99. See Kiyose's arguments in IMTFE, *Proceedings*, pp. 17,078; 17,086.
76. IMTFE, *Proceedings*, pp. 41, 701–702, 196ff.
77. Takayanagi, "Tokio Trials," p. 2; *Stars and Stripes* (Tokyo), April 18, 1948.
78. The court, argued defense counsel, was "unfair" in its refusal to allow the defendants "to know what is said touching their lives and liberty" —see *London Times*, November 11, 13, 1948.
79. IMTFE, *Judgment*.
80. Ibid., pp. 25–26.
81. Ibid., p. 82.
82. Ibid., p. 27.
83. Ibid., p. 994.
84. Ibid., pp. 34, 36.
85. Ibid., p. 10.
86. Ibid., pp. 991–1,000.
87. For evidence relating to conventional war crimes, see ibid., pp. 1,000–1,136.
88. Ibid., pp. 1,001–1,002.
89. Upon long deliberation, the IMTFE justices determined that the original charge had been drawn too broadly; no concrete evidence had appeared to prove serious Japanese designs "to attempt to secure the domination of North and South America." See ibid., pp. 1,142, 1,143–1,144.

90. Ibid., pp. 1,141–1,142.
91. For individual verdicts and sentences, see ibid., pp. 1,146–1,218.
92. Sir William Webb, International Military Tribunal for the Far East, "Separate Opinion of the President," November 1, 1948, pp. 8–9.
93. Ibid., pp. 14–17.
94. *New York Herald Tribune*, November 14, 1948; Webb, "Separate Opinion," pp. 18–20, 21. To be sure, Webb withdrew his original 650-page separate judgment because, he believed, "it now appears that in most matters the majority judgment is the same as mine." He substituted a 21-page "Separate Opinion,"—see letter, May 12, 1976, from Australian Acting Senior Archivist to author.
95. Delfin Jaranilla, "International Military Tribunal for the Far East. Concurring Opinion by the Honorable Mr. Justice Delfin Jaranilla, Member from the Republic of the Philippines. 1 November 1948," pp. 16–17.
96. Henri Bernard, "Dissenting Judgment of the Member from France of the International Military Tribunal for the Far East. November 12, 1948," pp. 1–4, 8–11, 18; Bernard V. A. Röling, "Opinion of Mr. Justice Röling, Member for the Netherlands. International Military Tribunal for the Far East. November 12, 1948," pp. 4–5, 7–10, 47.
97. Bernard, "Dissenting Judgment," pp. 1–4; Röling, "Opinion," p. 47.
98. Bernard, "Dissenting Judgment," pp. 18–20.
99. Ibid., pp. 20–22.
100. Röling, "Opinion," pp. 26–32, 44–45.
101. Ibid., pp. 48–49.
102. Ibid., p. 178.
103. Ibid., pp. 228–241.
104. Ibid., pp. 244–248.
105. Radhabinod Pal, *International Military Tribunal for the Far East. Dissentient Judgment* (Calcutta, 1953), p. 103.
106. Ibid., pp. 116–118, 121, 491, 512.
107. Ibid., pp. 381–382.
108. Ibid., pp. 595, 628, 665, 693.
109. Ibid., pp. 599, 620–621.
110. Ibid., pp. 217, 405–406, 408.
111. Ibid., pp. 67–68, 83, 99.
112. Ibid., p. 697.
113. William Sebald with Russell Brines, *With McArthur in Japan: A Personal History of the Occupation* (New York, 1965), pp. 167–169; Courtney Whitney, *MacArthur: His Rendezvous with History* (New York, 1956), pp. 281–282.
114. Justice Murphy dissented; Rutledge reserved decision; Douglas issued a separate concurring opinion; and Jackson abstained; United States Supreme Court, *Hirota* vs. *MacArthur*, 338 U.S. 197 (1948), and *New York Times*, December 21, 1948.

3. United States: Procedure and Machinery

1. On early U.S. warnings to Japan, see chapter 1.
2. Lord Robert A. Wright, *The History of the United Nations War Crimes Commission and the Development of the Laws of War* (London, 1948), pp. 2, 105, 127, 129–131, 151–152.
3. Far Eastern Commission, "Activities: Report by the Secretary General, February 26, 1946–July 10, 1947" (Washington, D.C., 1947), p. 2.
4. Ibid., p. 8, also appendix 39, pp. 97–100.
5. *Law Reports of the Trials of War Criminals*, 15 vols. Selected and prepared by the UNWCC (London, 1947–1949), v. 1, annex 2, p. 111.
6. *Ex parte Quirin*, 317 U.S. 1 (1942), 63 Sup. Ct., 87 L. Ed.; also, see James J. A. Daly, "The Yamashita Case and Martial Courts," *Connecticut Bar Journal*, v. 21, 1947, pp. 218–219.
7. *Law Reports*, v. 1, annex 2, pp. 112–113.
8. Ibid., p. 114.
9. Supreme Commander for the Allied Powers, *Trials of Class "B" and "C" War Criminals. History of the Non-Military Activities of the Occupation of Japan* (Tokyo, 1952), Monograph 5, appendix 2, pp. 215–216.
10. Ibid., pp. 215–216.
11. Ibid.
12. Ibid., pp. 216–217; Robert W. Miller, "War Crimes Trials at Yokohama," *Brooklyn Law Review*, v. 15, no. 2, 1949, p. 194, n. 12.
13. SCAP, *Trials of Class "B" and "C" War Criminals*, appendix 2, pp. 215, 217.
14. Ibid., pp. 217–218, 221–222.
15. For the reviewing procedure, see ibid., pp. 205–207, 222; and articles by two reviewers, Albert Lyman, "Yokohama War Crimes Trials: A Review," *Journal of the Bar Association of Washington, D.C.*, v. 17, 1950, pp. 268–269, and Paul E. Spurlock, "The Yokohama War Crimes Trials: The Truth about a Misunderstood Subject," *American Bar Association Journal*, v. 36, 1950, pp. 388–389, 436–437.
16. SCAP, *Trials of Class "B" and "C" War Criminals*, appendix 2, pp. 218–220. FDR's proclamation of July 2, 1942, included the provision that: "Such evidence shall be admitted as would, in the opinion of the President of the Commission, have probative value to a reasonable man." The influence on the SCAP regulations is obvious.
17. Ibid., appendix 3, pp. 227–234.
18. Ibid., p. 223; see also *Law Reports*, v. 1, annex 2, pp. 118–119. In actual practice, only the Netherlands prosecuted "criminal groups and organizations" in the East. See chapter 10.
19. SCAP, *Trials of Class "B" and "C" War Criminals*, appendix 2, p. 220.
20. A U.S. commission "may state the reasons in which the judgment is

based," in ibid., p. 221. Also, see *Law Reports*, v. 15, pp. x–xi, 2, 20.

21. See *Law Reports*, v. 1, annex 2, p. 116; also, G. W. Paton, "The War Trials and International Law," *Res Judicatae*, v. 3, 1947, p. 129.

22. *Law Reports*, v. 3, annex 3, pp. 105, 107–108. For China regulations, see ibid., pp. 105–112. Also, U.S. Department of the Army, *Report of the Judge Advocate, United States Forces, China Theater*, United States Army Forces China, Nanking Headquarters Command and Advisory Group, 1 January 1945 to 10 June 1947, pp. 113–119, 24.

23. SCAP, *Trials of Class "B" and "C" War Criminals*, p. 41.

24. Wright, *History of UNWCC*, p. 383; see also FEC, "Activities," appendix 39, pp. 97–100.

25. Wright, *History of UNWCC*, p. 383; also, SCAP, *Trials of Class "B" and "C" War Criminals*, pp. 41–42.

26. SCAP, *Trials of Class "B" and "C" War Criminals*, p. 43; Wright, *History of UNWCC*, p. 384. Also, U.S. Department of the Army, *Report of the Judge Advocate*, pp. 21–22.

27. U.S. Department of the Army, *Report of the Judge Advocate*, p. 22 and exhibit 19, p. 112; Wright, *History of UNWCC*, pp. 382–384.

28. U.S. Department of State, *Foreign Relations of the United States, 1946* (Washington, D.C., 1971), July 22, p. 439; Wright, *History of UNWCC*, pp. 385–386.

29. U.S. Department of the Navy, *Final Report of Navy War Crimes Program in the Pacific*, Submitted by the Director of War Crimes, U.S. Pacific Fleet to the Secretary of the Navy, 1 December 1949, v. 1, pp. 43, 58–59, 66–68, 91.

30. U.S. Department of the Army, *Terminal Report—War Crimes Trial Division, 1947. Philippine-Ryukyus Command*, (Washington, D.C., 1947) p. 1; U.S. Department of the Army, *Report of the Judge Advocate*, p. 26.

31. Lyman, "Yokohama War Crimes Trials," p. 272; Spurlock, "Yokohama War Crimes Trials," p. 388. Also, some hundred army lawyers worked in the background at Yokohama—see *Stars and Stripes* (Tokyo), December 14, 1945.

32. U.S. Department of the Navy, *Final Report*, vol. 1, pp. 90–92, 97–101; U.S. Department of the Army, *Terminal Report*, Philippine, pp. 1–2; U.S. Department of the Army, *Report of the Judge Advocate*, pp. 21–22.

33. U.S. Department of the Navy, *Final Report*, vol. 1, pp. 92, 98, 100–101; George E. Erickson, Jr., "United States Navy War Crimes Trials (1945–1949)," *Washburn Law Journal*, v. 5, 1965, pp. 96–98; Lyman, "Yokohama War Crimes Trials," pp. 268–270. Japanese interpreters first underwent careful screening by SCAP. On the whole their performances were considered trustworthy and "highly satisfactory throughout," U.S. Department of the Navy, *Final Report*, vol. 1, p. 101. Language responsibilities at Manila trials were handled by an American chief interpreter, a *Nisei* group (six officers, forty en-

listed men), five Japanese-American civilians and twenty-one Filipinos, U.S. Department of the Army, *Terminal Report*, Philippine,
tabulation B, chart 5.

34. *New York Times*, September 6, 1945; *London Times*, September 4,
1945.

35. *New York Times*, editorial, September 6, 1945; SCAP, *Trials of Class
"B" and "C" War Criminals*, pp. 3–4. Also, all political parties in
Japan were "carefully scrutinized to see that Japanese war criminals
[did] not hide behind the facade of legality and rise to power again,"
said Brig. Gen. E. R. Thorpe, chief of Allied Intelligence, Tokyo—see
Stars and Stripes (Shanghai), November 21, 1945.

36. *New York Times*, September 15, 1945.

37. See, for example, "Opening Statement" of judge advocate in trial of
Hara Chuichi, vice admiral, Imperial Japanese Navy, Navy Case No.
48; the U.S. Navy's Pacific war crimes program's "purpose was primarily one of deterrence. . . ."—see U.S. Department of the Navy,
Final Report, vol. 1, pp. 29, 80, 202.

38. SCAP, *Trials of Class "B" and "C" War Criminals*, pp. 3–4; U.S.
Department of the Navy, *Final Report*, vol. 1, p. 123.

39. SCAP, *Trials of Class "B" and "C" War Criminals*, pp. 46–49, 67–
68; *London Times*, September 14, 1945; *New York Herald Tribune*,
December 5, 1945.

40. *New York Times*, September 12, 13, November 19, 1945; *Stars and
Stripes* (Shanghai), October 19, November 21, December 1, 1945;
Stars and Stripes (Tokyo), November 10, December 4, 7, 11, 1945;
January 19, February 7, 8, 1946; SCAP, *Trials of Class "B" and "C"
War Criminals*, pp. 45–51, 67–68.

41. U.S. Department of State, *Occupation of Japan: Policy and Progress*,
Publication 2671 (Washington, D.C., 1947), p. 27. MacArthur's in-
structions as reported in a speech by Hugh Baillie, president of the
United Press, in *New York Times*, December 6, 1945.

42. SCAP, *Trials of Class "B" and "C" War Criminals*, p. 49.

43. The phrase belongs to Herbert Feis, *From Trust to Terror* (New York,
1970), p. ix.

44. James F. Byrnes, *Speaking Frankly* (New York, 1947), p. 105; *China
(Shanghai) Press*, March 20, 1949.

45. For the two statements, see *New York Times*, September 22, 1945;
MacArthur Memo, March 21, 1947, in U.S. Department of State, *Foreign Relations of the United States, 1947* (Washington, D.C., 1972),
pp. 454–456.

46. Eichelberger's remarks in *China Press*, November 12, December 3,
1947; George F. Kennan, *Memoirs, 1925–1950* (New York, 1967),
p. 381.

47. On this point, see Edwin O. Reischauer, *Japan: The Story of a Nation* (New York, 1970), pp. 233–235.

48. As of March 1, 1948, the U.S. had tried 574 Japanese, convicting 520;

the Allies, overall, had tried 2,794, convicting 2,379. See Wright, *History of UNWCC*, appendix 4, p. 518. On impatience with war crimes trials, see, for example, Kennan conversation with MacArthur, March 21, 1948, in U.S. Department of State, *Foreign Relations of the United States, 1948* (Washington, D.C., 1974), p. 718; *Sydney Morning Herald*, May 7, and editorial, June 16, 1948; *Straits Times* (Singapore), editorial, February 6, 1947. On disinterest in the trials, see, for example, *New York Times*, editorial, January 26, 1947; and A. Frederick Mignone, "After Nuremberg, Tokyo," *Texas Law Review*, v. 25, 1947, p. 490.

49. Kennan, *Memoirs*, p. 391; *Stars and Stripes* (Tokyo), October 5, 1948; see Shigeru Yoshida, *The Yoshida Memoirs*, translated by Kenichi Yoshida (Boston, 1962), p. 251.

50. U.S. Department of State, *Foreign Relations of the U.S., 1948*, March 1, p. 675; *New York Herald Tribune*, November 14, 1948.

51. SCAP released class "A" suspects, explained Alva C. Carpenter, chief of SCAP HQ's Legal Section, because by judging certain of the accused not guilty of committing conventional war crimes and/or crimes against peace, the IMTFE had "made it highly improbable that guilt could be established in additional cases." See *New York Times*, December 24, 1948; also, see *New York Times*, March 16, 1949; Far Eastern Commission, "Third Report by the Secretary General, December 24, 1948–June 30, 1950," Publication 3945 (Washington, D.C., 1950), pp. 4–5.

4. United States Trials—Yamashita and Homma: The Philippines

1. Brig. Gen. Courtney Whitney, "The Case of General Yamashita. A Memorandum," November 22, 1949, GHQ, SCAP, Government Section, p. 16; J. Gordon Feldhaus, "The Trial of Yamashita," *Current Legal Thought*, v. 13, 1947, p. 253; A. Frank Reel, *The Case of General Yamashita* (Rpt., New York, 1971), p. 62. Note that Feldhaus and Reel served as defense counsel for Yamashita.

2. Feldhaus, "Trial of Yamashita," p. 254; Reel, *Case of Yamashita*, p. 63.

3. Whitney, "Yamashita Memorandum," pp. 16–17; Feldhaus, "Trial of Yamashita," p. 254.

4. For description of the violence and damage, see *United States of America* vs. *Tomoyuki Yamashita*, United States Army Forces, Western Pacific, Exhibits (Manila [?], 1945).

5. *Law Reports of the Trials of War Criminals*, 15 vols. Selected and prepared by the UNWCC (London, 1947–1949), v. 4, case no. 21, pp. 3–4.

6. Ibid., pp. 11–12; Feldhaus, "Trial of Yamashita," p. 256.

7. Feldhaus, "Trial of Yamashita," p. 255; Whitney, "Yamashita Mem-

orandum," p. 19; George F. Guy, "The Defense of Yamashita," *Wyoming Law Journal*, v. 4, 1949, p. 161.

8. *Law Reports*, v. 4, pp. 10–11, 16.

9. Paul Katona, "Japanese War Crimes Trials," *Free World*, v. 12, 1946, p. 38; *Stars and Stripes* (Shanghai), October 30, 31, 1945; *Straits Times* (Singapore), October 30, 31, 1945; Feldhaus, "Trial of Yamashita," pp. 255–256.

10. John Deane Potter, *A Soldier Must Hang: The Biography of an Oriental General* (London, 1963), p. 170.

11. *Law Reports*, v. 4, pp. 18–20, 29–33; *Stars and Stripes* (Shanghai), October 31, November 1–3, 5, 7, 13, 14, 16, 21; *China* (Shanghai) *Press*, *New York Times*, *New York Herald Tribune*, October 31–November 21, 1945, *passim*.

12. *Stars and Stripes* (Shanghai), November 1, 1945.

13. *New York Herald Tribune*, November 6, 8, 1945.

14. *New York Times*, November 6, 1945; *London Times*, November 8, 1945; *China Press*, November 4, 1945; *Straits Times*, November 5, 1945.

15. As reported in Feldhaus, "Trial of Yamashita," pp. 252–253.

16. *Law Reports*, v. 4, opening and closing prosecution statements, case no. 21, pp. 17, 29–33; *New York Times*, November 20, 21, 1945; see also Whitney, "Yamashita Memorandum," pp. 16, 19.

17. *Law Reports*, v. 4, pp. 18, 23; Guy, "Defense of Yamashita," pp. 158–161.

18. Guy, "Defense of Yamashita," pp. 163–166; *Law Reports*, v. 4, pp. 23–29; Whitney, "Yamashita Memorandum," pp. 16–17.

19. *Law Reports*, v. 4, pp. 21–24; *New York Herald Tribune*, November 18, 22, 1945; see also remarks of a Yamashita military aide in Aubrey S. Kenworthy, *The Tiger of Malaya* (New York, 1953), pp. 15–16, 67.

20. *Law Reports*, v. 4, p. 24.

21. Everyone, it seemed, who came into prolonged contact with Yamashita was impressed by his deportment and sincerity. See, for example, Guy, "Defense of Yamashita," pp. 156–157; Potter, *A Soldier Must Hang*, pp. 170–172, 196–197; Kenworthy, *Tiger of Malaya*, pp. 55–56, 64–65.

22. *Law Reports*, v. 4, pp. 27, 29.

23. *Stars and Stripes* (Shanghai), November 30, 1945.

24. *Law Reports*, v. 4, p. 24; Guy, "Defense of Yamashita," p. 167.

25. *Law Reports*, v. 4, pp. 26–29; *New York Times*, November 27, 1945.

26. *Law Reports*, v. 4, pp. 33–35; Whitney, "Yamashita Memorandum," pp. 76–82.

27. *Law Reports*, v. 4, p. 37. The Philippine Court ruled that it lacked jurisdiction, and that the military commission had been "legally constituted." See *New York Times*, November 28, 1945.

28.   United States Supreme Court, *In re Yamashita*, 327 U.S. 1 (1946), at pp. 1–2.

29.   *New York Herald Tribune*, January 9, 1946; *New York Times*, December 7, 1945.

30.   U.S. Supreme Court, *In re Yamashita* (1946). Aside from Justices Murphy and Rutledge and defense counsel, most authorities have agreed with the Court's ruling, that is, that "the matter was one for review by higher military authority rather than the Supreme Court." See, for example, George E. Erickson, Jr., "United States Navy War Crimes Trials (1945–1949)," *Washburn Law Journal*, v. 5, 1965, p. 99, n. 40; John T. Ganoe, "The Yamashita Case and the Constitution," *Oregon Law Review*, v. 25, 1946, pp. 151–153; Daly, "Yamashita Case," pp. 218–219; Quincy Wright, "Due Process and International Law," *American Journal of International Law*, v. 40, no. 2, 1946, pp. 399, 405–406.

31.   For the complete statement, see Douglas MacArthur, *Reminiscences* (New York, 1964), pp. 295–296; *New York Herald Tribune*, February 9, 1946.

32.   Whitney, "Yamashita Memorandum," p. 76; Q. Wright, "Due Process," p. 404; Kenneth A. Howard, "Command Responsibility for War Crimes," *Journal of Public Law*, v. 21, 1972, pp. 16–17. Others who have agreed include Charles Fairman, "The Supreme Court on Military Jurisdiction: Martial Rule in Hawaii and the Yamashita Case," *Harvard Law Review*, v. 59, no. 6, 1946, p. 869; Adamin A. Tallow, *Command Responsibility: Its Legal Aspect* (Manila, 1965), p. 3.

33.   Guy, "Defense of Yamashita," p. 157. For a mere sampling of those who recognized the unprecedented nature of the Yamashita decision, see *New York Times*, editorial, March 5, 1946; *New York Herald Tribune*, editorial, December 8, 1945; F. E. Meek, "War Crimes Trials in the Pacific," *Idaho State Bar*, v. 21, 1947, p. 41; Bernard V. Röling, "The Law of War and the National Jurisdiction since 1945," *Recueil des Cours, Académie de Droit International*, v. 100, 1961, pp. 379–380.

34.   Kenworthy, *Tiger of Malaya*, p. 44; Potter, *A Soldier Must Hang*, p. 172. One author has suggested that the Supreme Court, too, by its decision to deny Yamashita's appeal, "was interested in setting a precedent." See Ganoe, "Yamashita Case," p. 157.

35.   *Law Reports*, v. 4, pp. 10–11, 16; Reel, *Case of General Yamashita*, pp. 84–86; Feldhaus, "Trial of Yamashita," pp. 255–256, 259.

36.   U.S. Supreme Court, *In re Yamashita* (1946); Charles S. Lyon, "Book Review: The Case of General Yamashita. By A. Frank Reel," *Columbia Law Review*, v. 50, 1950, p. 398; also, see Q. Wright, "Due Process," p. 406, and Fairman, "Supreme Court," pp. 870–871.

37.   *New York Herald Tribune*, November 8, 1945.

38.   *New York Herald Tribune*, November 27, 1945; see report of *London*

Daily Express, cited in Potter, *A Soldier Must Hang,* pp. 180–181; also see Reel, *Case of General Yamashita,* p. 94.

39. Tallow, *Command Responsibility,* pp. 201–202; see Perfecto's later criticism, in *China Press,* June 14, 1948.

40. U.S. Supreme Court, *In re Yamashita* (1946).

41. Guy, "Defense of Yamashita," pp. 158–159, 163; *New York Herald Tribune,* November 24, 1945; Reel, *Case of General Yamashita,* pp. 87, 91–92, 94, 241; Katona, "Japanese War Crimes Trials," p. 38. One author felt the trial constituted "a horrible display of racial discrimination" against a member of the "Yellow Race." See F. J. P. Veale, *Advance to Barbarism: The Development of Total Warfare from Sarajevo to Hiroshima,* 3rd ed. (London, 1968), pp. 307–308.

42. Erickson, "United States Navy War Crimes Trials," p. 343; Q. Wright, "Due Process," pp. 399, 406. Also, see "Majority Opinion," U.S. Supreme Court, *In re Yamashita* (1946).

43. U.S. Supreme Court, *Johnson* vs. *Eisentrager,* 339 U.S. 763 (1950), 70 Sup. Ct. 936 at pp. 946–947, 94 1. Ed. 1255. Interestingly, defending the accused and opposing Jackson's view in this case was A. Frank Reel, one of Yamashita's lawyers.

44. *New York Times,* editorials, December 8, 1945; March 5, 1946; *New York Herald Tribune,* editorials, December 8, 1945; February 24, 1946; *Nippon Times,* editorial, February 10, 1946; *Yomiuri Hochi* and *Mainichi,* as quoted in *Straits Times,* February 11, 1946: Arthur H. Kuhn, "International Law and National Legislation in the Trial of War Criminals: The Yamashita Case," *American Journal of International Law,* v. 44, 1950, pp. 561–562; John A. Appleman, *Military Tribunals and International Crimes* (Indianapolis, 1954), pp. 339–344.

45. See, for example, statements by U.S. Navy Captain J. J. Robinson, November 1, 1949, and the ruling of the five-man Military Review Board, in Whitney, "Yamashita Memorandum," pp. 20, 76–81; Meck, "War Crimes Trails in the Pacific," pp. 37–38; *Army and Navy Journal,* editorial, February 9, 1946, p. 744.

46. Yamashita expected to be found guilty, in Kenworthy, *Tiger of Malaya,* p. 30; *Nippon Times,* December 9, 1945; *China Press,* December 8, 1945.

47. *Law Reports,* v. 14, annex, p. 158; also, v. 11, annex, p. 100. Indeed, during the trial Chinese army spokespersons editorialized in the Japanese-language *Reform Daily News* (Shanghai) that "legal technicalities cannot and should not alter the death sentence given General Yamashita." Should Yamashita escape death, they argued, a precedent would be set which would preclude trying Japanese commanders for allowing atrocities in Nanking and other Chinese cities. Thus "there will be no war criminals among the Japanese." See *China Press,* January 1, 1946.

48. See, for example, chapter 7, "Australia"; chapter 9, "China," especially note 37; chapter 11, "The Philippines."

49. Said Chief Prosecutor Robert Jackson in his opening address at Nuremberg: "We must never forget that the record on which we judge these defendants today is the record on which history will judge us tomorrow." See Robert H. Jackson, *The Nürnberg Case* (New York, 1947), pp. 33–34; also, Telford Taylor, *Nuremberg and Vietnam: An American Tragedy* (New York, 1970), p. 94.

50. U.S. Department of the Army, United States Army Field Manual, *The Law of Land Warfare* (Washington, D.C., 1956), chapter 8, section 2, clause 501.

51. Howard, "Command Responsibility," pp. 16–17, 20.

52. U.S. Supreme Court, *In re Yamashita* (1946); Röling, "Law of War," pp. 380–382; see also "Two Japanese War Criminals," *New Republic*, v. 114, February 25, 1946; *China Press*, editorial, "Justice and Vengeance," February 13, 1946.

53. Taylor, *Nuremberg and Vietnam*, pp. 181–182; Richard A. Falk, *A Global Approach to National Policy* (Cambridge, Mass., 1975), p. 146. Similar conclusions have been drawn by Japanese critics: see, for example, *Asahi Shimbun*, Staff, *The Pacific Rivals* (New York, 1972), pp. 180–182.

54. Whitney, "Yamashita Memorandum," p. 20.

55. See, for example, *Straits Times*, October 5, 1945. Dr. Bu Lan, at a FEAC meeting, made an appeal to have Yamashita extradited to stand trial in Singapore—see *Straits Times*, January 25, 1946. Later a British foreign officer assured that if Yamashita's appeal to the U.S. Supreme Court had proven successful, immediate application would have been made to "have him turned over to British military authorities" for allowing atrocities "committed on British subjects in Singapore"—see *Straits Times*, February 8, 1946.

56. Cited in Potter, *A Soldier Must Hang*, pp. 195–196.

57. Richard A. Falk, Gabriel Kolko and Robert J. Lifton (eds.), *Crimes of War* (New York, 1971), p. 9.

58. Taylor, *Nuremberg and Vietnam*, p. 94. Also see chapter 4.

59. Bradley F. Smith, *Reaching Judgment at Nuremberg* (New York, 1977), p. 216.

60. Katona, "Japanese War Crimes Trials," p. 38; Kenworthy, *Tiger of Malaya*, p. 42. Emphasis added.

61. *New York Times*, editorial, September 15, 1945. See, for example, *Straits Times*, editorial, February 6, 1947.

62. Cited in Kenworthy, *Tiger of Malaya*, p. 67.

63. Supreme Commander for the Allied Powers. *Trials of Class "B" and "C" War Criminals, History of the Non-Military Activities of the Occupation of Japan* (Tokyo, 1952, Monograph No. 5, pp. 94–95.

64. *New York Times*, December 15, 1945; January 22, 1946; SCAP. *Trials of Class "B" and "C" War Criminals*, p. 92.

65. *New York Times*, January 10, 13, 16, 22, February 6, 1946; *New York Herald Tribune*, February 6, 1946; *Straits Times*, January 6, 1946; SCAP, *Trials of Class "B" and "C" War Criminals*, pp. 93–94.

66. Furness, George A., "Notes of Speech by George A. Furness, Asiatic Society of Japan (Tokyo)," *Bulletin*, no. 6, June 1976.

67. Concluding arguments by defense and prosecution, in Tallow, *Command Responsibility*, pp. 451–453; *New York Times*, February 5, 6, 7, 1946.

68. *New York Herald Tribune*, February 12, 1946.

69. U.S. Supreme Court, *Homma vs. Styer*, 327 U.S. 759 (1946); MacArthur, *Reminiscences*, pp. 296–298; *New York Times*, April 3, 1946.

70. John H. Skeen, Jr., Homma's chief defense counsel, labeled the hearing "a highly irregular trial, conducted in an atmosphere that left no doubt as to what the ultimate outcome would be," quoted in John Toland, *The Rising Sun* (New York, 1970), p. 320, note. Also, see "Two Japanese War Criminals," *New Republic*, p. 269. Some, though, criticized the critics: see J. Keenan's response to Murphy's and Rutledge's dissents, in *New York Herald Tribune*, February 14, 1946. For praise of the critics see *China Press*, April 14, 1946; MacArthur, *Reminiscences*, p. 298, emphasis added.

71. See, for example, *Stars and Stripes* (Tokyo), February 3, 20, 1946; *Straits Times*, January 11, 1946.

72. U.S. Department of the Army, *Terminal Report-War Crimes Trial Division, 1947. Philippine-Ryukyus Command*, table A, pp. 1–11, case no. 4.

73. Ibid., table A, pp. 1–11.

74. Ibid., table A, p. 1; for trial coverage see *Straits Times*, January 6, 11, 1946, and *China Press*, December 18, 1945; January 4, 6, 1946; also *Law Reports*, v. 4, p. 86.

75. See *China Press*, June 10, 1947. For statistics, see Appleman, *Military Tribunals*, p. 267.

5. Other United States Trials: China, the Pacific Islands and Yokohama

1. U.S. Department of the Army, *Report of the Judge Advocate, United States Forces, China Theater*, United States Army Forces China, Nanking Headquarters Command and Advisory Group China, 1 January 1945 to 10 June 1947, p. 21; U.S. Department of State, *Foreign Relations of the United States, 1946* (Washington, D.C., 1971), July 22, pp. 410.

2. U.S. Department of the Army, *Report of the Judge Advocate*, p. 22; *China* (Shanghai) *Press*, October 29, 1945.

3. U.S. Department of the Army, *Report of the Judge Advocate*, p. 22.

4. Ibid., see exhibits nos. 17–1, 17–2, pp. 107–109. For U.S. "advisory and operational assistance" rendered to the Pacific Sub-Commission and the Chinese, see p. 21.

5. Ibid., pp. 22, 27.

6. Ibid., p. 24.

7. *China Press*, December 15, 1945; January 4, 1946; *Law Reports of the Trials of War Criminals*, 15 vols. Selected and prepared by the UNWCC (London, 1947–1949), v. 5, case no. 25, pp. 2–3.

8. For trial presentation and coverage, see *China Press*, October 30, November 26, December 15, 1945; January 25, 1946.

9. *China Press*, February 27, 1946.

10. *China Press*, March 1, 9, 1946. For Wedemeyer's review, see April 5, 1946.

11. *China Press*, March 18, 19, 1946.

12. *Law Reports*, v. 5, p. 1.

13. *China Press*, March 26, 1946.

14. *China Press*, April 2, 1946.

15. *China Press*, April 16, 1946; *Law Reports*, v. 5, pp. 7–8.

16. *Law Reports*, v. 5, pp. 11, 13; *China Press*, April 16, 1946.

17. *Law Reports*, v. 5, case no. 32, p. 60.

18. Ibid., pp. 61–65; *China Press*, July 26, 1946.

19. *Law Reports*, v. 5, case no. 33, pp. 66–71.

20. *China Press*, May 11, March 5, 12, 25, 1946.

21. *China Press*, March 5, 12, September 17, 1946.

22. John A. Appleman, *Military Tribunals and International Crimes* (Indianapolis, 1954), p. 267.

23. U.S. Department of the Navy, *Final Report of Navy War Crimes Program in the Pacific*, Submitted by the Director of War Crimes, U.S. Pacific Fleet to the Secretary of the Navy, 1 December 1949, v. 1, pp. 80–85. Also, see George E. Erickson, Jr., "United States Navy War Crimes Trials (1945–1949)," *Washburn Law Journal*, v. 5, 1965, pp. 93, 96.

24. U.S. Department of the Navy, *Final Report*, v. 1, pp. 95, 163–164.

25. Ibid., v. 1, pp. 93a, 94, 97, 194.

26. Ibid., v. 1, p. 203.

27. Ibid., v. 1, pp. 67, 86, 122.

28. Ibid., v. 1, pp. 64–65, 76–78, 147–148, 180; and vol. 2, appendix B, case nos. 15 and 16, pp. 19–20.

29. Ibid., v. 1, pp. 122, 201.

30. *Law Reports*, v. 1, case no. 6, pp. 71–72; U.S. Department of the Navy, *Final Report*, v. 2, appendix B, case no. 25, p. 30.

31. *Law Reports*, v. 1, pp. 72–80, *passim*; also, *China Press*, December 14, 1945.

32. U.S. Department of the Navy, *Final Report*, v. 2, case no. 36, appendix B, pp. 38–40.

33. Ibid., v. 1, pp. 184, 187; *Stars and Stripes* (Tokyo), September 27, 1947. Erickson, "United States Navy War Crimes Trials," pp. 107–108.

34. *Law Reports*, v. 4, pp. 86–87.
35. *China Press*, September 4, 1947; *Stars and Stripes* (Tokyo), September 5, 1947. Descriptions in this case of Japanese use of bacteria or of germ-related war crimes resemble closely those brought forth by Soviet prosecutors at the Khabarovsk trial. See chapter 8.
36. U.S. Department of the Navy, *Final Report*, v. 2, case no. 39, appendix B, pp. 46–47; *China Press*, September 4, 6, 1947; January 20, 1949.
37. *China Press*, February 18, 1948; *New York Times*, March 26, 1948.
38. U.S. Department of the Navy, *Final Report*, v. 2, case no. 26, appendix B, p. 31; *Stars and Stripes* (Shanghai), December 28, 1945; *London Times*, December 27, 1945.
39. U.S. Department of the Navy, *Final Report*, v. 2—see, for example, case no. 37, appendix B, p. 44.
40. *China Press*, August 8, 1948.
41. Erickson, "United States Navy War Crimes Trials," pp. 89, 99; U.S. Department of the Navy, *Final Report*, v. 1, p. 204.
42. U.S. Department of the Navy, *Final Report*, v. 1, pp. 103–110.
43. Supreme Commander for the Allied Powers. *Trials of Class "B" and "C" War Criminals*, p. 44; U.S. Department of the Navy, *Final Report*, v. 1, p. 64.
44. SCAP, *Trials of Class "B" and "C" War Criminals*, pp. 73–74; Albert Lyman, "Yokohama War Crimes Trials: A Review," *Journal of Bar Association of Washington, D.C.*, v. 17, 1950, p. 267.
45. SCAP, *Trials of Class "B" and "C" War Criminals*, p. 2.
46. Ibid., see, for example, pp. 95 109.
47. Ibid., pp. 113–115; for other examples, see pp. 110–112, 116–125; *Stars and Stripes* (Tokyo), March 23, 1946.
48. See, for example, *Stars and Stripes* (Tokyo), December 18, 19, 28, 1945; January 8, 26, February 3, 7, March 14, 23, 25, 1946.
49. *Stars and Stripes*, December 18, 1945; February 14, 1946; *New York Times*, October 19, 1946. Another measure aimed at "speeding up" trials, which never materialized, proposed to offer Japanese accused "lesser sentences should they plead guilty." Such "plea bargaining" would relieve the burden of "overworked" military commissions. See *New York Times*, October 19, 1946.
50. SCAP, *Trials of Class "B" and "C" War Criminals*, p. 162. See, for example, *Stars and Stripes* (Tokyo), March 14, 1946; May 10, 1947.
51. SCAP, *Trials of Class "B" and "C" War Criminals*, pp. 164–177.
52. Ibid., pp. 137–150; *Stars and Stripes* (Tokyo), October 30, 1947.
53. *Stars and Stripes* (Tokyo), April 7, 1950; *Sydney Morning Herald*, March 17, 1948, U.S. Department of State, *Foreign Relations of the United States, 1948*, October 17, 1948, p. 873.
54. SCAP, *Trials of Class "B" and "C" War Criminals*, pp. 178–182.
55. Ibid., pp. 183–193, also, pp. 194–201.

56. *Stars and Stripes* (Tokyo), March 25, 1946; February 18, 1948.
57. *Malay Mail*, May 25, 1949.
58. See, for example, the remarks of Major Robert T. Dwyer, U.S. legal officer, in *China Press*, December 19, 1946; *Stars and Stripes* (Tokyo), August 31, 1948.
59. *China Press*, May 29, June 26, July 15, October 7, 1948.
60. SCAP, *Trials of Class "B" and "C" War Criminals*, chapter 3, "Statistics," pp. 202ff.
61. See, for example, SCAP, *Trials of Class "B" and "C" War Criminals*, p. 96. See statements by Colonel A. C. Carpenter in *Stars and Stripes* (Tokyo), December 14, 1945; Paul E. Spurlock, "The Yokohama War Crimes Trials: The Truth about a Misunderstood Subject," *American Bar Association Journal*, v. 36, 1950, pp. 388–389.
62. See chapter 4.
63. Lyman, "Yokohama War Crimes Trials," pp. 268, 272.
64. Appleman, *Military Tribunals*, pp. 330–331; U.S. Department of the Navy, *Final Report*, v. 1, p. 99.
65. Robert W. Miller, "War Crimes Trials at Yokohama," *Brooklyn Law Review*, v. 15, no. 2, 1949, pp. 208–209.
66. Spurlock, "Yokohama War Crimes Trials," p. 436; U.S. Department of the Navy, *Final Report*, v. 1, p. 98. For example: Japanese were "given the best defense possible," said an American officer of the Judge Advocate General's Office, in the *China Press*, December 19, 1946; Erickson, "United States Navy War Crimes Trials," pp. 97–99; F. E. Meek, "War Crimes Trials in the Pacific," *Idaho State Bar*, v. 21, 1947, p. 37.
67. R. John Pritchard, "The Nature and Significance of British Post-War Trials of Japanese War Criminals, 1946–1948," Paper read at Conference of the British Association for Japanese Studies (1977), p. 15—I am indebted to Mr. Pritchard for providing me with an advanced copy of his paper; U.S. Department of the Army, *Terminal Report—War Crimes Trial Division, 1947. Philippine-Ryukyus Command* (Washington, D.C., 1947), p. 4.
68. U.S. Department of the Navy, *Final Report*, v. 1, pp. 99–101; *Law Reports*, v. 15, pp. 193–195.
69. Spurlock, "Yokohama War Crimes Trials," p. 436; Lyman, "Yokohama War Crimes Trials," pp. 269–270.
70. Lyman, "Yokohama War Crimes Trials," p. 270; Appleman, *Military Tribunals*, pp. 269, 322, 331; Kennan to MacArthur, March 21, 1948, in U.S. Department of State, *Foreign Relations of the United States, 1948*, p. 717; Charles Fairman, "The Supreme Court on Military Jurisdiction: Martial Rule in Hawaii and the Yamashita Case," *Harvard Law Review*, v. 59., no. 6, 1946, pp. 881–882, 879. Also, see Erickson, "United States Navy War Crimes Trials," p. 99; and Spurlock, "Yokohama War Crimes Trials," p. 437.

71. See, for example, Appleman, *Military Tribunals*, pp. 318–319, 322, 333; Miller, "War Crimes Trials at Yokohama," pp. 198–200.
72. Figures have been determined from chart in Appleman, *Military Tribunals*, p. 267, after amendment of Yokohama figures according to those in SCAP, *Trials of Class "B" and "C" War Criminals*, pp. 202–204, and those in U.S. Department of the Navy, *Final Report*, v. 1, pp. 103–110. Compare these total figures with those provided by a reputable Japanese source, Epilogue, note 10.

6. Britain

1. See, for example, Foreign Minister Eden's report, March 10, 1942, in Great Britain, *Parliamentary Debates* (Hansard), Fifth Series, House of Commons, v. 378, p. 390.
2. Churchill "associated" the British government with a previous FDR "warning" on September 8, 1942; Wright, *The History of the United Nations War Crimes Commission and the Development of the Laws of War* (London, 1948), pp. 93–94, 127.
3. Great Britain, *Parliamentary Debates*, House of Lords, 1945, pp. 663, 678; 1946, p. 2163; M. E. Bathurst, "The United Nations War Crimes Commission," *American Journal of International Law*, v. 39, 1945, p. 568.
4. For a mere sampling of British concern, official and private, that justice be steadfastly upheld at Eastern war crimes trials, see *London Times*, "Far Eastern War Crimes," July 31, 1946; May 20, 1949; *Straits Times* (Singapore), September 30, 1945; May 15, July 7, August 1, 1946.
5. For the initial British position, see chapter 2, note 1.
6. Great Britain, Royal Warrant, 14th June 1945, Army Order 81/1945, with Amendments, HMSO, 1945. Also, see *Law Reports of Trials of War Criminals*, 15 vols. Selected and prepared by the UNWCC. (London, 1947–1949), v. 1, annex 1, p. 105.
7. Royal Warrant, regulation 1; Frederick H. Maugham, *U.N.O. and War Crimes* (London, 1951), pp. 98–99.
8. Royal Warrant, regulation 2.
9. Ibid., regulation 5.
10. Ibid.; see also, *Law Reports*, v. 1, annex 1, p. 106.
11. *Law Reports*, v. 1, annex 1, p. 107; Royal Warrant, regulation 5.
12. L. C. Green, "The Trials of Some Minor War Criminals," *Indian Law Review*, v. 4, 1950, p. 250; *Law Reports*, v. 15, p. 165, note 3.
13. Royal Warrant, regulation 3.
14. *Law Reports*, v. 1, annex 1, pp. 107–108.
15. Ibid., p. 108.
16. Royal Warrant, regulation 8a–f.
17. See chapter 2.
18. G. Brand, "The War Crimes Trials and the Laws of War," *British*

Yearbook of International Law, 1949 (London, 1949), p. 416; see statements by Lords Maugham and Roche in Great Britain, *Parliamentary Debates*, House of Lords, 1945, pp. 663, 678.

19.   Royal Warrant, regulation 7. Letter from former British war crimes court president, and currently attorney general of England, Samuel Charles Silkin, to author, March 23, 1977.

20.   Royal Warrant, regulation 8, provisions 4–6; *Law Reports*, v. 1, annex 1, pp. 109–110.

21.   Royal Warrant, regulation 9.

22.   *Law Reports*, v. 15, pp. x–xi, 20. Britain and America, on rare occasions, departed from this rule. See chapter 6, British action in the Gozawa trial, and chapter 4 for U.S. action in the Yamashita trial. On differences between U.S. and British military court procedure, see G. W. Paton, "The War Trials and International Law," *Res Judicatae*, v. 3, 1947, p. 129.

23.   For example, see British action in trial of Chusaburo Yamamoto, *Law Reports*, v. 3, case no. 20, pp. 79–80; also, v. 15, p. 8.

24.   Ibid., v. 15, p. 21.

25.   *Straits Times*, September 1, 1946.

26.   Wright, *History of UNWCC*, p. 380.

27.   Ibid., pp. 380–381.

28.   "Mounting indignation" in England was accompanied by "angry protest," *Straits Times*, September 22, 1945.

29.   *Straits Times*, September 19, 30, 1945.

30.   See statement by secretary of state for war, Mr. Lawson, in Great Britain, *Parliamentary Debates*, House of Lords, October 25, 1945, v. 414, p. 2,163.

31.   *Straits Times*, November 13, 15, 1945; *New York Times*, December 28, 1945; *London Times*, July 31, 1946; Wright, *History of UNWCC*, p. 381.

32.   Wright, *History of UNWCC*, p. 381; *London Times*, July 31, 1946.

33.   *London Times*, July 31, 1946.

34.   *Straits Times*, December 28, 1945; January 25, 27, 1946; *Malay Mail*, July 19, 21, 1947.

35.   *London Times*, July 31, 1946; Wright, *History of UNWCC*, p. 382.

36.   See Britain's official expression of gratitude for American cooperation in this affair, in U.S. Department of the Army, *Report of the Judge Advocate, United States Forces, China Theater*, United States Army Forces China, Nanking Headquarters Command and Advisory Group, 1 January 1945 to 10 June 1947, exhibit 19, p. 112. Papers of General Thomas Blamey, cables from Secretary of State for Dominion Affairs, London, to Australian Government, November 10, 15, 1945, "Japanese War Crimes," SC 477, CRS A1066 File No. H45/590/1, Australian War Memorial. Australia, for example, "modelled" its War Crimes Act on the British Royal Warrant, see chapter 7, note 20. Beyond this, Canberra followed London's lead in its decision to try Japanese war

criminals before military courts, see Blamey Papers, Memo No. 32291 from Secretary, War Crimes Commission (K. G. Brennan) to Acting Secretary, Department of External Affairs, "Establishment of Courts for Trial of War Criminals," March 9, 1945, CRS A1066 File No. H45/580/2.

37. Wright, *History of UNWCC*, p. 382; *London Times*, July 31, 1946; Great Britain, *Parliamentary Debates*, House of Lords, v. 415, November 2, 1945, p. 783; U.S. Department of the Army, *Report of the Judge Advocate*, p. 24.

38. *London Times*, October 6, 1945; see Mountbatten's "Foreword" to Colin Sleeman, (ed.), *Trial of Gozawa Sadaichi and Nine Others* (London, 1948), pp. xiii–xiv.

39. Blamey Papers, Department of External Affairs, cablegram, December 14, 1945, CRS A1066, Item H45/580/6/2.

40. Sleeman, *Trial of Gozawa*, p. 4; *Straits Times*, January 22, 1946.

41. Such was the opinion of the defense counsel at the trial, Colonel Sleeman, in Sleeman, *Trial of Gozawa*, p. xlii. Compare Green's assertion that the trial was intended to cast dishonor on so-called "Indian patriots," currently on trial in Delhi, by demonstrating their "collaboration" with Japanese, in Green, "Minor War Criminals," pp. 249–250.

42. Sleeman, *Trial of Gozawa*, p. 3.

43. Public interest was active in Southeast Asia, not in England. The "opening of British Far Eastern War Crimes Trials was totally ignored by the British Press," ibid., p. xlii. See *Straits Times*, January 22–February 2, 1946.

44. Sleeman, *Trial of Gozawa*, p. 5.

45. Ibid., p. 86.

46. Ibid., p. 3.

47. Ibid., pp. 57, 73, 81–84, 87–88, 132, 148, 184, 218, 221–222, 226.

48. For example, ibid., pp. 46, 57, 62, 73, 118–119.

49. For example, ibid., pp. 50, 57, 73, 81–84, 85, 185.

50. For example, ibid., pp. 145, 154, 182, 190.

51. Ibid., p. 145.

52. Ibid., pp. 198, lxiv.

53. Ibid., pp. 81–85.

54. *Straits Times*, February 2, 1946.

55. Sleeman, *Trial of Gozawa*, pp. 230–231; *Law Reports*, v. 15, pp. 158–159, 175.

56. See note 43. Ironically, the trial was covered in the American press—see *New York Times*, February 2, 1946.

57. See, for example, Green, who, while conceding the existence of criticism, deemed the trial report clear proof "that the accused received a fair trial," in "Minor War Criminals," p. 252; for a positive evaluation of early British trials, see *London Times*, July 31, 1946; Sleeman, *Trial of Gozawa*, p. 205. A former court president at the early trials

believes today that his court "was fair," in letter from S. C. Silkin to author, March 23, 1977.

58.   *Straits Times*, January 20, February 3, April 27, July 17, 1946; *Stars and Stripes* (Shanghai), March 9, 1946; *China* (Shanghai) *Press*, January 1, 1946.

59.   *Law Reports*, v. 3, case no. 20, pp. 76, 79–80.

60.   *Straits Times*, March 12, 1946.

61.   *Straits Times*, February 20, 22, 1946.

62.   *Straits Times*, April 27, July 2, August 31, September 25, 29, 1946.

63.   *Straits Times*, February 19, 1946; *China Press*, April 12, 1946.

64.   *London Times*, March 29, 1946.

65.   Colin Sleeman and S. C. Silkin, (eds.), *Trial of Sumida Haruzo and Twenty Others (The "Double Tenth" Trial)* (London, 1951), pp. xxxi, 258; *Straits Times*, April 16, 1946.

66.   *Straits Times*, August 10, 16, 20, September 1, October 6, 10, 11, 1946.

67.   *Straits Times*, August 20, 1946.

68.   *Straits Times*, August 22, 1946.

69.   *Straits Times*, February 9, 1946.

70.   *Straits Times*, February 6, 1946; *Malay Mail*, November 5, 1947; *China Press*, August 12, 1947.

71.   *Malay Mail*, October 9, 1947; *Straits Times*, February 8, 1946.

72.   *Malay Mail*, June 25, 1947.

73.   *Straits Times*, April 4, 1946.

74.   The appointment of Allied members to British military courts was not compulsory, even in cases where Allied nationals had been the victims. See Royal Warrant, regulation 5; *Law Reports*, v. 2, pp. 127–128.

75.   *Straits Times*, May 30, October 17, 1946; *Malay Mail*, October 14, 1947.

76.   *Straits Times*, February 8, 1946. For reliance on Yamashita precedent, see *Malay Mail*, June 10, 1947; and *China Press*, October 26, 1948.

77.   *London Times*, June 7, 1946.

78.   For coverage of the trial, see *passim*, *Straits Times*, October 22, 29, 31, November 1, 8, 19, 20, December 3, 4, 1946.

79.   For coverage of the trial, see *passim*, *Straits Times*, August 23, 28–31, September 3–5, 11, 12, 1946.

80.   *Straits Times*, July 3, 1946.

81.   *Malay Mail*, May 6, 1947.

82.   *Malay Mail*, May 1, 1947.

83.   *Straits Times*, February 27, 1946.

84.   See, for example, *China Press*, March 18, 1947; *Straits Times*, February 20, 1946; March 18, 1947.

85.   *Straits Times*, May 3, March 1, 8, August 1, 1946.

86.   *Straits Times*, October 5, 1946; *London Times*, April 3, 1947.

87.   *Straits Times*, February 2, October 18, 1946.

88. See *Law Reports*, v. 15, pp. 156–157; also *Straits Times*, February 22, April 4, June 13, August 28, October 5, 18, November 19, 1946; *Malay Mail*, October 14, 1947.

89. R. John Pritchard, "The Nature and Significance of British Post-War Trials of Japanese War Criminals, 1946–1948," Paper read at Conference of the British Association for Japanese Studies, 1977, pp. 14–15; letter from S. C. Silkin to author, March 23, 1977.

90. *Straits Times*, June 7, 1946; also, Sleeman, *Trial of Gozawa*, p. 205.

91. Sleeman, *Trial of Gozawa*, p. lxviii; *Straits Times*, June 7, 1946.

92. *Straits Times*, May 15, July 24, August 1, 1946.

93. See, for example, letter from ex-POW to editor, *London Times*, January 1, 1947.

94. See editorial, *Straits Times*, January 13, 1946; also letters to editor, September 7, 9, 1946.

95. See reports of debate in *London Times*, June 30, July 12, 27, 1948.

96. As reported in *China Press*, December 29, 1946.

97. *New York Times*, April 2, 1948.

98. *London Times*, December 16, 1946; *Straits Times*, December 20, 1946.

99. *London Times*, May 20, 1949. See also Lord Hankey, *Politics, Trials and Errors* (Chicago, 1950).

100. *Straits Times*, September 13, 1946.

101. For letters see *Straits Times*, September 14, 16, 17, 19, 1946.

102. See letters to editor, *London Times*, January 1, 9, 1947.

103. *London Times*, January 10, 1947.

104. *Straits Times*, September 7, 1946.

105. *Straits Times*, March 12, 1946; *China Press*, October 18, 1946.

106. See editorial, *Straits Times*, February 6, 1947.

107. Far Eastern Commission, "Third Report by the Secretary General, Dec. 24, 1948–June 30, 1950" (Washington, D.C., 1950), pp. 4–5; also, *New York Times*, March 16, 1949; *London Times*, June 16, 1948.

108. See, for example, M. A. Fitzsimons, *The Foreign Policy of the British Labour Government: 1945–1951* (Notre Dame, Indiana, 1953), p. 28; W. N. Medlicott, *British Foreign Policy since Versailles, 1919–1963* (London, 1968), p. 270. The state of Anglo-Soviet relations was "causing much heart-searching concern in London," *Straits Times*, October 25, 1945.

109. See above, note 43; for example, between July and September 1946 the *London Times* contained but one brief reference to the IMTFE; for dying interest in Southeast Asian trials, see editorial, *Straits Times*, February 6, 1947; see statement by Secretary of State for War Bellenger, *London Times*, January 30, 1947.

110. See *London Times*, January 15, 1947; July 12, 27, 1948; *New York Times*, April 2, 1948.

111. On Britain's postwar economic and commercial interest in Japan, see A. S. B. Olver, *Outline of British Policy in East and Southeast Asia,*

1945–May 1950 (London, 1950), pp. 1–2, 8, 11, 15; *Malay Mail,* May 27, June 27, October 11, 1949.

112. As reported in Pritchard, "British Post-War Trials," tables A, B and D; also, p. 19. Compare these figures with those given by a reputable Japanese source, Epilogue, note 10. Greater validity is attributed to Pritchard's figures for several reasons. First, they provide a case-by-case breakdown of trial results in all British theaters. Second, they are more recent. Third, Pritchard states that he has taken into account the factor of duplication, that is, that a substantial number of Japanese stood charged before more than one military court.

7. Australia and Other Commonwealth Trials (Canada, New Zealand)

1. Lord Robert A. Wright, *The History of the United Nations War Crimes Commission and the Development of the Laws of War* (London, 1948), pp. 120, 127, 144.

2. See reports in *Straits Times* (Singapore), September 22, 1945, and *New York Herald Tribune,* October 29, 1945.

3. For Webb Commission, see Australia, *Parliamentary Debates,* Senate and House of Representatives, Sydney, October 4, 1945, p. 6,510; April 10, 1946, pp. 1,294–1,297.

4. Australia, *Parliamentary Debates,* 1945; see, for example, September 18, 20, 21, 25, 27–28, October 4, 5, 1945, v. 185, pp. 5,485, 5,681, 5,765, 5,778–5,779, 5,811, 6,109, 6,642–6,643.

5. See speech, September 10, 1945, in Herbert V. Evatt, *Australia in World Affairs* (Sydney, 1946), p. 66; also, Australia, Department of External Affairs, *Current Notes on International Affairs,* Sydney, v. 16, 1945, pp. 219–220; Australia, *Parliamentary Debates,* v. 185, September 18, 20, 26, 1945, pp. 5,485, 5,681, 5,929; Papers of General Thomas Blamey, statement made by the Acting Minister for External Affairs (Mr. Makin) to the press, September 21, 1945, Department of External Affairs, "Japanese War Criminals," CRS A1066, Item H45/578, Australian War Memorial.

6. Herbert V. Evatt, "Has the Menace of Japan Been Removed?" *New York Times Magazine,* February 3, 1946; Australia, Department of External Affairs, *Current Notes,* v. 17, no. 3, March 1946, p. 134; Evatt, *Australia in World Affairs,* p. 66; Australia, *Parliamentary Debates,* v. 185, September 18, 20, 26, 1945, pp. 5,485, 5,681, 5,929.

7. See above, note 4.

8. N. D. Harper, *Australia and the Peace Settlement with Japan* (Sydney, 1950), p. 22; Australia, *Parliamentary Debates,* v. 192, June 5, 6, 1947, p. 3,687.

9. See, for example, Australia, *Parliamentary Debates,* v. 189, November 14, 1946, p. 269; v. 196, April 8, 1948, p. 747; *Sydney Morning Herald,* October 1, 1948. Australia was "less concerned" with Russia,

feeling that the U.S. would protect it—see Frederick S. Dunn, *Peacemaking and the Settlement with Japan* (Princeton, N.J., 1963), p. 128; as late as June 24, 1949, Australians feared a renewed war with Japan, in *Malay Mail*, June 24, 1949.

10. Australia, Department of External Affairs, *Current Notes*, v. 17, no. 3, March 1946, p. 134.

11. Ibid., p. 136; Australia, *Parliamentary Debates*, v. 189, November 14, 1946, p. 269.

12. Evatt, "Menace of Japan," p. 86; also, Australia, Department of External Affairs, *Current Notes*, v. 17, no. 3, March 1946, pp. 134, 136; Trevor R. Reese, *Australia, New Zealand and the United States: A Survey of International Relations, 1941–1968* (London, 1969), pp. 84–86; Dunn, *Peacemaking*, p. 109. Canberra worried that American proposals to lift economic restrictions from Japan would result in "the restoration of industries which might enable" re-armament, in Australia, *Parliamentary Debates*, v. 196, April 8, 1948, p. 747, and *Sydney Morning Herald*, October 1, 1948.

13. Blamey Papers, letter from Webb to Dr. J. D. L. Hood, Acting Secretary, Department of External Affairs, June 26, 1945, and from Hood to Webb, June 8, 1945, CRS A1066, Item H45/580/6/2.

14. Australia, *Parliamentary Debates*, v. 193, November 13, 1946, p. 162.

15. *New York Herald Tribune*, April 22, 1946. Indeed, Australia's and New Zealand's "casual approach" to their respective postwar Pacific defense contributions "was obviously founded on the assumption that the United States would maintain large forces in the Central Pacific and that in the event of war American protection, or at least assistance, could be counted upon." See Reese, *Australia, New Zealand and the United States*, pp. 66–67, 108–109.

16. See, for example, the assertion in *New York Times*, September 17, 1945, that Allied policy in the Far East "means American policy in the Far East"; Australia, *Parliamentary Debates*, v. 204, October 5, 1949, p. 947.

17. *New York Herald Tribune*, January 17, 1946; see also, for example, Evatt, *Australia in World Affairs*, p. 141; U.S. Department of State, *Foreign Relations of the United States, 1946* (Washington, D.C., 1971), pp. 384, 386–387.

18. See, for example, U.S. Department of State, *Foreign Relations of the United States, 1946*, pp. 395–397; *New York Times*, January 18, 1946; "Joseph Keenan Meets the Press," *American Mercury*, v. 70, 1950, pp. 456–458. Also, see chapter 2.

19. Sir William Webb, International Military Tribunal for the Far East, "Separate Opinion of the President, November 1, 1948," p. 19.

20. Australia, War Crimes Act 1945, Canberra, 1945. See discussion of War Crimes Act in Australia, *Parliamentary Debates*, October 4,

1945, pp. 6,510–6,512. Also, see *Law Reports of the Trials of War Criminals*, 15 vols. Selected and prepared by the UNWCC (London, 1947–1949), v. 6, annex, pp. 94ff. Indeed, Australia "modelled" its War Crimes Act after the Royal Warrant, in Blamey Papers, "Australian Trials of Japanese War Criminals," November 10, 1945, CRS A1066 File No. H45/590/1, submission to the Acting Minister for External Affairs, unsigned. For the Royal Warrant, see chapter 6.

21.   No. 1 read: "Planning, preparation, initiation or waging of a war of aggression, or a war in violation of international treaties, agreements or assurances, or participation in a common plan or conspiracy for the accomplishment of any of the foregoing."—*Law Reports*, v. 6, annex, p. 95.

22.   Ibid., pp. 95–97.

23.   War Crimes Act, section 12; *Law Reports*, v. 6, annex, p. 98.

24.   War Crimes Act, sections 5, 6; also, Australia, *Parliamentary Debates*, October 4, 1945, pp. 6,510–6,511.

25.   *Law Reports*, v. 6, annex, pp. 98–99.

26.   Ibid., p. 99; on the judge advocate, see ibid., v. 15, p. 165.

27.   War Crimes Act, sections 9(1), 10.

28.   Ibid., sections 11(1), (3); *Law Reports*, v. 6, pp. 100–101.

29.   *Law Reports*, v. 6, p. 101.

30.   See, for example, Australian cases at Rabaul, in *Law Reports*, v. 15, "Supplemental Cases," p. 8; also *Straits Times*, October 2, 1946.

31.   *Law Reports*, v. 5, p. 27; v. 15, pp. 20–21.

32.   Wright, *History of UNWCC*, pp. 386–387; Blamey Papers, Secretary, Department of the Army Melbourne to Secretary, Department of External Affairs, December 6, 1945; CRS A1066 File No. A45/590/1.

33.   Wright, *History of UNWCC*, p. 387.

34.   Ibid., pp. 387–388. For cooperation with Dutch authorities, see Australia, Department of External Affairs, *Current Notes*, v. 17, no. 1, January 1946, p. 4.

35.   Wright, *History of UNWCC*, p. 388. See, for example, *London Times*, January 4, 8, 18, 1946; March 22, April 9, May 17, 1947.

36.   Wright, *History of UNWCC*, p. 389.

37.   Ibid., pp. 387–390; *Law Reports*, v. 11, pp. 60, 62; Australia, *Parliamentary Debates*, v. 186, April 10, 1946, pp. 1,295–1,296; Blamey Papers, memo from J. Oldham, "Interrogation in Regard to War Crimes," June 18, 1945, CRS A1066 File No. H45/580/2.

38.   As reported in *Daily Telegraph* (London), October 16, 1945.

39.   *New York Times*, November 5, 1945.

40.   For trial coverage, see ibid.; also, *New York Herald Tribune*, December 2, 1945; *Stars and Stripes* (Shanghai), December 4, 1945.

41.   Wright, *History of UNWCC*, pp. 389–390.

42.   *New York Times*, December 6, 1945; *China* (Shanghai) *Press*, December 15, 1945.

43. *London Times,* December 12, 1945.

44. *London Times,* January 4, 1946. For other mass trials, see *London Times,* December 15, 1945; *Stars and Stripes* (Shanghai), January 23, 1946; *Straits Times,* September 17, 1946.

45. Wright, *History of UNWCC,* p. 389; "War Crimes Trials," *Australian Encyclopaedia* (Sydney, 1958), p. 150.

46. *Law Reports,* v. 5, p. 76, note 4.

47. See, for example, ibid., cases nos. 27, pp. 32–36, and 28, pp. 37–38.

48. Ibid., case no. 26, p. 25.

49. Ibid., pp. 26, 30–31.

50. Ibid., v. 11, case no. 60, p. 56.

51. Ibid.

52. Ibid., pp. 56–57.

53. Ibid., p. 58.

54. Ibid., pp. 58–59.

55. Ibid., p. 59.

56. Ibid., pp. 59–60; *London Times,* April 9, 15, 24, May 17, 1947; *New York Times,* April 15, 1945.

57. *London Times,* December 15, 1945; George Dickinson, "Manus Island Trials," *Royal Australian Historical Society,* v. 38, 1952, p. 67.

58. See, for example, *Stars and Stripes* (Shanghai), January 23, 1946; *London Times,* January 15, 1946; May 17, 1947.

59. *London Times,* October 2, 1946; *Straits Times,* October 2, 1946.

60. The president of the court had based his judgment on an amendment in the *Manual of Military Law* (Australian edition) which held that such a defense applies only when a superior order is not "obviously unlawful." See *Straits Times,* October 2, 1946; also, see George Dickinson, "Japanese War Trials," *Australian Quarterly,* v. 24, 1952, p. 72.

61. See, for example, Dickinson, "Japanese War Trials," p. 75.

62. *Straits Times,* January 12, 1946.

63. *Straits Times,* June 28, July 2, 1946.

64. *Straits Times,* July 2, 1946.

65. *China Press,* November 16, 1947.

66. See, for example, *Sydney Morning Herald,* January 15, 26, 1948; *New York Times,* March 17, 1948.

67. See, Australia, *Parliamentary Debates,* v. 207, February 24, 1950, p. 100. Australia had tried 259 cases, involving 769 Japanese, as of March 1, 1948, in Wright, *History of UNWCC,* appendix 4, p. 518.

68. Australia, *Parliamentary Debates,* v. 207, March 16, 1950, pp. 882–883.

69. U.S. Department of State, *Foreign Relations of the United States, 1948,* p. 822; *New York Herald Tribune,* November 14, 1948; *New York Times,* December 24, 1948.

70. *London Times,* June 16, 1948; Far Eastern Commission, "Third Re-

port by the Secretary General, Dec. 24, 1948–June 30, 1950" (Washington, D.C., 1950), pp. 4–5.

71. See, for example, Australia, Department of External Affairs, *Current Notes*, v. 19, no. 5, May 1948, p. 267; *Sydney Morning Herald*, May 7, and editorial, June 16, 1948.

72. Australia, *Parliamentary Debates*, v. 207, March 16, 1950, pp. 882–899 *passim*; *London Times*, February 25, 1950.

73. Australia, *Parliamentary Debates*, v. 207, February 24, 1950, pp. 100–101; March 16, 1950, pp. 882–883, 888, 890, 893. There were also those who agreed with American policy: "As an alley of the U.S.A. in the occupation of Japan," said one, "surely we should coordinate our policy with theirs," ibid., v. 204, October 2, 1949, p. 947.

74. Ibid., v. 207, March 16, 1950, pp. 884–885, 894–895; *London Times*, December 5, 1949.

75. *London Times*, February 25, 1950; Australia, *Parliamentary Debates*, v. 207, February 24, 1950, p. 101.

76. Australia, Department of External Affairs, *Current Notes*, v. 21, no. 3, March 1950, p. 229; Dickinson, "Manus Island Trials," pp. 67 ff.

77. See, for example, Australia, Department of External Affairs, *Current Notes*, v. 17, no. 3, March 1946, pp. 134, 136; and v. 18, no. 6, June 16, 1947, p. 396.

78. See, for example, editorials in *Sydney Morning Herald*, April 30, July 30, 1948.

79. Shigeru Yoshida, *The Yoshida Memoirs*, translated by Kenichi Yoshida (Boston, 1962), p. 251. Another indication that Americans felt this way may be found in the scant—virtually negligible—coverage afforded the Manus Island trials by the U.S. press. See *New York Times* and *New York Herald Tribune*, June 1950–May 1951.

80. On Soviet intransigence, see above, chapter 8.

81. Dunn, *Peacemaking*, pp. 174, 178–181.

82. See, for example, Australia, *Parliamentary Debates*, v. 189, December 4, 1946, p. 971; v. 198, October 5, 1948, p. 1,113.

83. Ibid., v. 186, March 20, 1946, p. 415; v. 207, March 16, 1950, pp. 882–888. See also, Harold Wakefield, *New Paths for Japan* (New York, 1948), pp. 173–174.

84. In this regard, note the frequent government reports on the status of the trials: for example, Australia, Department of External Affairs, *Current Notes*, v. 16, 1945, pp. 219–220; v. 17, 1947, p. 124; v. 19, no. 5, 1948, p. 267; Australia, *Parliamentary Debates*, v. 186, March 20, 1946, p. 415; v. 189, December 5, 6, 1946, p. 1,173; v. 207, February 24, 1950, pp. 100–101; v. 208, June 6, 1950, pp. 3,711–3,712, June 7, p. 3,839.

85. Australia, *Parliamentary Debates*, v. 207, February 24, 1950, p. 100; also, March 16, 1950, pp. 889–890.

86. Ibid., v. 208, June 6, 7, 1950, pp. 3,711–3,712, 3,839.

87. Wakefield, *New Paths for Japan*, p. 173.

88. *New York Times*, December 6, 1945.

89. Dickinson, "Japanese War Trials," pp. 69–71.

90. George E. Erickson, Jr., "United States Navy War Crimes Trials (1945–1949)," *Washburn Law Journal*, v. 5, 1965, p. 99, note 40; Dickinson, "Japanese War Trials," p. 71.

91. "War Crimes Trials," *Australian Encyclopaedia*, table 2, p. 156. Compare these figures with those provided by a reputable Japanese source, Epilogue, note 10.

92. These regulations re-enacted the war crimes regulations (Canada) which were made by Order in Council on August 30, 1945. See *Law Reports*, v. 4, annex, p. 125.

93. Ibid.

94. Ibid., pp. 125, 126.

95. Ibid., pp. 126–127.

96. Ibid., p. 130.

97. Alexander Brady and F. R. Scott (eds.), *Canada after the War* (Toronto, 1944), p. 146.

98. Canada, "Report of the Department of National Defence for the Fiscal Year Ending Mar. 31, 1946" (Ottawa, 1946), p. 65; Canada, "Report of the Department of External Affairs, Canada 1948" (Ottawa, 1949), p. 55.

99. See Ian Brownlie, *International Law and the Use of Force by States* (Oxford, 1963), p. 175.

100. U.S. Department of State, *Foreign Relations of the United States, 1946*, pp. 394–395. The U.S. approved the Canadian proposals in February, ibid., p. 416.

101. Ibid., pp. 394–395; Canada, *Parliamentary Debates*, House of Commons, 1946 (Ottawa, 1946), v. 1, April 12, 1946, p. 809.

102. Canada, *Parliamentary Debates*, v. 1, April 12, 1946, p. 809; also, see *China Press*, April 25, 1946.

103. Canada, *Parliamentary Debates*, v. 1, April 12, 1946, pp. 809–810.

104. D. H. Gardner, *Canadian Interests and Policies in the Far East since World War II* (Toronto, 1950), p. 5; *Stars and Stripes* (Tokyo), May 25, 1947.

105. New Zealand, War History Branch, Department of Internal Affairs, *Prisoners of War. Official History of New Zealand in the Second World War 1939–1945* (Wellington, 1954), pp. x, 188–189, 522; Samuel Leatham, *New Zealand's Interests and Policies in the Far East* (Wellington, 1950), pp. 7, 11–12.

106. New Zealand, Department of External Affairs, "Annual Report of the Department of External Affairs, Year Ended March 31, 1949" (Wellington, 1949), p. 19; *Dominion* (Wellington), January 18, 1946.

107. Letter, April 12, 1976, from New Zealand, National Archives, Department of Internal Affairs, to author.

108. New Zealand, *Parliamentary Debates*, Legislative Council and House of Representatives (Wellington, 1948), v. 278, September 26, 1947, pp. 649–650.

109. The IMTFE, said one critic, in process over two years, "had become a complete farce," ibid., p. 649.

110. Leatham, "New Zealand's Interests," pp. 3–7, 11–12, 21.

111. New Zealanders, like Australians, often heatedly disputed certain aspects of U.S. Pacific policy—its plans to revive the Japanese economy, for one. But, in general, they found a sense of security in the American presence in the Far East. See Dunn, *Peacemaking*, pp. 81–82, 109–110, 115, 128, 150–151, 156.

8. Russia

1. See Robert J. C. Butow, *Japan's Decision to Surrender* (Stanford, 1954), pp. 154–159.

2. *Punishment for War Crimes*: The Inter-Allied Declaration Signed at St. James' Palace, London, on 13 January 1942, and Relative Documents (London, 1942), p. 15.

3. M. E. Bathurst, "The United Nations War Crimes Commission," *American Journal of International Law*, v. 39, 1945, pp. 567–568.

4. For the Moscow Declaration, see Lord Robert A. Wright, *The History of the United Nations War Crimes Commission and the Development of the Laws of War* (London, 1948), pp. 107–108.

5. See "War Crimes: Work of the United Nations Commission," by a legal correspondent in *London Times*, December 18, 1946; Bathurst, "UNWCC," pp. 567–568.

6. Wright, *History of UNWCC*, p. 158.

7. *London Times*, December 18, 1946; Wright, *History of UNWCC*, p. 159.

8. United Nations Information Organization, *Information Paper No. 1*, 1946, p. 10.

9. Bathurst, "UNWCC," p. 570.

10. Potsdam Declaration, July 26, 1945. For the USSR's part in the preceding, see Adam B. Ulam, *Expansion and Coexistence: Soviet Foreign Policy, 1917–1973*, 2nd ed. (New York, 1974), pp. 378–388, 390–394.

11. Far Eastern Commission, "Activities: Report by the Secretary General, February 26, 1946–July 10, 1947" (Washington, D.C., 1947), p. 2.

12. See *New York Times*, September 17, 30, 1945; Edwin O. Reischauer, *Japan: The Story of a Nation* (New York, 1970), pp. 221–222; Akira Iriye, *The Cold War in Asia* (Englewood Cliffs, N.J., 1974), p. 126.

13. U.S. Department of State, *Foreign Relations of the United States, 1946* (Washington, D.C., 1971), January 8, p. 386.

14. This "official silence" in the USSR regarding the Far East was "rapidly approaching the point where it will resemble a loud noise," *New York Herald Tribune*, November 16, 1945.

15. U.S. Department of State, *Foreign Relations of the United States, 1946*, January 13, pp. 388–389.

16. Ibid., January 26, 1946, pp. 397–399.

17. Ibid., January 13, 30, 1946, pp. 388–389, 399.

18. See Harry S. Truman, *Year of Decisions* (New York, 1955), pp. 440–444; also Ulam, *Expansion and Coexistence*, pp. 396–397.

19. Ulam, *Expansion and Coexistence*, pp. 397–398; also, Frederick S. Dunn, *Peacemaking and the Settlement with Japan* (Princeton, N.J., 1963), pp. xi–xii.

20. As reported in the *Straits Times* (Singapore), and *Stars and Stripes* (Shanghai), October 27, 1945.

21. M. Markov, "The Approaching Trial of the Major Japanese War Criminals," *New Times*, no. 8, April 15, 1946, pp. 7–10. Emphasis added.

22. Also, said the diplomat, "The Soviet Union has never had a free or independent-minded press. When something is published in *Pravda* or *Izvestia* or a provincial newspaper or even a scientific weekly, everybody assumes that it is the official pronouncement of the Party or government." See Tad Szulc, *Czechoslovakia since World War II* (New York, 1971), p. 348.

23. S. Golunsky, "Trial of the Japanese War Criminals," *New Times*, no. 18, May 1, 1947, p. 6; also, A. Trainin, "From Nuremberg to Tokyo," *New Times*, no. 12, March 17, 1948, pp. 11–13; V. Berezhkov, "The Tokyo Trial," *New Times*, no. 5, January 28, 1948, p. 6.

24. Trainin, "From Nuremberg to Tokyo," p. 14.

25. See, for example, ibid., p. 12; Golunsky, "Japanese War Criminals," pp. 6–7.

26. M. Raginsky and S. Rozenblit, "What People Expect of the International Military Tribunal in Tokyo" (from *Pravda*), *Soviet Press Translations*, 3, no. 14, July 15, 1948, p. 421.

27. Golunsky, "Japanese War Criminals," p. 7; Raginsky and Rozenblit, "What People Expect of IMT," pp. 421–424.

28. Berezhkov, "Tokyo Trial," p. 9.

29. M. Markov, "Falsification of History at the Tokyo Trial," *New Times*, no. 17, April 21, 1948, p. 10.

30. See, for example, M. Marinin, "Remilitarization of Japan," *Current Digest of the Soviet Press* (*CDSP*), 2, no. 48, January 13, 1951, p. 26; Max Beloff, *Soviet Policy in the Far East, 1944–1951* (London, 1953), pp. 122–125.

31. Solis Horwitz, "The Tokyo Trial," *International Conciliation*, 1950, p. 496. Cited in Richard H. Minear, *Victors' Justice: The Tokyo War Crimes Trial* (Princeton, N.J., 1971), pp. 107–109, note 70.

32. Shigemitsu's indictment and conviction caused substantial disconcertion in Allied circles, where many believed him to be an able and honest diplomat, and a man of peace. See, for example, Joseph C. Grew's affidavit, which defense counsel tried, unsuccessfully, to submit as evidence at the IMTFE, *Stars and Stripes* (Tokyo), November

13, 1946; protest by four members of Britain's House of Lords, *Stars and Stripes*, May 21, 1949; *Washington Post* editorial, December 23, 1948; Lord Hankey, *Politics, Trials and Errors* (Chicago, 1950), pp. 82–84, 91–94, 98–102. "The prosecution," Keenan said after the trial, "is ashamed at the sentence given Shigemitsu," *London Times*, November 22, 1948.

33. See above, chapter 2. Also, wrote Donihi: "Minear's source [Kojima] is totally wrong," and "I'm sure he wouldn't have a means of learning of any consent by Keenan and MacArthur 'under threat of a Soviet walkout,'" letter to author, May 31, 1977; U.S. Department of State, *Foreign Relations of the United States, 1946*, January 2, 8, pp. 382, 386.

34. *New York Herald Tribune*, April 22, 1946.

35. Brendan F. Brown, "Red China, the Tokyo Trial, and Aggressive War," *Louisiana Bar Journal*, v. 3, 1956, pp. 152–153; Joseph B. Keenan and Brendan F. Brown, *Crimes against International Law* (Washington, D.C., 1950), p. vii.

36. Most likely, the Soviets held additional Japanese war crimes trials. During the IMTFE the Russian prosecutor on several occasions alluded to such trials, as when he refused to produce witnesses—currently "under investigation by the Russians on war crimes charges"—for the Tokyo Tribunal—see *Stars and Stripes* (Tokyo), November 7, 11, 1947. Also, the U.S. Navy director of war crimes, citing in December 1949 the absence of figures for Soviet-conducted Eastern war crimes trials, added that they nonetheless "are believed to have been extensive in number"—see U.S. Department of the Navy, *Final Report of Navy War Crimes Program in the Pacific*, submitted by the Director of War Crimes, U.S. Pacific Fleet to the Secretary of the Navy, 1 December 1949, v. 1, p. 27. Despite these factors, the adverse international reaction to the Khabarovsk trial, its decidedly political nature and Moscow's subsequent classification of some 300,000 Japanese POWs as "war criminals" and consequent refusal to repatriate them render any further publicizing of Russian-conducted Japanese trials highly improbable.

37. Dean Acheson, *Present at the Creation* (New York, 1969), p. 429; also, see Dunn, *Peacemaking*, p. 91.

38. *Malay Mail*, May 9, 1949.

39. See, for example, *Malay Mail*, May 9, 23, June 21, August 15, November 22, 1949; also, Russell Brines, *MacArthur's Japan* (Philadelphia, 1948), p. 260.

40. See, for example, *China Press*, December 2, 1947; articles by Lindsay Parrott in *New York Times*, June 28, 29, December 4, 1949; June 15, 1951: also, see *New York Times*, June 28, 1949.

41. On Soviet motives at this time, see *London Times*, February 3, 1950; *New York Times*, June 29, 1949; *Malay Mail*, December 31, 1949; Peter Calvocoressi, *Survey of International Affairs, 1949–1950* (Lon-

don, 1953), pp. 454–455; Far Eastern Commission, "Third Report by the Secretary General. Dec. 24, 1948–June 30, 1950" (Washington, D.C., 1950), pp. 4–5.

42. USSR, *Materials on the Trial of Former Servicemen of the Japanese Army Charged with Manufacturing and Employing Bacteriological Weapons* (Moscow, 1950), indictment, p. 7.

43. Ibid., p. 5. See, for example, brief notation that there was to be such a trial, in *New York Times*, December 24, 1949.

44. USSR, *Materials*, pp. 5–6.

45. Ibid., p. 244.

46. Ibid., pp. 38, 239.

47. Ibid., pp. 243–244.

48. Ibid., pp. 7–9.

49. Ibid., pp. 9–12.

50. Ibid., pp. 15–22; also, pp. 426, 437.

51. Ibid., pp. 396–404.

52. Ibid., p. 469.

53. Ibid., pp. 475–476.

54. Ibid., p. 471.

55. Ibid., pp. 477–478.

56. Ibid., pp. 220, 311, 406–408, 443. Compare Keenan's assertion that, as regarded evidence bearing on bacteriological warfare, "none whatever" was introduced at the IMTFE. He labeled as "false" any Soviet claims that he had offered or been offered any such evidence. See "Joseph Keenan Meets the Press," *American Mercury*, v. 70, 1950, pp. 457–458. Also, the *Tokyo Shimbun* called Soviet allegations a "ruse by Moscow," as reported in *Malay Mail*, December 31, 1949.

57. USSR, *Materials*, pp. 409–410, 466.

58. Ibid., pp. 276, 405, 411–412, 415, 447, 466. It is interesting to note that historians have generally regarded the Kwantung Army at the time of the Soviet invasion as "nothing more than an empty shell"— see Butow, *Japan's Decision to Surrender*, p. 154.

59. See, for example, USSR, *Materials*, pp. 242, 244, 247, 359, 390–393.

60. Ibid., pp. 245–247.

61. Ibid., see, for example, pp. 263ff.

62. Ibid., see, for example, pp. 272, 284, 292, 307, 321, 325, 334, 345.

63. Ibid., pp. 515–522.

64. In this matter, see the "Findings" of the Soviet medical experts, ibid., pp. 396–404. For verdict and sentences, see ibid., pp. 525–530, 534–535.

65. USSR, *Information Bulletin*, published by the Embassy of the Union of Soviet Socialist Republics in the U.S.A., vol. 6, no. 60, September 11, 1946, p. 23.

66. M. Raginsky, "Monstrous Atrocities of the Japanese Imperialists," *New Times*, no. 2, January 8, 1950, pp. 3–7.

67. V. Mayevsky, "Monstrous Crimes Committed by Japanese Barbarians," *USSR Information Bulletin*, 10, no. 3, February 10, 1950, pp. 21–27; and "American Occupation Authorities Protect Japanese War Criminals," *CDSP*, v. 3, no. 23, July 21, 1951, p. 14.

68. "Advocate of Plague," *CDSP*, v. 2, no. 9, April 15, 1950, pp. 28–29.

69. "Bring the War Criminals to Justice!" *New Times*, no. 6, February 8, 1950, pp. 3–5; "Ill-Starred Defenders of War Criminals," *CDSP*, v. 2, no. 11, April 29, 1950, pp. 22–23.

70. M. Markov, "America's 'New Policy' in the Far East," *New Times*, no. 12, April 3, 1950, pp. 6–9; Marinin, "Remilitarization of Japan," *CDSP*, v. 2, no. 48, January 13, 1951, p. 26.

71. See, for example, articles in *Soviet Press Translations*: "Chinese Public Demands Punishment of Japanese War Criminals," v. 5, no. 8, April 3, 15, 1950; "The Chinese People Protest the Illegal Acts of the American Authorities in Japan," v. 5, no. 13, July 1, 1950; "Declaration of Chou En-lai," v. 5, no. 22, December 15, 1950; *London Times*, May 18, 1950; *New York Times*, February 9, November 28, 1950.

72. Frederick H. Maugham, *U.N.O. and War Crimes* (London, 1951), p. 28; Lord Hankey, *Politics, Trials and Errors*, p. 9.

73. A. N. Vasilyev, "On the Results of the Tokio War Crimes Trials," *CDSP*, v. 1, no. 25, July 19, 1949, pp. 11–15. See, for example, Trainin, "From Nuremberg to Tokyo," pp. 12–14.

74. USSR, *Materials*, p. 447.

75. Bernard V. A. Röling, "The Law of War and the National Jurisdiction since 1945," Recueil des Cours, *Académie de Droit International*, v. 100 (Leyde, the Netherlands, 1961), p. 431, note 6.

76. Calvocoressi, *Survey of International Affairs*, pp. 454–455.

77. As reported in *Malay Mail*, December 31, 1949.

78. Quoted in David Rees, *Korea: The Limited War* (New York, 1964), pp. 338, 352–354, 361–362.

79. As reported in John C. Clews, *Communist Propaganda Techniques* (London, 1964), p. 265; *New York Times*, August 19, 1961.

80. See front page story, "Japan Accused of World War II Germ Deaths," in *Washington Post*, November 19, 1976.

81. See *Malay Mail*, May 9, 23, June 21, August 15, 1949; *New York Times*, June 15, October 17, 1951; Brines, *MacArthur's Japan*, p. 260; Australia, Department of External Affairs, *Current Notes on International Affairs*, Sydney, v. 23, no. 1, January 1952, p. 48; *London Times*, July 30, 1952.

82. *New York Times*, October 17, 1951.

83. *New York Times*, October 22, 1951.

84. Reischauer, *Japan: The Story of a Nation*, p. 277.

85. Armin H. Meyer, *Assignment: Tokyo* (Indianapolis, 1974), pp. 145–146.

86. *New York Times*, January 11, 1976.

9. China

1. Lord Robert A. Wright, *The History of the United Nations War Crimes Commission and the Development of the Laws of War* (London, 1948), p. 380; F. F. Liu, *A Military History of Modern China, 1924–1949* (Princeton, N.J., 1956), pp. 226–227. The Chinese government was trying "to negotiate a surrender" with 100,000 Japanese troops in Manchuria as of November 27, 1946—see *China* (Shanghai) *Press*.

2. Walter L. Riley, "The International Military Tribunal for the Far East and the Law of the Tribunal as Revealed by the Judgment and the Concurring and Dissenting Opinions," Ph.D. dissertation, University of Washington, 1957, pp. 11–12.

3. The Sub-Committee's creation followed the UNWCC's "adoption" of a Chinese proposal, Wright, *History of UNWCC*, pp. 127, 129–131; Far Eastern Commission, "Activities: Report by the Secretary General, February 26, 1946–July 10, 1947" (Washington, D.C., 1947), pp. 2, 8. Also, Far Eastern Commission, "Second Report by the Secretary General. July 10, 1947–Dec. 23, 1948" (Washington, D.C., 1949), p. 51.

4. *China Press*, January 8, May 28, 1946.

5. Wright, *History of UNWCC*, pp. 5, 121–122, 380.

6. *Law Reports of the Trials of War Criminals*, 15 vols. Selected and prepared by the UNWCC (London, 1947–1949), v. 14, annex, p. 152.

7. Ibid.

8. Ibid., pp. 152–153.

9. Ibid., pp. 153–155.

10. Ibid., p. 155. Also, see Ian Brownlie, *International Law and the Use of Force by States* (Oxford, 1963), p. 182.

11. *Law Reports*, v. 14, annex, p. 155.

12. Ibid., pp. 155–156.

13. Ibid., p. 156.

14. Ibid., p. 159.

15. See, for example, *China Press*, March 3, 16, 1946.

16. *Law Reports*, v. 14, annex, pp. 157–158.

17. Ibid., pp. 158–159.

18. Ibid., pp. 159–160.

19. See, for example, *New York Times*, January 24, 1946; *China Press*, January 4, 25, 27, February 28, March 1, 1946.

20. On American impatience with Chinese inactivity, see *New York Times*, September 22, 1945. On U.S.-Chinese cooperation vis-à-vis the trials, see statement by General Wedemeyer in *Straits Times* (Singapore), September 18, 1945; *Stars and Stripes* (Shanghai), October 31, December 19, 1945. On British assistance, see *China Press*, October 29, 30, December 15, 1945; September 18, 1946.

21. *Stars and Stripes* (Shanghai), November 30, 1945; *China Press*, December 25, 1945; January 24, 1946.
22. *China Press*, March 3, 12, 1946.
23. *China Press*, March 3, 16, 1946.
24. *China Press*, March 15, 16, 27, April 4, 9, 1946.
25. *China Press*, April 9, 1946.
26. *China Press*, April 18, 1946. All Chinese trials held before enactment of the Law of October 24, 1946, were conducted under the terms of Chinese rules governing war crimes trials then in effect. Basically, the same principles applied. See *Law Reports*, v. 14, annex, case no. 83, p. 3.
27. See, for example, *China Press*, April 18, May 24, 1946; January 7, February 3, August 15, September 23, December 11, 17, 19, 1947; January 27, May 18, 28, June 8, September 2, 1948; *Malay Mail*, July 26, 1949.
28. *London Times*, July 23, 1947.
29. *Law Reports*, v. 15, p. 20.
30. *Malay Mail*, July 26, 1947.
31. *China Press*, February 6–8, 1947; *Straits Times*, February 7, 1947.
32. *China Press*, March 11, April 2, 27, 1947.
33. *China Press*, June 1, 1948.
34. See, for example, *China Press*, June 2, July 16, August 3, 1948.
35. *China Press*, December 22, 1947.
36. *China Press*, for example, October 27, 1946; June 1, 1948.
37. See *Law Reports*, v. 14, annex, p. 158, note 1. For other trials dealing with doctrine of command responsibility, see, for example, *China Press*, June 1, 2, 8, 25, 1948.
38. *Law Reports*, v. 14, p. 1.
39. Ibid., pp. 1–2.
40. Brownlie, *International Law*, p. 182. Also, see *Law Reports*, v. 14, p. 4.
41. *Law Reports*, v. 14, p. 5.
42. Ibid.
43. Ibid., pp. 6–7.
44. *China Press*, September 14, 1946; *Straits Times*, September 15, 1946.
45. *China Press*, August 3, 14, 1948; December 22, 1945.
46. *China Press*, August 3, 11, 14, 1948.
47. *China Press*, August 15, 1948.
48. *China Press*, August 3, 11, 1948.
49. *China Press*, August 24, 1948.
50. *China Press*, September 25, November 9, 1948.
51. The court's decision was not verbatim, but as reported in the *China Press*, January 27, 1949. Compare the decision reached by a U.S. military commission in the Yamashita case, involving somewhat similar principles, above, chapter 4.

52. *London Times*, January 31, 1949.
53. Confusion abounds in this matter. In early February 1949 SCAP took over from China 260 "convicted Japanese war criminals," at the "request" of the Nationalist government. These men were to finish their terms of imprisonment at Sugamo Prison, in Tokyo. One newspaper implied that Okamura was one of the 260; another that the Communists believed him to be. Yet, as shown, Okamura had been acquitted. See *China Press*, February 1, 5, 1949; *New York Times*, January 31, February 5, 1949.
54. *China Press*, January 24, 1946; July 3, 1947.
55. *China Press*, editorial, December 7, 1945; *Malay Mail*, October 7, 1947.
56. See official statements, for example, in *China Press*, April 9, 1946; August 15, 1948.
57. *China Press*, April 25, 1946.
58. *China Press*, July 19, 1947.
59. *China Press*, October 27, 1946.
60. See, for example, *China Press*, March 3, 1946; August 5, 11, 1948; *Stars and Stripes* (Tokyo), August 20, 1948.
61. *China Press*, November 13, March 20, 1946.
62. *China Press*, September 5, 1946.
63. *China Press*, November 27, 1947. See, for example, March 4, October 13, 1948.
64. *China Press*, September 27, 1946.
65. Papers of General Thomas Blamey, memo to the Chancery, Australian Legation, Chungking, March 7, 1945, CRS A1066 File No. H45/580/2; and Department of External Affairs to Australian Legation, Chungking, September 6, 1945, and memo to Acting Minister, "War Crimes," September 24, 1945, CRS A1066 File No. H45/580/6/2, Australian War Memorial.
66. U.S. Department of State, *The China White Paper, August 1949* (Stanford, Cal., 1967), p. 130; Herbert Feis, *The China Tangle* (Princeton, N.J., 1953), p. 377.
67. These "puppet" trials received considerably more press coverage than those of war criminals. For example, from September 1945 to June 1946 a lead story relating to puppet trials appeared nearly every day in the *China Press*.
68. For the declining military fortunes of the Nationalists after 1947, see U.S. Department of State, *China White Paper*, pp. 318–323, 334–336.
69. *China Press*, December 27, 1947; March 31, 1948.
70. *Sydney Morning Herald*, August 26, 27, 1948.
71. *New York Herald Tribune*, editorial, November 12, 1948; see, for example, *China Press*, April 21, June 2, 1948; January 27, 1949.
72. For Chinese efforts to "wind down" war crimes trials, see, for example, *China Press*, December 27, 1947; March 31, April 21, June 2,

1948; January 27, 1949. For SCAP recommendation, see *New York Herald Tribune*, November 14, 1948; for FEC recommendation, see *New York Times*, March 16, 1949.

73.   *China Press*, February 1, 1949.

74.   Lawrence Olson, *Japan in Postwar Asia* (New York, 1970), pp. 82–83.

75.   U.S. Department of State, *China White Paper*, p. 354; U.S. Department of State, *Foreign Relations of the United States, 1946* (Washington, D.C., 1971), July 22, p. 410.

76.   *New York Herald Tribune*, November 6, 9, 1945.

77.   *China Press*, editorial, September 5, 1948; *New York Times* September 17, 1945; also, September 30, 1945.

78.   *Malay Mail*, October 7, 1947; for Mei's statement, see *China Press*, November 15, 1948. Mei, incidentally, later converted to the Chinese Communist cause.

79.   *China Press*, March 25, 1946.

80.   *China Press*, December 22, 1945; *London Times*, January 31, 1949.

81.   *China Press*, January 14, 1947.

82.   See, for example, *London Times*, January 31, February 7, 1949.

83.   *New York Times*, January 31, February 5, 1949.

84.   *London Times*, May 18, 1950; "The Chinese People Protest the Illegal Acts of the American Authorities in Japan," *Soviet Press Translations*, v. 15, no. 13, July 1950, p. 415.

85.   Hsinhua News Agency, as reported in *Soviet Press Translations*, v. 5, no. 22, December 1950, pp. 693–694.

86.   "Chinese Public Demands Punishment of Japanese War Criminals," *Soviet Press Translations*, v. 5, no. 8, April 1950, pp. 254–255.

87.   *London Times*, August 6, 1952.

88.   Homu Daijin Kanbo Shiho Hosei Chosabu, *Senso hanzai saiban gaishi yo (General History of Trials of War Crimes)*, (Tokyo, 1973), "Table of Trials' Results of War Criminals (B & C Classes)," p. 266.

10. The Netherlands

1.   *Punishment for War Crimes*: The Inter-Allied Declaration Signed at St. James' Palace, London, on 13 January 1942, and Relative Documents (London, 1942), p. 3. Also, M. E. Bathurst, "The United Nations War Crimes Commission," *American Journal of International Law*, v. 39, 1945, pp. 565–566, 568–569; Lord Robert A. Wright, *The History of the United Nations War Crimes Commission and the Development of the Laws of War* (London, 1948), pp. 127, 129–131.

2.   Far Eastern Commission, "Activities: Report by the Secretary General. February 26, 1946–July 10, 1947" (Washington, D.C., 1947), p. 2; *New York Times*, August 18, 1945.

3.   Eventually, Dutch authorities amended metropolitan legislation more in the direction of NEI legislation: rules of international law were made applicable to acts punishable by Dutch courts as war crimes against humanity. See *Law Reports of the Trials of War Crim-*

inals, 15 vols. Selected and prepared by the UNWCC (London, 1947–1949), v. 11, annex, pp. 86–88; also, v. 15, p. 34.

4. Ibid., v. 15, p. 34; also, v. 11, annex, pp. 87–88, 91.
5. Ibid., p. 93.
6. Ibid., pp. 93–94.
7. There were three types of Dutch courts-martial. But the temporary courts-martial "appear to be in practice the only ones to be used for war crimes trials," ibid., pp. 97; 106–107.
8. Ibid., pp. 106–108.
9. Ibid., p. 98.
10. See ibid., v. 14, annex, pp. 152–153; Supreme Commander for the Allied Powers, *Trials of Class "B" and "C" War Criminals* (Tokyo, 1952), appendix 2, p. 216; also, *Law Reports*, v. 15, pp. 90–92. And while they were empowered to do so, U.S. authorities refrained from trying any Japanese for major, or class "A," offenses at lesser trials.
11. *Law Reports*, v. 11, annex, p. 103. Chinese law, too, prescribed set punishments; China's punishments, though, were far more categorized according to the crime itself. See above, chapter 9.
12. *Law Reports*, v. 11, annex, pp. 98, 100.
13. Ibid., p. 102.
14. Ibid., pp. 101–102. Prosecution of "criminal groups" is to be distinguished from "joint" or "mass" trials, commonly held by Allied nations in the East. In the former, the crime charged is committed in such a way that it "can be ascribed to the group as a whole," and is "considered to have been committed by that group." In the latter, all accused are charged merely with committing similar (or the same) crimes. See ibid., p. 101; also, v. 13, case no. 79, pp. 140–142.
15. *Law Reports*, v. 11, annex, p. 108. Compare, for example, this provision with the following: Great Britain, The War Office, Royal Warrant, 14th June 1945, Army Order 81/1945, with Amendments.
16. *Law Reports*, v. 11, annex, pp. 108–109. Also, v. 15, pp. x–xi, 20.
17. Ibid., v. 11, annex, pp. 106–107, 109–110.
18. See Wright, *History of UNWCC*, pp. 381–382; also above, chapter 6, pp. 130–131; *London Times* article, "Far Eastern War Crimes," July 31, 1946.
19. See Wright, *History of UNWCC*, pp. 382, 385; Australia, Department of External Affairs, *Current Notes on International Affairs*, Sydney, v. 17, no. 1, January 1946, p. 4.
20. Wright, *History of UNWCC*, pp. 384–386; *Stars and Stripes* (Tokyo), January 19, 1950.
21. Wright, *History of UNWCC*, p. 389.
22. *Straits Times* (Singapore), December 15, 1945.
23. *New York Times*, September 7, 1946.
24. Great Britain, *Parliamentary Debates*, House of Lords, January 28, 1947, p. 174.
25. *Law Reports*, v. 13, case no. 76, p. 122.

26. Ibid., pp. 122–123, 124–125.
27. Ibid., v. 11, case no. 59, p. 1.
28. Ibid., pp. 2–4.
29. Ibid., v. 13, case no. 77, p. 126.
30. Ibid., pp. 126, 128.
31. Ibid., pp. 127–128.
32. Ibid., pp. 128–129; also, v. 15, p. 87.
33. Ibid., v. 13, pp. 127–129, 130.
34. Ibid., p. 110; also, v. 15, p. 113, note 8.
35. *New York Times*, October 19, 1947.
36. *Malay Mail*, May 2, 1947.
37. *New York Times*, December 16, 1948; *Stars and Stripes* (Tokyo), January 19, 1950.
38. See, for example, *Stars and Stripes* (Tokyo), March 17, 1949; also *Straits Times*, December 15, 1945.
39. *Law Reports*, v. 13, case no. 79, pp. 138, 140.
40. Ibid., pp. 140, 144–145.
41. *New York Times*, June 25, 1946.
42. *Law Reports*, v. 15, "Supplemental Cases," p. 132.
43. *Stars and Stripes* (Tokyo), March 3, 1949; *Malay Mail*, December 6, 1949.
44. *Stars and Stripes* (Tokyo), January 19, 1950.
45. Homu Daijin Kanbo Shiho Hosei Chosabu, *Senso hanzai saiban gaishi yo* (*General History of Trials of War Crimes*) (Tokyo, 1973), "Table of Trials' Results of War Criminals (B & C Classes)," p. 266.
46. Compare these figures with those of "unverified Japanese press accounts" of 1948 which said that Dutch courts acquitted 55% of all those accused, in Russell Brines, *MacArthur's Japan* (Philadelphia, 1948), p. 117. The latter figures are palpably incorrect.
47. For British, Australian, Chinese and Philippine statistics, see appropriate sections of chapters 5, 6, 9 and 11.
48. Bernard V. A. Röling, "The Law of War and the National Jurisdiction since 1945," Recueil des Cours, *Académie de Droit International* (Leyde, the Netherlands, 1961), v. 100, pp. 329–330, note 2.
49. *Stars and Stripes* (Tokyo), January 14, 1950.

11. The Philippines

1. Far Eastern Commission, "Activities: Report by the Secretary General, February 26, 1946–July 10, 1947" (Washington, D.C., 1947), pp. 2–5, 8; also, Far Eastern Commission, "Second Report by the Secretary General, July 10, 1947–December 23, 1948" (Washington, D.C., 1949), p. 51.
2. Delfin Jaranilla, "International Military Tribunal for the Far East. Concurring Opinion by the Honorable Mr. Justice Delfin Jaranilla, Member from the Republic of the Philippines 1 November 1948."
3. Supreme Commander for the Allied Powers, *Trials of Class "B" and*

"C" War Criminals (Tokyo, 1952), pp. 41–42. Also, see Manuel Lim, "Highlights of the Yamashita and Homma Trials," *Philippine Law Journal*, v. 22, 1947, p. 9.

4. Lord Robert A. Wright, *The History of the United Nations War Crimes Commission and the Development of the Laws of War* (London, 1948), p. 5.

5. Adamin A. Tallow, *Command Responsibility: Its Legal Aspect* (Manila, 1965), pp. x–xi. Also, Lim, "Yamashita and Homma," pp. 5–6.

6. See, for example, *China* (Shanghai) *Press*, June 10, 1947; Wright, *History of UNWCC*, p. 383.

7. Philippines, executive order No. 68, "Establishing a National War Crimes Office and Prescribing Rules and Regulations Governing the Trials of Accused War Criminals," July 29, 1947, sec. 1, National Archives, Manila.

8. Ibid., sec. 3, a–e; also, letter of May 17, 1976, from Chief, National Archives, Republic of the Philippines, to author.

9. Philippines, executive order No. 68, secs. 4, 5; *China Press*, November 22, 1947, January 16, 1948.

10. Tallow, *Command Responsibility*, p. 374; Philippines, executive order no. 68, sec. 2 (1–3).

11. Philippines, executive order No. 68, sec. 5, d (1, 2, 4), g, h. See, for example, *China Press*, July 28, 1948; February 16, 20, 1949.

12. Philippines, executive order No. 68, Section 5 b.

13. See statement by Colonel A. C. Carpenter. While this remark referred to American-held trials in the Philippines, the same reasoning certainly applied to Filipino-conducted trials—see *Stars and Stripes* (Tokyo), December 14, 1945.

14. *China Press*, June 10, 1947; Lim, "Yamashita and Homma," p. 6.

15. *New York Times*, September 21, 1949.

16. *China Press*, November 5, 1947; February 16, 1949.

17. *China Press*, November 22, 1947.

18. *China Press*, November 23, 1947.

19. *China Press*, January 16, 1948.

20. *China Press*, February 25, 1948.

21. For trial coverage, see *China Press*, September 15, 23, November 9, 1948.

22. *Malay Mail*, December 16, 1949.

23. For trial coverage, see, for example, *China Press*, December 3, 1948; *Stars and Stripes* (Tokyo), August 14, 1948; July 15, 1949; *New York Times*, July 14, 1949.

24. *Stars and Stripes* (Tokyo), July 15, 1949.

25. *New York Times*, editorial, September 15, 1945.

26. Tallow, *Command Responsibility*, pp. 3, 40–41, 59.

27. See, for example, *China Press*, January 23, February 20, 1949; *Stars and Stripes* (Tokyo), August 10, 1948; June 28, October 27, 1949.

28. *China Press*, February 20, 1949; *New York Times*, February 19, 1949.

29. *China Press*, March 22, 1949; *Stars and Stripes* (Tokyo), October 28, 1949.

30. *Stars and Stripes* (Tokyo), August 10, 1948.

31. *Stars and Stripes* (Tokyo), June 28, 1949; *Malay Mail*, December 16, 1949.

32. *Stars and Stripes* (Tokyo), October 28, 31, 1949.

33. Marcial P. Lichauo, *Roxas: The Story of a Great Filipino and of the Political Era in Which He Lived* (Manila, 1952), pp. 234–236.

34. *Malay Mail*, December 30, 1949.

35. Tallow, *Command Responsibility*, pp. 201–202; *China Press*, June 14, 1948.

36. Quoted in Tallow, *Command Responsibility*, pp. 200–201.

37. Eugene A. Hessel, "Let the Judges Do the Hanging!" *Christian Century*, v. 66, 1949, pp. 984–986.

38. Tallow, *Command Responsibility*, p. 200.

39. *China Press*, January 16, 1948.

40. As reported in *China Press*, November 10, 1947.

41. Tallow, *Command Responsibility*, p. 374.

42. As reported in Homu Daijin Kanbo Shiho Hosei Chosabu, *Senso hanzai saiban gaishi yo* (*General History of Trials of War Crimes*) (Tokyo, 1973), "Table of Trials' Results of War Criminals (B & C Classes)," p. 266.

43. Indeed, collaboration "remains an explosive issue in the Philippines even a generation afterward," in David Joel Steinberg, *Philippine Collaboration in World War II* (Ann Arbor, Mich., 1967), pp. vii, 32–33, 37–38.

44. Ibid., pp. 123–127; *New York Times*, September 11, 1945.

45. See, for example, the long and fiery debates, in Republic of the Philippines, *Congressional Record*, House of Representatives, Manila, 1945–1948, 1, September 15, 1945, 1,118–1,119; 3, nos. 12–14, February 9, 11, 12, 1948, pp. 209–228, 241–262, 277–325; February 13, 1948, pp. 329–423.

46. Russell H. Fifield, *Americans in Southeast Asia: The Roots of Commitment* (New York, 1973), p. 78.

47. Press coverage of the nascent and then widespread civil war was extensive. See, for example, *China Press*, September 1, 13, 1946; January 4, 14, 1947.

48. Fifield, *Americans in Southeast Asia*, pp. 77–79.

49. Steinberg, *Philippine Collaboration*, pp. 114, 122–123.

50. Harry S. Truman, *Year of Decisions* (New York, 1955), pp. 65–66; *New York Herald Tribune*, May 1, 1946; Fifield, *Americans in Southeast Asia*, p. 78.

51. Lim, "Yamashita and Homma," p. 6.

52. *Stars and Stripes* (Tokyo), December 15, 1948.

53. *China Press*, April 1, 1948.

54. Such dissent and, specifically, demands for Hirohito's trial, were

either extremely isolated or deliberately screened from press coverage. See, for example, Philippines, *Congressional Record*, v. 1, no. 8, August 22, 1945, p. 685; and *Stars and Stripes* (Shanghai), October 23, 1945. The Filipino representative at the IMTFE, Justice Delfin Jaranilla, delivered a separate "Concurring Opinion." His major disagreement was that the tribunal "acted with so much leniency in favor of the accused" in treatment afforded and sentences awarded them. See Jaranilla, "Concurring Opinion," pp. 17, 34.

55. For FEC "recommendation" of March 31, 1949, see Far Eastern Commission, "Third Report by the Secretary General, Dec. 24, 1948–June 30, 1950" (Washington, D.C., 1950), pp. 5, appendix II, p. 17.

56. *New York Times*, June 4, 1946.

57. *China Press*, July 28, 1948.

58. *Stars and Stripes* (Tokyo), August 5, 1948.

12. France

1. "From the moment that agreement" between Vichy and Tokyo was signed in early 1941, "it was obvious that French sovereignty over Indochina had become a farce." See Bernard Fall, *The Two Viet-Nams: A Political and Military Analysis*, 2nd rev. ed. (New York, 1967), p. 45.

2. *Punishment for War Crimes*: The Inter-Allied Declaration Signed at St. James' Palace, London, on 13 January 1942, and Relative Documents (London, 1942), p. 12; M. E. Bathurst, "The United Nations War Crimes Commission," *American Journal of International Law*, v. 39, 1945, pp. 565–568; Lord Robert A. Wright, *The History of the United Nations War Crimes Commission and the Development of the Laws of War* (London, 1948), pp. 127, 129–131.

3. *New York Times*, February 25, 1945.

4. *New York Times* May 13, 1945.

5. *New York Times*, September 11, 1945.

6. Far Eastern Commission, "Activities: Report by the Secretary General, February 26, 1946–July 10, 1947" (Washington, D.C., 1947), pp. 1–3; Henri Bernard, "Dissenting Judgment of the Member from France of the International Military Tribunal for the Far East. November 12, 1948."

7. *Law Reports of the Trials of War Criminals*, 15 vols. Selected and prepared by the UNWCC (London, 1947–1949), v. 3, annex 2, pp. 93–94. Emphasis added.

8. Ibid., pp. 93, 95. Also, see v. 15, pp. 9–10. For de Menthon's statement, see United Nations Information Organization, *Information Paper No. 1*, 1946, p. 2.

9. *Law Reports*, v. 3, pp. 94, 99.

10. Ibid., pp. 98–99.

11. Decisions by majority vote prevailed only in "wartime." In peacetime decisions had to be at least by a 5–2 vote (the commission having

been expanded by one member in peacetime). France was technically still at war with Japan until the ratification of the San Francisco Peace Treaty in September 1951.

12. *Law Reports*, v. 3, p. 99; also, v. 15, pp. 2, 20.

13. Ibid., v. 3, pp. 97, 99–100.

14. The author has tried in vain to obtain relevant French government documents, beyond those already cited. Ostensibly, they are not yet available to the public. Furthermore, the French commenced their Eastern trials in 1947, the same year that the UNWCC decided to "wind down" its activities. Detailed coverage by that body of French trials in Saigon was therefore precluded. Finally, press coverage of French Indochinese trials was spotty, frequently inconsequential and nearly always inconclusive.

15. *Law Reports*, v. 3, p. 93.

16. Wright, *History of UNWCC*, p. 381.

17. Ibid., pp. 383–384, 386; *Stars and Stripes* (Tokyo), December 9, 1949.

18. *China* (Shanghai) *Press*, January 10, 1948.

19. *Law Reports*, v. 3, pp. 95–96.

20. *London Times*, February 17, 1947; *China Press*, February 17, 1947. Indeed, considering the relatively few trials (39) conducted by French authorities, and the number of Japanese involved (230), it would appear logical to conclude that France relied more regularly on mass trials than most other Allied nations. For figures, see note 27.

21. *China Press*, November 4, 1946; February 17, April 16, 1947.

22. *Straits Times* (Singapore), February 20, 1947; *London Times*, March 20, 1951.

23. *Stars and Stripes* (Tokyo), December 9, 1949.

24. *Law Reports*, v. 15, pp. 156–157; v. 3, p. 96.

25. Ibid., v. 3, p. 94.

26. See *Malay Mail*, December 6, 1949; *London Times*, March 20, 1951.

27. Homu Daijin Kanbo Shiho Hosei Chosabu, *Senso hanzai saiban gaishi yo* (*General History of the Trials of War Crimes*) (Tokyo, 1973), "Table of Trials' Results of War Criminals (B & C Classes)," p. 266.

Epilogue: Ideals Upheld

1. Eugene Davidson, *The Nuremberg Fallacy: Wars and War Crimes since World War II* (New York, 1973), p. 291.

2. For a brief, but devastating, account of Japanese war atrocities, see Edward F. L. Russell, *The Knights of Bushido: A Short History of Japanese War Crimes* (London, 1958).

3. Hannah Arendt, *Eichmann in Jerusalem: A Report on the Banality of Evil* (New York, 1963), p. 232.

4. For example, a host of lawyers, political scientists and historians shared to various, but often considerable, extent Tojo's assessment of the IMTFE: "I can only say it was a victor's trial" (*Nippon Times*, November 13, 1948). See, for a mere sampling, H. A. Hauxhurst,

Owen Cunningham, Charles F. Wennerstrum, James T. Brand, "Forum on War Crimes Trials (Addresses)," *American Bar Association, Comparative and International Law Section*, 1948, p. 34; statement by J. N. Freeman, IMTFE defense counsel, in *China* (Shanghai) *Press*, February 8, 1949; George F. Kennan, U.S. Department of State, *Foreign Relations of the United States, 1948* (Washington, D.C., 1974), March 21, p. 718; U.S. Supreme Court Justice William O. Douglas' separate opinion, *Hirota* vs. *MacArthur* 338 U.S. 197 (1948), at p. 215; Lord Hankey, *Politics, Trials and Errors* (Chicago, 1950), pp. 111, 114; Richard H. Minear, *Victors' Justice: The Tokyo War Crimes Trial* (Princeton, N.J., 1971).

An equally qualified array of individuals, on the other hand, praised the IMTFE for its enforcement and expansion of international law and universal principles of justice. See, for example, Lord Robert A. Wright (UNWCC chairman), "War Crimes under International Law," *The Law Quarterly Review*, 1946, p. 550; John A. Appleman, *Military Tribunals and International Crimes* (Indianapolis, 1954), p. 12; A. Frederick Mignone, "After Nuremberg, Tokyo," *Texas Law Review*, v. 25, 1947, pp. 476–477; Gordon Walker, in *Christian Science Monitor*, November 12, 1948; R. Q. Quentin-Baxter, "The Task of the International Military Tribunal at Tokyo," *New Zealand Law Journal*, v. 25, 1949, pp. 133–134.

5. On the indefinability of "aggressive war," then and now, see, for example, C. A. Pompe, *Aggressive War: An International Crime* (The Hague, 1953), pp. 30–33, 70; Enrico Serra, *L'Aggressione internazionale* (Milan, 1946), p. 173; United Nations, General Assembly, "Report of the Special Committee on the Question of Defining Aggression," New York, 1973. Also, see John G. Stoessinger, *The Might of Nations* (New York, 1963), pp. 246, 257.

6. Richard A. Falk, *A Global Approach to National Policy* (Cambridge, Mass., 1975), p. 153; Arthur M. Schlesinger, Jr., "The Necessary Amorality of Foreign Affairs," *Harper's Magazine*, August 1971, p. 73.

7. George F. Kennan, *Memoirs, 1925–1950* (Boston, 1967), p. 260.

8. United Nations, *Yearbook, 1946–1947* (New York, 1947), p. 254.

9. Georg Schwarzenberger, *A Manual of International Law*, 5th ed. (New York, 1967), p. 211. Also, see *New York Times*, editorial, May 14, 1946.

10. The figures of 2,200 trials and 5,700 defendants are minimal ones at best, considering that Soviet trials have not been taken into account.

   Beyond this, certain discrepancies in the total trial statistics are to be found. Two separate tables of final statistics, consequently, are offered. Table A, that is, is a reproduction of the "Table of the Results of the Trials of Class B and C War Criminals," provided by a Japanese source: Homu Daijin Kanbo Shiho Hosei Chosabu, *Senso hanzai saiban gaishi yo* (*General History of Trials of War Crimes*) (Tokyo, 1973), p. 266. This tabulation, K. Suyama, Director of the Di-

Table A

Judging nation	No. of trials	Accused	Con-victed	Death	Life	Ac-quitted	Others
America	456	1,453	1,176	143	162	188	89
Britain	330	978	779	223	54	116	83
Australia	294	949	646	153	38	276	36
Netherlands	448	1,038	969	236	28	55	14
France	39	230	198	63	23	31	1
Philippines	72	169	133	17	87	11	27
China	605	883	504	149	83	350	29
Total	2,244	5,700	4,405	984	475	1,027	279

Table B

Judging nation	No. of trials	Accused	Con-victed	Death	Life	Ac-quitted	Others
America	474	1,409	1,229	163	—	180	—
Britain	306	920	811	265	55	107	2
Australia	296	924	644	148	39	280	—
Netherlands	448	1,038	969	236	28	55	14
France	39	230	198	63	23	31	1
Philippines	72	169	133	17	87	11	27
China	605	883	504	149	83	350	29
Total	2,240	5,573	4,488	1,041	—	1,014	—

vision of Interlibrary Services, National Diet Library, assured the author, "is most accurate" (Letter, September 7, 1977). Accordingly, its totals for Dutch, Chinese, Philippine and French trials—where no conflicting or better figures have been located—have been relied upon in the text.

Where what were considered equally or more authoritative sources existed, as in the cases of American, British and Australian trial results, *Senso hanzai* . . . has been accorded secondary importance. Table B therefore contains figures from *Senso hanzai* . . . for Dutch, Chinese, Philippine and French trials, added to those contained in respective governmental sources for American, British and

Australian trials. Sources for the latter figures may be found in the appropriate sections of the respective chapters.

Further inexactitude surrounds the number of Japanese lesser war criminals executed by the Allied nations, again excluding Soviet trials. As may be seen, table A gives a sum figure of 984; table B, 1,041. However, the figure of 920 Japanese executed is offered by Noboru Kojima, *Tokyo Saiban*, 2 vols. (Tokyo, 1971), v. 2, p. 225. Said Richard Minear on this matter: "Kojima gives no source for his figures. . . . But Tadao Inoue of the Japanese Government's Ministry of Justice (War Crimes Materials room) confirms the correctness of Kojima's figures," *Victors' Justice*, p. 6, note 3. (Kojima, noteworthily, also agreed with *Senso hanzai* . . . 's figure of 5,700 Japanese accused brought to trial by Allied minor war crimes courts.) Also, the staff of the *Asahi Shimbun* concurred with the total figure of 920 Japanese executed, *The Pacific Rivals* (New York, 1971), p. 182. Yet, still another Japanese source, *Seiki no isho* (*The Last Testament of the Century*), edited by Sugamo Isho Hensankai (Tokyo, 1954), appendix, p. 1, concluded that 901 class "B" and "C" war criminals were executed by Allied forces in the East.

One final word of caution: it is not entirely clear, except in the case of Britain, whether the factor of duplication—that is, where an accused stood charged and received sentencing at more than one trial—has been taken into account in any of these figures.

11. U.S. Department of State, *Foreign Relations of the United States, 1948* (Washington, D.C., 1974), March 21, pp. 717–718.

12. On this point, see *Law Reports of the Trials of War Criminals*, 15 vols. Selected and prepared by the UNWCC (London, 1947–1949), v. 15, pp. 193–195.

13. U.S. Supreme Court, *In re Yamashita*, 327 U.S. 1 (1946).

Bibliography

Official Proceedings, Documents and Government Publications

Australia. Department of External Affairs. *Current Notes on International Affairs*. Sydney, 1945–1952.

———. File 54.6 Atrocities. Papers of General Thomas Blamey, Australian War Memorial.

———. *Parliamentary Debates*. Senate and House of Representatives. Sydney, 1945–1951.

———. War Crimes Act 1945, Canberra, 1945.

Bernard, Henri. "Dissenting Judgment of the Member from France of the International Military Tribunal for the Far East. November 12, 1948." IMTFE, Tokyo.

Canada. *Parliamentary Debates*, House of Commons. 1946. Ottawa: Controller of Stationery, 1946.

———. "Report of the Department of External Affairs, Canada 1948." Ottawa: Controller of the Stationery, 1949.

———. "Report of the Department of National Defence for the Fiscal Year Ending March 31, 1946." Ottawa: Controller of Stationery, 1947.

———. "Report of the Department of National Defence for the Fiscal Year Ending March 31, 1947." Ottawa: Controller of the Stationery, 1947.

———. "Report of the Secretary of State for External Affairs for the Fiscal Year Ended December 31, 1946." Ottawa: Controller of the Stationery, 1947.

Far Eastern Commission, "Activities: Report by the Secretary General. February 26, 1946–July 10, 1947." Publication 2888. Washington, D.C.: GPO, 1947.

———. "Second Report by the Secretary General. July 10, 1947–Dec. 23, 1948." Publication 3420. Washington, D.C.: GPO, 1949.

———. "Third Report by the Secretary General, Dec. 24, 1948–June 30, 1950." Publication 3945. Washington, D.C.: GPO, 1950.

The Far Eastern Commission: A Study in International Cooperation, 1945–1952. Dr. George H. Blakeslee. Publication 5138, Washington, D.C.: GPO, 1953.

General Tomoyuki Yamashita vs. *Lieutenant General Wilhelm Styer.*

United States Supreme Court Records. Lawyers' edition, 327, October 1945.

Great Britain. *Parliamentary Debates.* (Hansard). Fifth Series. House of Commons. Official Report. Vols. 378, 414–432, 1945–1947. London, HMSO.

———. *Parliamentary Debates.* (Hansard). Fifth Series. House of Lords, v. 142, 1945–1946. London, HMSO.

———. The War Office. Royal Warrant. Regulations for the Trial of War Criminals. 14th June 1945, Army Order 81/1945, with Amendments. HMSO, 1945.

Instrument of Surrender (Japan). September 2, 1945.

International Military Tribunal for the Far East. *Judgment.* Tokyo, November 1948.

International Military Tribunal for the Far East. *Proceedings.* Tokyo, May 3, 1946–April 16, 1948.

Jaranilla, Delfin. "International Military Tribunal for the Far East. Concurring Opinion by the Honorable Mr. Justice Delfin Jaranilla, Member from the Republic of the Philippines. 1 November 1948." IMTFE, Tokyo.

Law Reports of the Trials of War Criminals. 15 vols. Selected and prepared by the United Nations War Crimes Commission. London: HMSO, 1947–1949.

New Zealand. Department of External Affairs. "Annual Report of the Department of External Affairs." Wellington, 1948–1951. Publications 65–97.

———. *Parliamentary Debates.* Legislative Council and House of Representatives. Wellington, 1945–1949.

———. War History Branch, Department of Internal Affairs. *Prisoners of War.* W. Wynne Mason. *Official History of New Zealand in the Second World War 1939–1945.* Wellington, 1954.

Pal, Radhabinod. *International Military Tribunal for the Far East, Dissentient Judgment.* Calcutta: Sanyal & Co., 1953.

Philippines, Republic of the. *Congressional Record.* House of Representatives. Vols. 1–3, 1945–1948. Manila.

———. Executive Order No. 68, "Establishing a National War Crimes Office and Prescribing Rules and Regulations Governing the Trials of Accused War Criminals." July 29, 1947. National Archives, Manila.

Potsdam Declaration. July 26, 1945.

Punishment for War Crimes: The Inter-Allied Declaration Signed at St. James' Palace, London, on 13 January 1942, and Relative Documents. Issued by the Inter-Allied Information Committee, London, HMSO, 1942.

Röling, Bernard V. A. "Opinion of Mr. Justice Röling, Member for the Netherlands. International Military Tribunal for the Far East. November 12, 1948." IMTFE, Tokyo.

Sleeman, Colin, ed. with a foreword by Lord Mountbatten. *Trial of Gozawa*

Sadaichi and Nine Others. London: William Hodge and Co., Ltd. 1948.

———. and S. C. Silkin, eds. *Trial of Sumida Haruzo and Twenty Others (The "Double Tenth" Trial).* London: William Hodge and Co., Ltd., 1951.

Supreme Commander for the Allied Powers. "International Military Tribunal for the Far East, Established at Tokyo January 19, 1946." Washington, D.C.: GPO, 1947.

———. *Trials of Class "B" and "C" War Criminals. History of the Non-Military Activities of the Occupation of Japan.* Tokyo: SCAP, 1952. Monograph 5.

Takayanagi, Kenzo. "The Tokio Trials and International Law. Answer to the Prosecution's Argument Delivered at IMTFE on 3 and 4 March 1948." Tokyo, 1948.

Tojo, Hideki. "Affidavit of Hideki Tojo, Individual Defense." Tokyo, IMTFE, December 19, 1948.

Union of Soviet Socialist Republics. *Current Digest of the Soviet Press.* 1949–1951. Published by the Joint Committee on Slavic Studies.

———. *Information Bulletin.* Published by the Embassy of the Union of Soviet Socialist Republics in the U.S.A. 1946, 1950–1951.

———. *Materials on the Trial of Former Servicemen of the Japanese Army Charged with Manufacturing and Employing Bacteriological Weapons.* Foreign Languages Publishing House, Moscow, 1950.

———. *New Times.* 1946–1950.

———. *Soviet Press Translations.* Seattle: Far Eastern and Russian Institute, University of Washington, 1948–1950.

United Nations. General Assembly. "Report of the Special Committee on the Question of Defining Aggression." April 25–May 30, 1973. 28th Session, New York, 1973.

———. *Yearbook, 1946–1947.* New York, 1947.

United Nations Information Organization. *Information Paper No. 1.* Issued by the Reference Division of the UNIO, 1946.

United States of America vs. *Tomoyuki Yamashita.* Public trial before the military commission convened by the commanding general, United States Army Forces, Western Pacific, Exhibits. [Manila?] 1945. 5 vols.

United States Army Forces in the Pacific. "Regulations Governing the Trial of War Criminals." September 24, 1945–December 27, 1946.

United States. Department of the Army. *Report of the Judge Advocate, United States Forces, China Theater.* United States Army Forces China, Nanking Headquarters Command and Advisory Group China, 1 January 1945 to 10 June 1947.

———. Department of the Army. *Terminal Report—War Crimes Trial Division, 1947. Philippine-Ryukyus Command.* The Adjutant General's Office, Washington, D.C.

———. Department of the Army. United States Army Field Manual, *The Law of Land Warfare.* Washington, D.C., 1956.

————. Department of the Navy. *Final Report of Navy War Crimes Program in the Pacific*. Submitted by the Director of War Crimes, U.S. Pacific Fleet to the Secretary of the Navy, 1 December 1949. Navy Historical Center, Washington, D.C.

————. Department of State. *Bulletin*. "Answer to Soviet Protest on MacArthur Clemency Circular." 23 (July 10, 1950).

————. Department of State. *Bulletin*. "Apprehension, Trial, and Punishment of War Criminals in the Far East." 16 (May 4, 1947).

————. Department of State. *Bulletin*. "Non-Military Activities in Japan and Korea." 14 (May 12, 1946).

————. Department of State. *Bulletin*. "Trial of Far Eastern War Criminals." 14 (May 19, 1946).

————. Department of State. *Bulletin*. "Trial of Far Eastern War Criminals," 14 (March 10, 1946).

————. Department of State. *Bulletin*. "Trial of Japanese War Criminals." 20 (May 1, 1949).

————. Department of State. *Bulletin*. "USSR Motives on Trying Emperor of Japan Questioned." 22 (February 13, 1950).

————. Department of State. *The China White Paper, August 1949*. Stanford, Cal.: Stanford University Press, 1967.

————. Department of State. *Foreign Relations of the United States, 1946*. 8. Washington, D.C.: GPO, 1971.

————. Department of State. *Foreign Relations of the United States, 1947*. 6. Washington, D.C.: GPO, 1972.

————. Department of State. *Foreign Relations of the United States, 1948*. 6. Washington, D.C.: GPO, 1974.

————. Department of State. "International Military Tribunal for the Far East Established at Tokyo January 19, 1946." Publication 2765. Washington, D.C.: GPO, 1946.

————. Department of State. "Moscow Meeting of Foreign Ministers, December 16–26, 1945." Publication 2448. Washington, D.C.: GPO, 1946.

————. Department of State. *Occupation of Japan: Policy and Progress*. Publication 2671. Washington, D.C.: GPO, 1947.

————. Department of State. "Trial of Japanese War Criminals." Publication 2613. Washington, D.C.: GPO, 1946.

————. Department of State. "United States Initial Post-Surrender Policy for Japan." August 29, 1945.

————. United States Supreme Court. *Ex parte Quirin*, 317 U.S. 1 (1942).

————. *Hirota* vs. *MacArthur*, 338 U.S. 197 (1948).

————. *Homma* vs. *Styer*, 327 U.S. 759 (1946).

————. *In re Yamashita*, 327 U.S. 1 (1946).

————. *Johnson* vs. *Eisentrager*, 339 U.S. 763 (1950).

Webb, Sir William. International Military Tribunal for the Far East. "Judgement of Sir William Webb." Australian War Memorial; Misc., DRL 2481 (3rd Series) Webb Collection.

———. International Military Tribunal for the Far East. "Separate Opinion of the President, November 1, 1948." IMTFE, Tokyo.

Whitney, Brig. Gen. Courtney, U.S. Army Chief, Government Section. "The Case of General Yamashita. A Memorandum." November 22, 1949. GHQ, SCAP, Government Section.

Wright, Lord Robert A. *The History of the United Nations War Crimes Commission and the Development of the Laws of War*. London: HMSO, 1948.

Memoirs, Books, Articles by Participants and Contemporaries

Acheson, Dean. *Present at the Creation*. New York: W. W. Norton, 1969.

Allen, Lafe Franklin. "Japan's Militarists Face the Music." *American Foreign Service Journal*. 24: August 1947.

———. "Judgment Day in Tokyo." *Military Government Journal*. 2: Fall 1949.

Blakeney, Ben Bruce. "International Military Tribunal." *American Bar Association Journal*. 32: August 1946.

Blewett, George F. "Victor's Injustice: The Tokyo War Crimes Trial." *American Perspective*. 4: Summer 1950.

Brines, Russell. *MacArthur's Japan*. Philadelphia: J. B. Lippincott, 1948.

Brown, Brendan F. "Red China, the Tokyo Trial, and Aggressive War." *Louisiana Bar Journal*. 3: January 1956.

Byrnes, James F. *Speaking Frankly*. New York: Harper & Brothers, 1947.

Churchill, Winston. *The Grand Alliance*. Boston: Houghton, Mifflin & Co., 1950.

Comyns-Carr, Arthur S. "The Judgment of the International Military Tribunal for the Far East." *Transactions of the Grotius Society*. 34: November 1948.

———. "The Tokyo War Crimes Trial." *Far Eastern Survey*. 18: May 18, 1949.

Dickinson, George. "Japanese War Trials." *Australian Quarterly*, 24: June 1952.

———. "Manus Island Trials." *Royal Australian Historical Society*. 38, part 2: July 1952.

Evans, Harold. "The Trial of Major Japanese War Criminals." *New Zealand Law Review*. 23: January–December 1947.

Evatt, Herbert V. *Australia in World Affairs*. Sydney: Angus and Robertson, 1946.

———. "Has the Menace of Japan Been Removed?" *New York Times Magazine*. February 3, 1946.

Feldhaus, J. Gordon. "The Trial of Yamashita." *Current Legal Thought*. 13: August 1947.

Furness, George A. "Notes of Speech by G. A. Furness, Asiatic Society of Japan (Tokyo)," *Bulletin*. 6: June 1976.

Guy, George F. "The Defense of Yamashita." *Wyoming Law Journal*. 4: Fall 1949.

Hanayama, Shinso. *The Way of Deliverance: Three Years With the Condemned Japanese War Criminals*. Translated by Hideo Suzuki, et al. New York: Scribner's, 1950.

Hankey, Lord. *Politics, Trials and Errors*. Chicago: Henry Regnery Company, 1950.

———. "Postscript," to Viscount Maugham. *U.N.O. and War Crimes*. London: John Murray, 1951.

Hauxhurst, H. A., Owen Cunningham, Charles F. Wennerstrum, James T. Brand. "Forum on War Crimes Trials (Addresses)." *American Bar Association*. Comparative and International Law Section. 1948–1949.

Hessel, Eugene A. "Let the Judges Do the Hanging!" *Christian Century*. 66: August 24, 1949.

Horwitz, Solis. "The Tokyo Trial." *International Conciliation*. 465: November 1950.

Hull, Cordell. *The Memoirs of Cordell Hull*. 2 vols. New York: MacMillan Company, 1948.

Ireland, Gordon. "Ex Post Facto from Rome to Tokyo." *Temple Law Quarterly*. 21: July 1947.

———. "Uncommon Law in Martial Tokyo." *Year Book of World Affairs*. 4: 1950.

Jackson, Robert H. *The Case against the Nazi War Criminals*. New York: Alfred Knopf, 1946.

———. *The Nürnberg Case*. New York: Alfred Knopf, 1947.

———. "Report of Robert H. Jackson, U.S. Representative to the International Conference on Military Trials, London, 1945." U.S. Department of State Publication 3080. Washington, D.C., 1949.

"Joseph Keenan Meets the Press." *American Mercury*. 70: April 1950.

Katona, Paul. "Japanese War Crimes Trials." *Free World*. 12: November 1946.

Keenan, Joseph B. "Observations and Lessons From International Criminal Trials." *University of Kansas City Law Review*. 17: 1949.

——— and Brendan F. Brown. *Crimes against International Law*. Washington, D.C.: Public Affairs Press, 1950.

Kennan, George F. *Memoirs, 1925–1950*. Boston: Little, Brown and Company, 1967.

Kenworthy, Aubrey S. *The Tiger of Malaya*. New York: Exposition, 1953.

Kodama, Yoshio. *Sugamo Diary*. Translated by Taro Fukuda. Japan: n.p. 1960.

Lim, Manuel. "Highlights of the Yamashita and Homma Trials." *Philippine Law Journal*. 22: January 1947.

Liu, James T. C. "The Tokyo Trial." *China Monthly*. 8: July 1947.

———. "The Tokyo Trial: Second Look." *China Monthly*. 8: August 1947.

Lyman, Albert. "Yokohama War Crimes Trials: A Review." *Journal of Bar Association of Washington, D.C.*. 17: June 1950.

MacArthur, Douglas. "General MacArthur's Review of the War Crimes

Sentences Issued on November 24, 1948." *Contemporary Japan.* 17: July/December 1948.

———. *Reminiscences.* New York: McGraw Hill, 1964.

McKenzie, Walter I. "The Japanese War Trials." *Journal of the National Association of Referees in Bankruptcy.* 21: July 1947.

Maugham, Viscount Frederick H. *U.N.O. and War Crimes.* London: John Murray, 1951.

Meek, F. E. "War Crimes Trials in the Pacific." *Idaho State Bar.* 21: 1947.

Mignone, A. Frederick. "After Nuremberg, Tokyo." *Texas Law Review.* 25: May 1947.

Reel, A. Frank. *The Case of General Yamashita.* Reprint. New York: Octagon Books, 1971.

———. "Even His Enemy." *Ohio Bar Association Report.* 19: June 3, 1946.

Röling, Bernard V. A. *International Law in an Expanded World.* Amsterdam: Djambatan, 1960.

———. "The Law of War and the National Jurisdiction since 1945." Recueil des Cours. *Académie de droit International.* 100: Leyde, The Netherlands, 1961.

———. "On Aggression, on International Criminal Law, on International Criminal Jurisdiction." *Netherlands International Law Review.* April 1955, July 1955. 2 parts.

———. "The Tokyo Trial in Retrospect." In Susumu Yamaguchi, ed. *Buddhism and Culture.* Kyoto: Nakano Press, 1960.

Scwelb, Egon. "Crimes Against Humanity." *The British Yearbook of International Law* London: Oxford University Press, 1946.

———. "The United Nations War Crimes Commission." *The British Yearbook of International Law.* London: Oxford University Press, 1946.

Sebald, William with Russell Brines. *With MacArthur in Japan: A Personal History of the Occupation.* New York: W. W. Norton, 1965.

Shigemitsu, Mamoru. *Japan and Her Destiny,* edited by F. S. Piggot. Translated by Oswald White. New York: E. P. Dutton, 1958.

Spurlock, Paul E. "The Yokohama War Crimes Trials: The Truth about a Misunderstood Subject." *American Bar Association Journal.* 36: May 1950.

Stimson, Henry L. "The Nuremberg Trial: Landmark in Law." *Foreign Affairs.* January 1947.

——— and McGeorge Bundy. *On Active Service.* New York: Harper and Brothers, 1948.

Sutton, David N. "The Trial of Tojo: The Most Important Trial in All History?" *American Bar Association Journal.* 36: February 1950.

Togo, Shigenori. *The Cause of Japan.* Translated by Fumihiko Togo and Ben Bruce Blakeney. New York: Simon and Schuster, 1956.

Truman, Harry S. *Year of Decisions.* New York: Doubleday, 1955.

Vasilyev, A. N. "The Soviet Trial of the Chief Japanese War Criminals." *Soviet Press Translations.* 3, no. 7: April 1, 1948.

Willkie, Wendell. *One World*. New York: Simon and Schuster, 1943.
Wright, Quincy. "Due Process and International Law." *American Journal of International Law*. 40, no. 2: April 1946.
Wright, Lord Robert A. "War Crimes under International Law." *The Law Quarterly Review*. January 1946.
Yoshida, Shigeru. *The Yoshida Memoirs*. Translated by Kenichi Yoshida. Boston: Houghton, Mifflin Company, 1962.

Newspapers and Magazines

China Press (Shanghai). October 1945–March 1949.
Christian Science Monitor. November 1948.
Daily Telegraph (London). October 16, 1945.
Dominion (Wellington). January 18, 1946.
London Times. 1945–1952.
Malay Mail. April 1947–December 31, 1947; April 1949–December 31, 1949.
Manila Times. June 1948.
New York Herald Tribune. 1945–1951.
New York Times. 1945–1951; August 19, 1961; January 11, 1976; February 13, 1977.
Nippon Times. December 9, 1945; February 10, 1946; November 13, 1948; May 7, 1956.
Stars and Stripes (Shanghai, China edition). 1945–1946.
Stars and Stripes (Tokyo, Japan edition). 1945–1950.
Straits Times (Singapore). September 1945–March 1947.
Sydney Morning Herald. January 1948–January 1949.
Time Magazine. January 3, 1949.
Washington Post. December 23, 1948; January 11, 1949; November 19, 1976.

Ph.D. Dissertations

Riley, Walter L. "The International Military Tribunal for the Far East and the Law of the Tribunal as Revealed by the Judgment and the Concurring and Dissenting Opinions." Ph.D. dissertation. University of Washington, 1957.
Wadsworth, Lawrence W., Jr. "A Short History of the Tokyo War Crimes Trials with Special Reference to Some Aspects of Procedures." Ph.D. dissertation. American University, 1955.

Secondary Materials: Articles and Book Reviews

"Advocate of Plague." *Current Digest of the Soviet Press*. 2, no. 9: April 15, 1950.
Albertson, Terry L. "Book Review: Victors' Justice: The Tokyo War Crimes Trial. By Richard H. Minear." *Harvard International Law Journal*. 13: Summer 1972.

"American Occupation Authorities Protect Japanese War Criminals." *Current Digest of the Soviet Press*. 3, no. 23: July 21, 1951.

Army and Navy Journal. Editorial, February 9, 1946.

Basu, K. K. "Tokio Trials." *Indian Law Review*. 3: 1949.

Bathurst, M. E. "The United Nations War Crimes Commission." *American Journal of International Law*. 39: 1945.

Baxter, R. R. "The Municipal and International Law Basis of Jurisdiction over War Crimes." *British Yearbook of International Affairs*. 28: 1951.

Berezhkov, V. "The Tokyo Trial." *New Times*. 5: January 28, 1948.

Brand, G. "The War Crimes Trials and the Laws of War." *British Yearbook of International Law, 1949*. London: Oxford University Press, 1949.

"Bring the War Criminals to Justice!" *New Times*. 6: February 8, 1950.

"The British Court for War Criminals," by "E." *The Law Journal*. 95: September 15, 1945.

Cantor, Milton. "Book Review: Victors' Justice: The Tokyo War Crimes Trial. By Richard H. Minear." *American Journal of Legal History*. 16: October 1972.

"The Chinese People Protest the Illegal Acts of the American Authorities in Japan." *Soviet Press Translations*. 15, no. 13: July 1, 1950.

"Chinese Public Demands Punishment of Japanese War Criminals." 5, no. 8: April 3, 15, 1950.

Cowles, Willard B. "Trial of War Criminals by Military Tribunals." *American Bar Association Journal*. June 1944.

Daly, James J. A. "The Yamashita Case and Martial Courts." *Connecticut Bar Journal*. 21: April–June 1947.

"Declaration of Chou En-lai." *Soviet Press Translations*. 5, no. 22: December 15, 1950.

Erickson, George E., Jr. "United States Navy War Crimes Trials (1945–1949)." *Washburn Law Journal*. 5: Winter 1965.

Fairman, Charles. "The Supreme Court on Military Jurisdiction: Martial Rule in Hawaii and the Yamashita Case." *Harvard Law Review*. 59, no. 6: July 1946.

Finch, George A. "The Punishment of War Criminals." *Inter-American Academy of Comparative and International Law*. 4: 1954.

Ganoe, John T. "The Yamashita Case and the Constitution." *Oregon Law Review*. 25: April 1946.

Garcia-Mora, Manuel R. "Crimes against Peace in International Law: From Nuremberg to the Present." *Kentucky Law Journal*. 53: 1964.

Glueck, Sheldon. "The Nuremberg Trial and Aggressive War." *Harvard Law Review*. 39: 1946.

Golunsky, S. "Trial of the Japanese War Criminals." *New Times*. 18: May 1, 1947.

Green, L. C. "The Trials of Some Minor War Criminals." *Indian Law Review*. 4: 1950.

Gregory, Tappan. "Murder Is Murder and the Guilty Can Be Punished." *American Bar Association Journal.* 32, no. 9: September 1946.

Harkelroad, Donald R. "Book Review: Victors' Justice: The Tokyo War Crimes Trial. By Richard H. Minear." *New York University Journal of International Law and Politics.* 5: Summer 1972.

"Have We Lost the Peace?" *Christian Century.* July 13, 1949.

Hogan, Willard N. "War Criminals." *South Atlantic Quarterly.* 45, no. 4: October 1946.

Howard, Kenneth A. "Command Responsibility for War Crimes." *Journal of Public Law.* 21: 1972.

"Ill-Starred Defenders of War Criminals." *Current Digest of the Soviet Press.* 2, no. 11: April 29, 1950.

"International Hangings." *The Commonweal.* 49: November 1948.

"International Law." *Encyclopaedia Britannica Book of the Year,* 1946. London, 1946.

"International Military Tribunal for the Far East." *International Organization.* 1: February 1947.

"International Military Tribunal for the Far East." *International Organization.* 3: February 1949.

Kudryavtsev, V. "The Verdict against Japanese Militarism." *Soviet Press Translations.* 4, no. 1: February 1, 1949.

Kuhn, Arthur H. "International Law and National Legislation in the Trial of War Criminals: The Yamashita Case." *American Journal of International Law.* 44: July 1950.

Liu, James T. C. "The Tokyo Trials: Source Materials." *Far Eastern Survey.* 17, no. 14: July 28, 1948.

Lyon, Charles S. "Book Review: The Case of General Yamashita. By A. Frank Reel." *Columbia Law Review.* 50: 1950.

Marinin, M. "Remilitarization of Japan." *Current Digest of the Soviet Press.* 2, no. 48: January 13, 1951.

Markov, M. "America's 'New Policy' in the Far East." *New Times.* 12: April 3, 1950.

———. "The Approaching Trial of the Major Japanese War Criminals." *New Times.* 8: April 15, 1946.

———. "Falsification of History at the Tokyo Trial." *New Times.* 17: April 21, 1948.

Mayevsky, V. "Monstrous Crimes Committed by Japanese Barbarians." *USSR Information Bulletin.* 10, no. 3: February 10, 1950.

Miller, Robert W. "War Crimes Trials at Yokohama." *Brooklyn Law Review.* 15, no. 2: April 1949.

Moon, Bucklin. "Book Review: The Case of General Yamashita. By A. Frank Reel." *New York Times Book Review.* October 9, 1949.

Paton, G. W. "The War Trials and International Law." *Res Judicatae.* 3: October 1947.

Pritchard, R. John. "The Nature and Significance of British Post-War Trials of Japanese War Criminals, 1946–1948." Paper read at Conference of the British Association for Japanese Studies, Spring 1977.

Quentin-Baxter, R. Q. "The Task of the International Military Tribunal at Tokyo." *New Zealand Law Journal*. 25: June 7, 1949.

Raginsky, M. "Monstrous Atrocities of the Japanese Imperialists." *New Times*. 2: January 8, 1950.

———— and S. Rozenblit. "What People Expect of the International Military Tribunal in Tokyo." *Soviet Press Translations*. 3, no. 14: July 15, 1948.

Rama, Rao T. S. "The Dissenting Judgment of Mr. Justice Pal at the Tokyo Trial." *Indian Year Book of International Affairs*. 2: 1953.

Rie, Robert. "The War Crimes Trials." *American Journal of International Law*. 48: 1954.

Schlesinger, Arthur M., Jr. "The Necessary Amorality of Foreign Affairs." *Harper's Magazine*. August 1971.

"Sentence Japanese War Criminals." *Christian Century*. 65: November 12, 1948.

Solow, Herbert. "A Rather Startling Result." *Fortune*. 39, no. 4: April 1949.

Tolman, Edgar B. "Review of Recent Supreme Court Decisions." *American Bar Association Journal*. 32: 1946.

Trainin, A. "From Nuremberg to Tokyo." *New Times*. 12: March 17, 1948.

"Two Japanese War Criminals." *New Republic*. 114: February 25, 1946.

Vasilyev, A. N. "On the Results of the Tokio War Crimes Trials." *Current Digest of the Soviet Press*. 1, no. 25: July 19, 1949.

Vasilyev, V. "The Atrocities of the Agressors Have Been Exposed!" *Soviet Press Translations*. 5, no. 13: July 1, 1950.

Walkinshaw, Robert B. "The Nuremberg and Tokyo Trials: Another Step toward International Justice." *American Bar Association Journal*. 35: April 1949.

"War Crimes Trials." *Australian Encyclopaedia*. Sydney: Angus and Robertson, 1958.

Secondary Materials: Books

Appleman, John A. *Military Tribunals and International Crimes*. Indianapolis: Bobbs-Merrill, 1954.

Arendt, Hannah. *Eichmann in Jerusalem: A Report on the Banality of Evil*. New York: Viking Press, 1963.

Asahi Shimbun, Staff. *The Pacific Rivals*. New York: Weatherhill, 1972.

Beloff, Max. *Soviet Policy in the Far East, 1944–1951*. London: Oxford University Press, 1953.

Bergamini, David. *Japan's Imperial Conspiracy*. New York: William Morrow, 1971.

Borg, Dorothy and Shumpei Okamoto, editors. *Pearl Harbor as History*. New York: Columbia University Press, 1973.

Brady, Alexander and F. R. Scott, editors. *Canada after the War*. Toronto: MacMillan of Canada, 1944.

Browne, Courtney. *Tojo: The Last Banzai*. New York: Holt, Rinehart and Winston, 1967.

Brownlie, Ian. *International Law and the Use of Force by States*. Oxford: The Clarendon Press: 1963.

Butow, Robert J. C. *Japan's Decision to Surrender*. Stanford, Cal.: Stanford University Press, 1954.

————. *Tojo and the Coming of the War*. Stanford, Cal.: Stanford University Press, 1961.

Buttinger, Joseph. *Vietnam: A Political History*. New York: Praeger, 1968.

Calvocoressi, Peter. *Survey of International Affairs, 1947–1948*. London: Oxford University Press, 1952.

————. *Survey of International Affairs, 1949–1950*. London: Oxford University Press, 1953.

Clews, John C. *Communist Propaganda Techniques*. London: Methuen & Co., 1964.

Davidson, Eugene. *The Nuremberg Fallacy: Wars and War Crimes since World War II*. New York: MacMillan, 1973.

Dinstein, Yoram. *The Defense of 'Obedience To Superior Orders' in International Law*. Leyden, The Netherlands: A. W. Sijthoff, 1965.

Dunn, Frederick S. *Peacemaking and the Settlement with Japan*. Princeton: Princeton University Press, 1963.

Falk, Richard A. *A Global Approach to National Policy*. Cambridge, Mass.: Harvard University Press, 1975.

————, Gabriel Kolko and Robert J. Lifton, editors. *Crimes of War*. New York: Random House, 1971.

Falk, Stanley L. *Bataan: The March of Death*. New York: Norton, 1962.

Fall, Bernard. *The Two Viet-Nams: A Political and Military Analysis*. 2nd rev. ed. New York: Praeger Publishers, 1967.

Feis, Herbert. *The China Tangle*. Princeton: Princeton University Press, 1953.

————. *From Trust to Terror*. New York: W. W. Norton, 1970.

Fifield, Russell H. *Americans in Southeast Asia: The Roots of Commitment*. New York: Crowell Company, 1973.

Fitzsimons, M. A. *The Foreign Policy of the British Labour Government, 1945–1951*. Notre Dame, Indiana: University of Notre Dame Press, 1953.

Gardner, D. H. *Canadian Interests and Policies in the Far East since World War II*. Eleventh Conference, Institute of Pacific Relations. Canadian Institute of International Affairs. Toronto, 1950.

Harper, N. D. *Australia and the Peace Settlement with Japan*. Sydney: Australian Institute of International Affairs, 1950.

Hinton, Harold C. *China's Turbulent Quest*. New York: MacMillan, 1970.

Homu Daijin Kanbo Shiho Hosei Chosabu. *Senso hanzai saiban gaishi yo (General History of Trials of War Crimes)*. Tokyo, 1973.

Iriye, Akira. *The Cold War in Asia*. Englewood Cliffs, N.J.: Prentice-Hall, 1974.

Jessup, Philip. *A Modern Law of Nations*. New York: MacMillan, 1958.

Kajima, Morinosuke. *Modern Japan's Foreign Policy*. Rutland, Vt.: Charles K. Tuttle, 1969.

Kaplan, Morton A. and Nicholas deB. Katzenbach. *The Political Foundations of International Law*. New York: John Wiley, 1961.

Kawai, Kazuo. *Japan's American Interlude*. Chicago: University of Chicago Press, 1960.

Kim, Sung Yong. *United States–Philippine Relations, 1946–1956*. Washington, D.C.: Public Affairs Press, 1968.

Kojima, Noboru. *Tokyo Saiban (Tokyo Trial)*. 2 vols. Tokyo, 1971.

Leatham, Samuel. *New Zealand's Interests and Policies in the Far East*. New Zealand Institute of International Affairs. Wellington, 1950.

Lichauo, Marcial P. *Roxas: The Story of a Great Filipino and of the Political Era in Which He Lived*. Manila: Kiko Printing Press, 1952.

Liu, F. F. *A Military History of Modern China, 1924–1949*. Princeton: Princeton University Press, 1956.

Medlicott, W. N. *British Foreign Policy since Versailles, 1919–1963*. London: Methuen, 1968.

Meyer, Armin H. *Assignment: Tokyo*. Indianapolis: Bobbs-Merrill, 1974.

Minear, Richard H. *Victors' Justice: The Tokyo War Crimes Trial*. Princeton, N.J.: Princeton University Press, 1971.

Olson, Lawrence. *Japan in Postwar Asia*. New York: Praeger, 1970.

Olver, A. S. B. *Outline of British Policy in East and Southeast Asia, 1945– May 1950*. London: Royal Institute of International Affairs, 1950.

Palmier, Leslie H. *Indonesia and the Dutch*. London: Oxford University Press, 1962.

Pompe, C. A. *Aggressive War: An International Crime*. The Hague: Martinus Nijhoff, 1953.

Potter, John Deane. *A Soldier Must Hang: The Biography of an Oriental General*. London: Frederick Muller, 1963.

Rees, David. *Korea: The Limited War*. New York: St. Martin's Press, 1964.

Reese, Trevor R. *Australia, New Zealand and the United States: A Survey of International Relations, 1941–1968*. London: Oxford University Press, 1969.

Reischauer, Edwin O. *Japan: The Story of a Nation*. New York: Alfred Knopf, 1970.

———. *The United States and Japan*. 3rd edition. New York: Viking Press, 1965.

Rosencrance, R. N. *Australian Diplomacy and Japan, 1945–1957*. London: Cambridge University Press, 1962.

Russell, Edward F. L. *The Knights of Bushido: A Short History of Japanese War Crimes*. London: Cassell & Co., 1958.

Schroeder, Paul W. *The Axis Alliance and Japanese-American Relations, 1941*. Ithaca, N.Y.: Cornell University Press, 1958.

Schurmann, Franz. *The Logic of World Power*. New York: Pantheon Books, 1974.

Schwarzenberger, Georg. *A Manual of International Law*. 5th edition. New York: Praeger, 1967.

Seiki no isho (*The Last Testament of the Century*). Sugamo Isho Hensankai, editor. Tokyo: Shiragikukai, 1954.

Serra, Enrico. *L'Aggressione internazionale*. Milan, 1946.

Sherwood, Robert E. *Roosevelt and Hopkins*. New York: Harper Brothers, 1948.

Shiroyama, Saburo. *War Criminal: The Life and Death of Hirota Koki*. New York: Kodansha International, 1977.

Smith, Bradley F. *Reaching Judgment at Nuremberg*. New York: Basic Books, 1977.

Steinberg, David Joel. *Philippine Collaboration in World War II*. Ann Arbor: University of Michigan Press, 1967.

Stoessinger, John G. *The Might of Nations*. New York: Random House, 1963.

Szulc, Tad. *Czechoslovakia since World War II*. New York: Grosset & Dunlap, 1971.

Tallow, Adamin A. *Command Responsibility: Its Legal Aspect*. Manila: By author, 1965.

Taylor, Telford. *Nuremberg and Vietnam: An American Tragedy*. New York: Quadrangle Books, 1970.

Toland, John. *The Rising Sun*. New York: Random House, 1970.

Ulam, Adam B. *Expansion and Coexistence: Soviet Foreign Policy, 1917–1973*. 2nd edition. New York: Praeger, 1974.

Veale, F. J. P. *Advance to Barbarism: The Development of Total Warfare from Serajevo to Hiroshima*. 3rd revised edition. London: Mitre Press, 1968.

Wakefield, Harold. *New Paths for Japan*. New York: Oxford University Press, 1948.

Whitney, Courtney. *MacArthur: His Rendezvous with History*. New York: Alfred Knopf, 1956.

Woetzel, Robert K. *The Nuremberg Trials in International Law*. New York: Praeger, 1960.

Correspondences Cited in Text

Australia. Australian Acting Senior Archivist. May 12, 1976.

Donihi, Robert. May 31, June 10, 1977. To third party, May 30, 1977.

New Zealand. National Archives. Department of Internal Affairs. April 12, 1976.

Philippines, the Republic of. Chief, National Archives. May 17, 1976.

Pritchard, R. John. July 13, 1977.

Silkin, Samuel Charles. March 23, 1977.

Suyama, K. Director of the Division of Interlibrary Services, National Diet Library, Tokyo. September 7, 1977.

Index